TEENAGE MUTANT NINJA TURTLES

KRANG WAR · VOL. 5

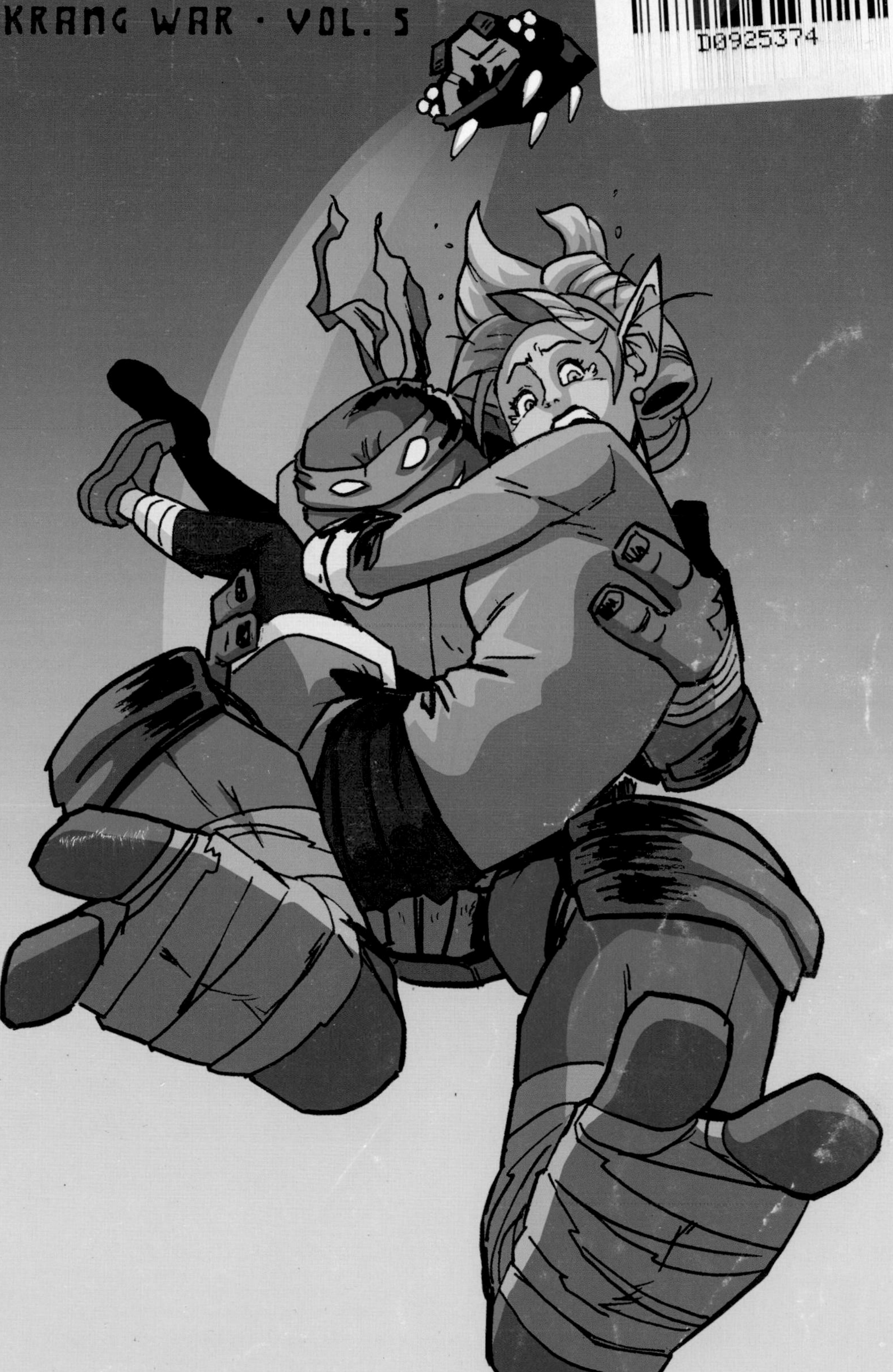

Story by Kevin Eastman & Tom Waltz · Script by Tom Waltz   Art by Ben Bates

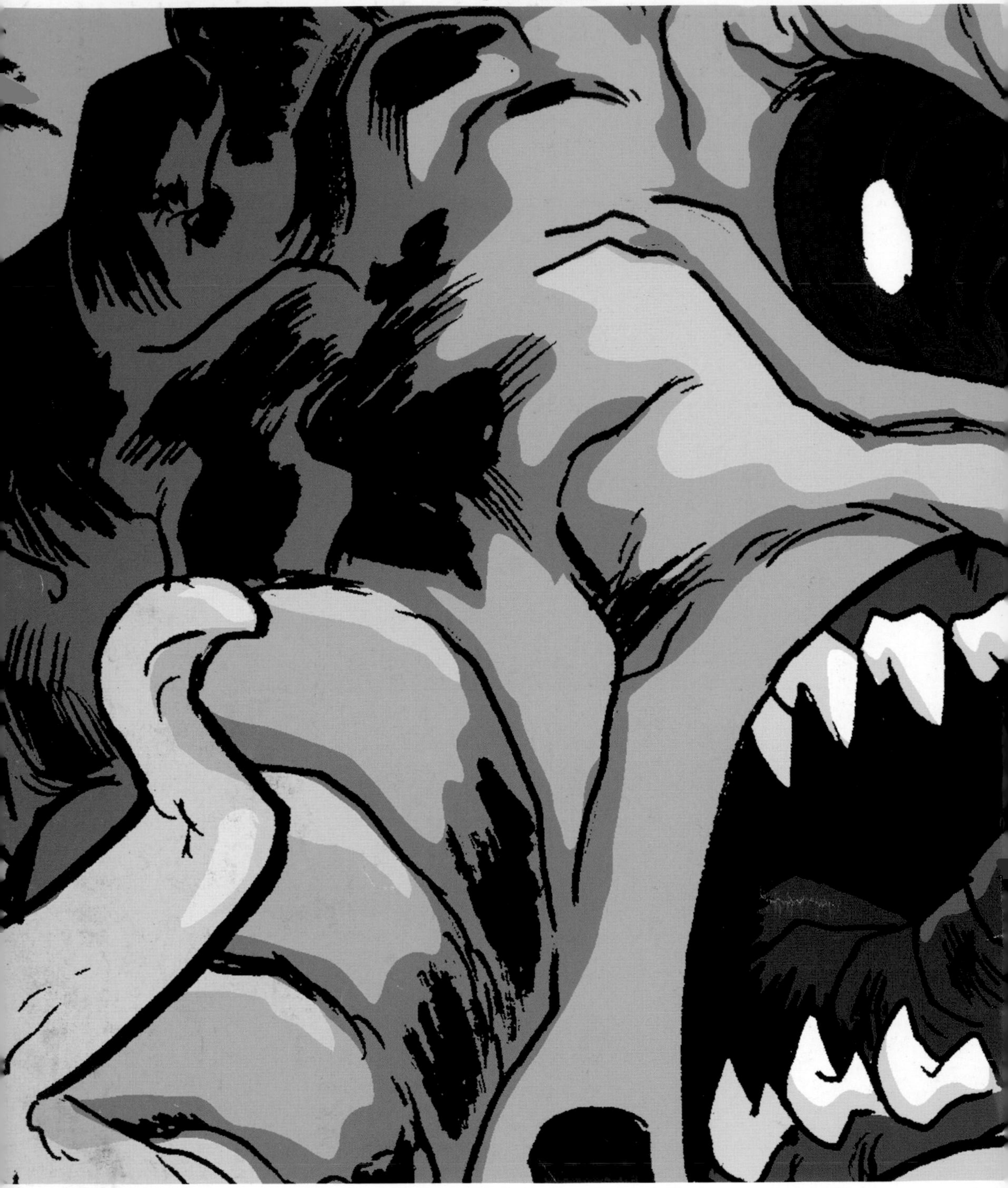

Special thanks to Joan Hilty, Linda Lee, and Kat van Dam for their invaluable assistance.

nickelodeon™

IDW founded by Ted Adams, Alex Garner, Kris Oprisko, and Robbie Robbins

ISBN: 978-1-61377-640-7

17 16 15 14   2 3 4 5

IDW®

Ted Adams, CEO & Publisher
Greg Goldstein, President & COO
Robbie Robbins, EVP/Sr. Graphic Artist
Chris Ryall, Chief Creative Officer/Editor-in-Chief
Matthew Ruzicka, CPA, Chief Financial Officer
Alan Payne, VP of Sales
Dirk Wood, VP of Marketing
Lorelei Bunjes, VP of Digital Services

Originally published as TEENAGE MUTANT NINJA TURTLES Issues #17-20.

Colors by Ronda Pattison • Letters by Shawn Lee Series Edits by Bobby Curnow

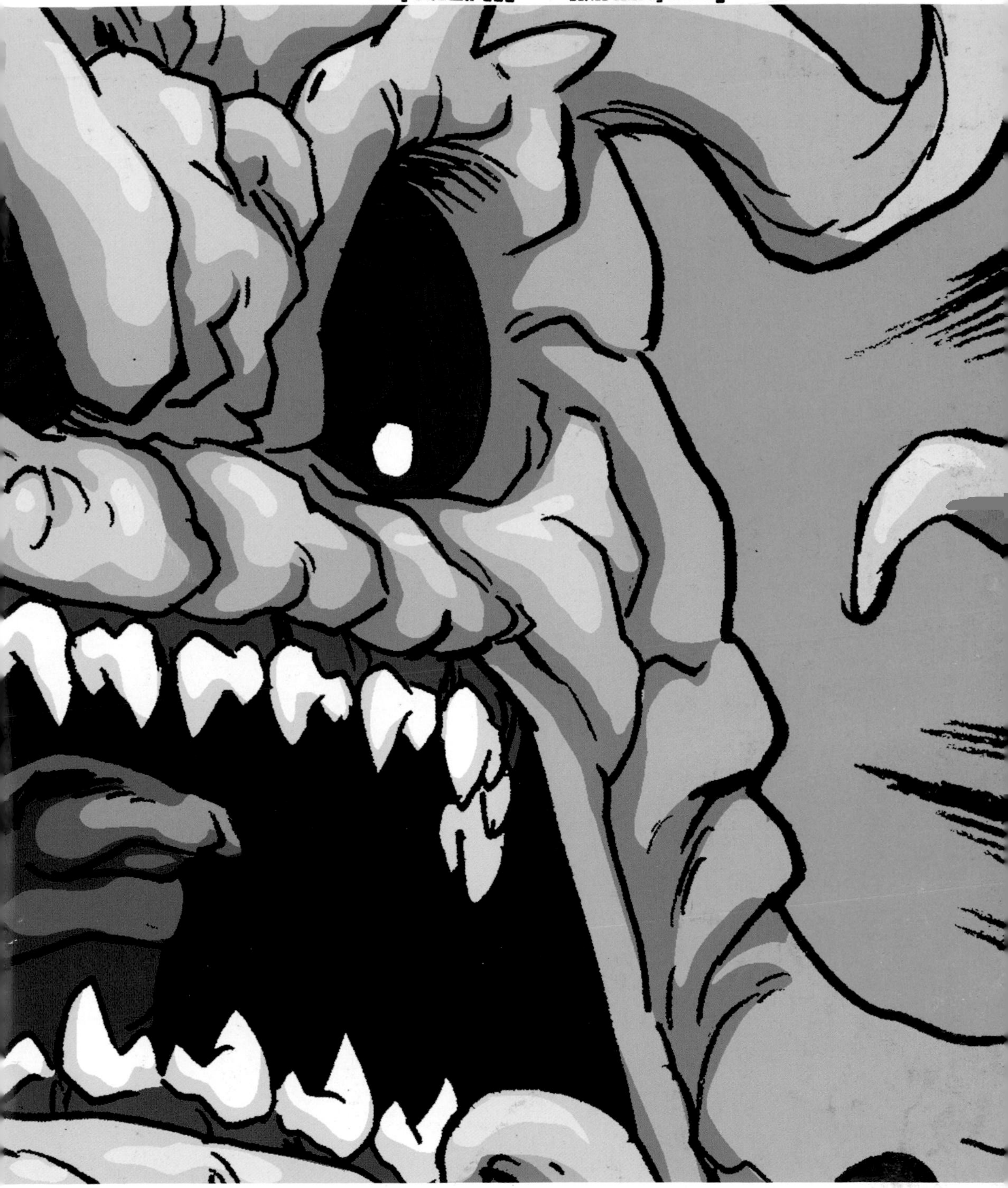

Collection Edits by Justin Eisinger & Alonzo Simon

Collection Design by Shawn Lee • Cover by Nick Pitarra • Colors by Megan Wilson

Based on characters created by Peter Laird and Kevin Eastman

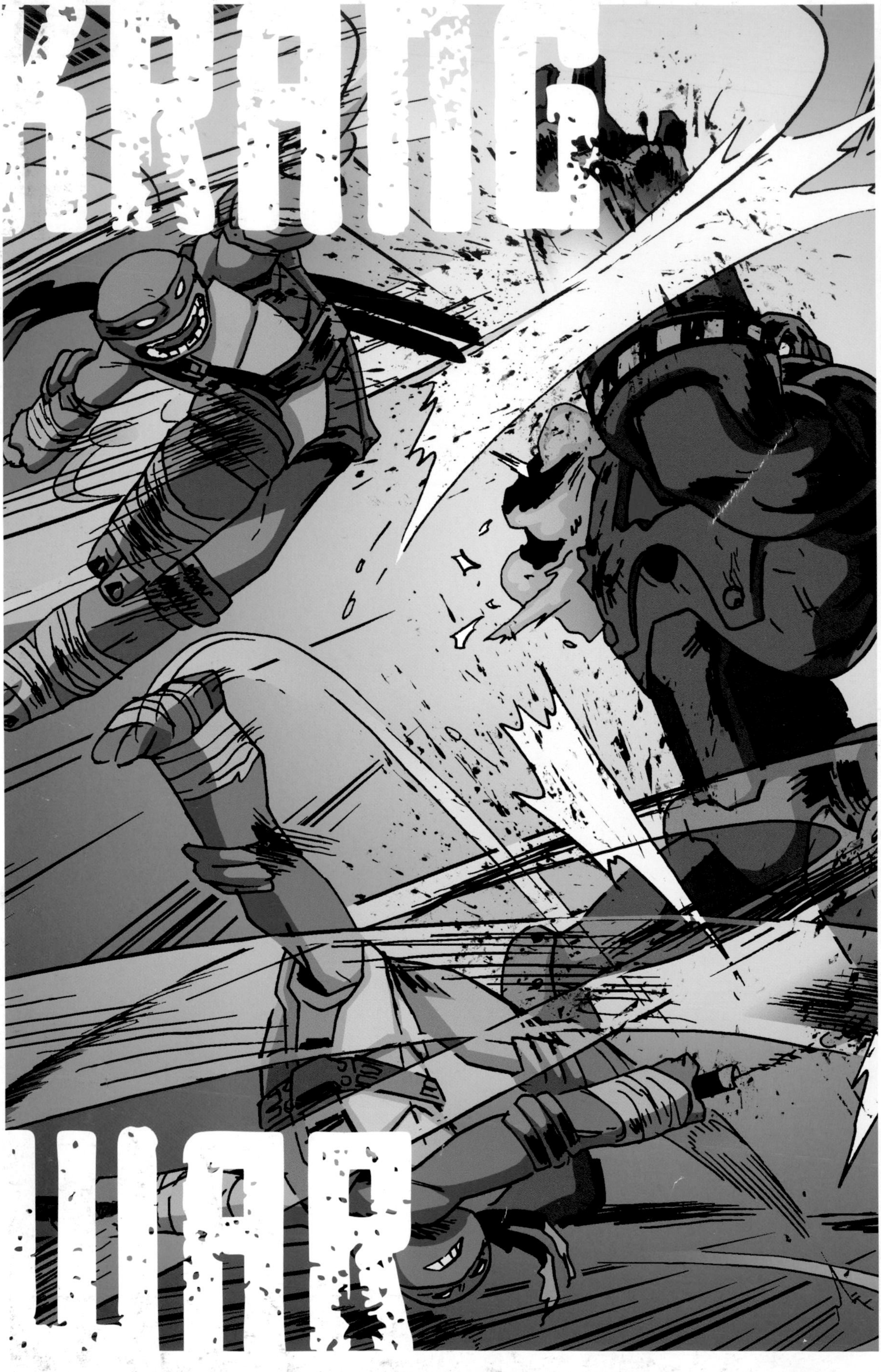
KRANG
WAR

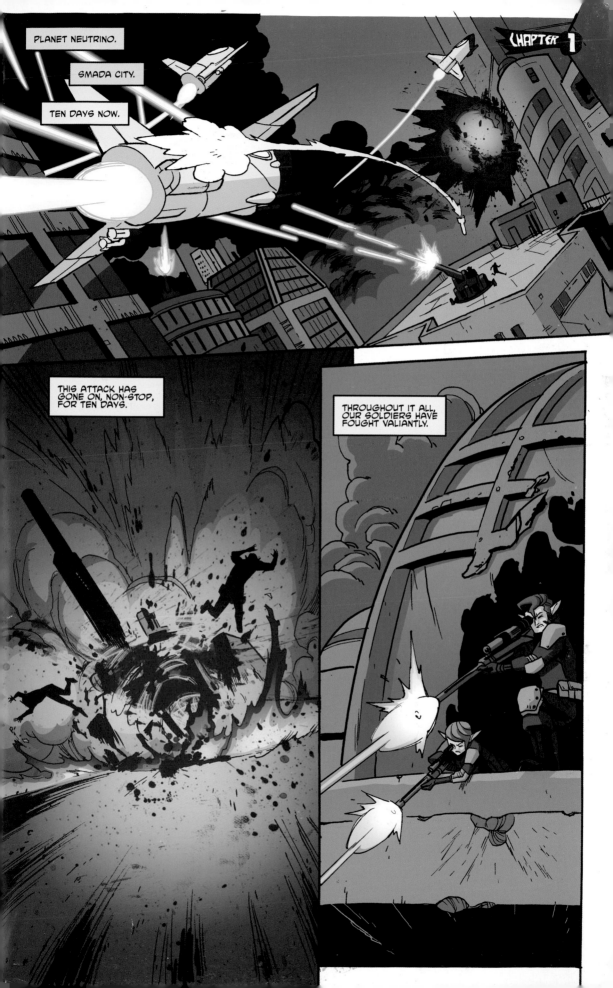

CHAPTER 1

PLANET NEUTRINO.

SMADA CITY.

TEN DAYS NOW.

THIS ATTACK HAS GONE ON, NON-STOP, FOR TEN DAYS.

THROUGHOUT IT ALL, OUR SOLDIERS HAVE FOUGHT VALIANTLY.

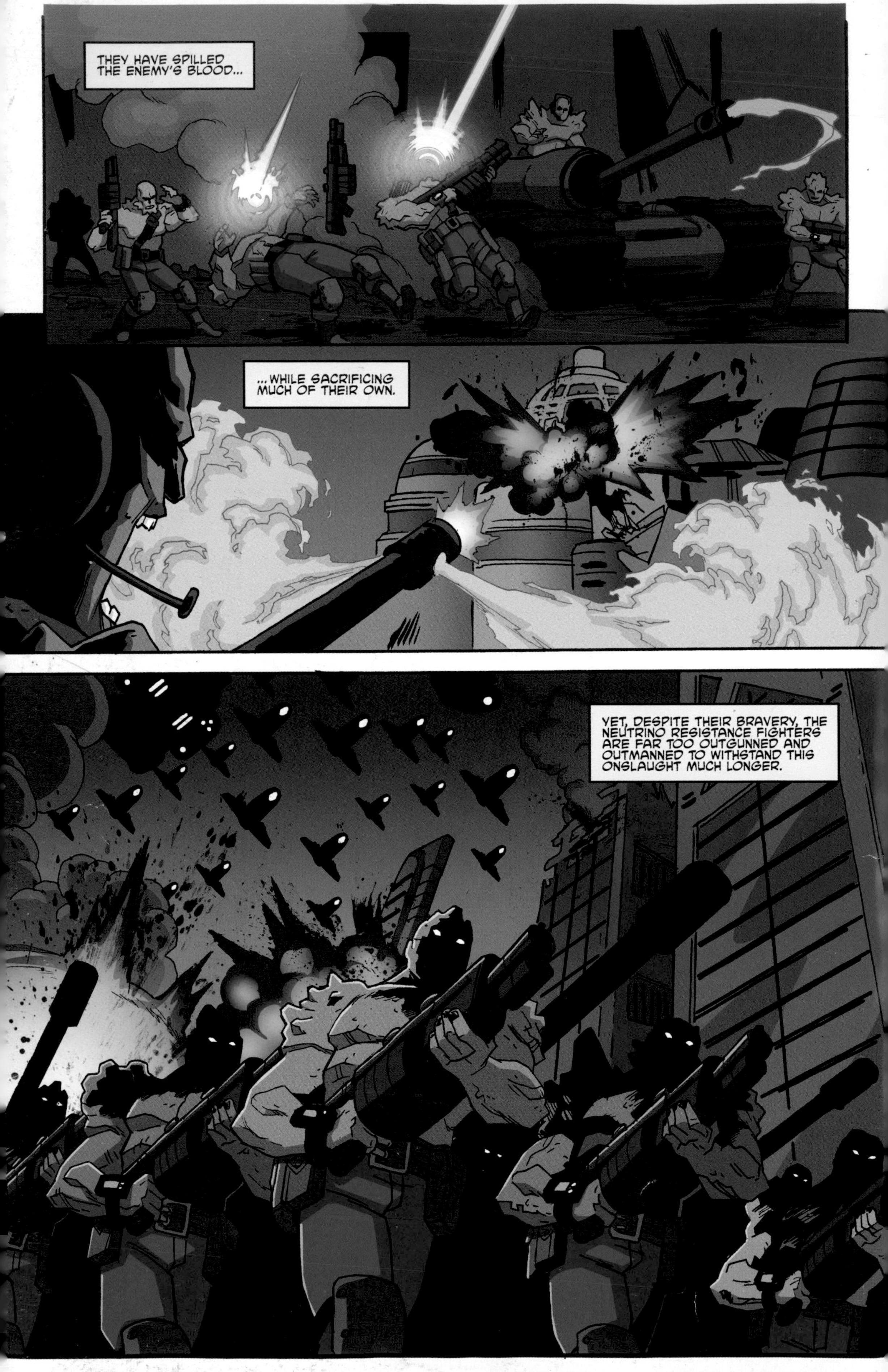
THEY HAVE SPILLED THE ENEMY'S BLOOD...
...WHILE SACRIFICING MUCH OF THEIR OWN.
YET, DESPITE THEIR BRAVERY, THE NEUTRINO RESISTANCE FIGHTERS ARE FAR TOO OUTGUNNED AND OUTMANNED TO WITHSTAND THIS ONSLAUGHT MUCH LONGER.

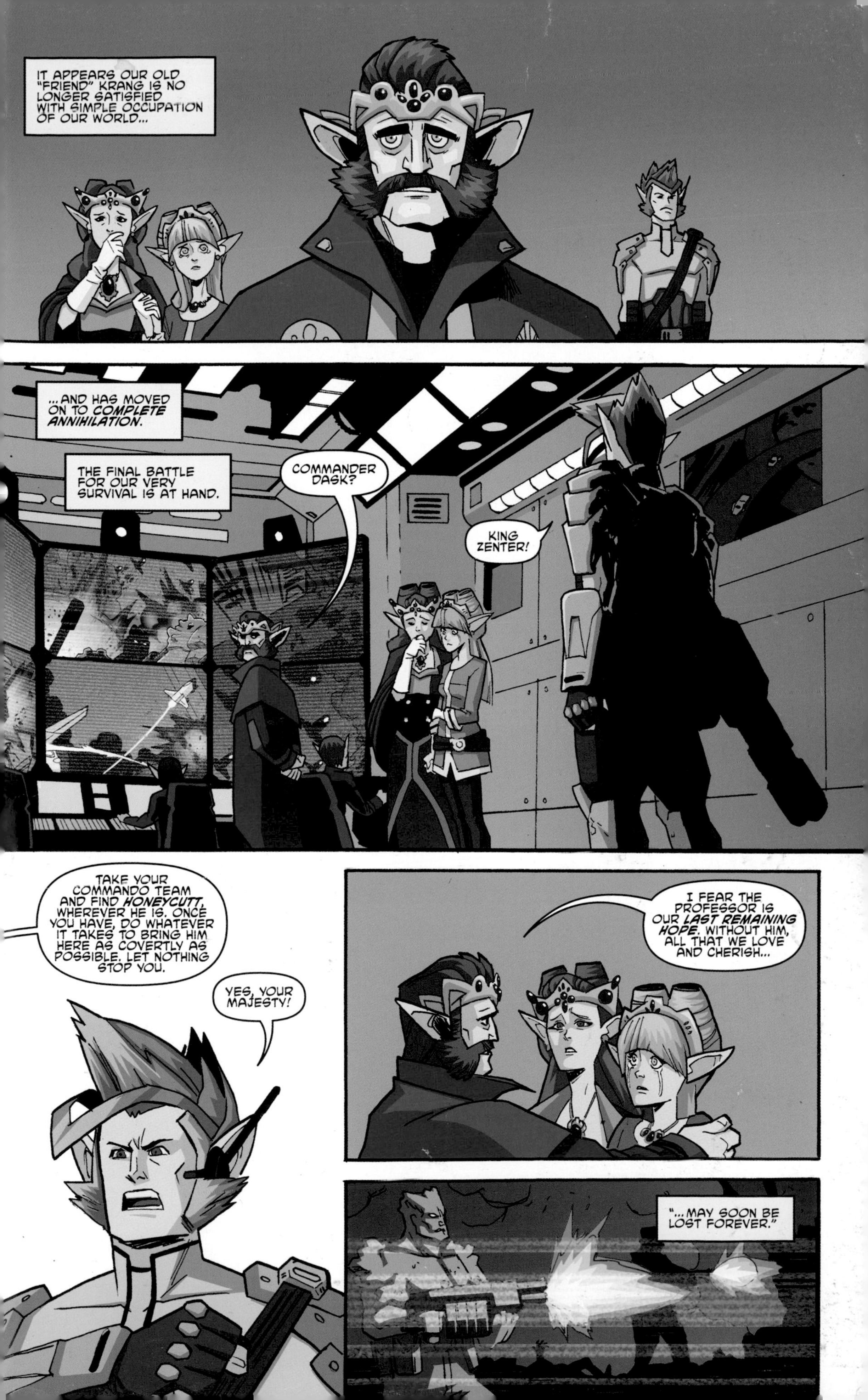

IT APPEARS OUR OLD "FRIEND" KRANG IS NO LONGER SATISFIED WITH SIMPLE OCCUPATION OF OUR WORLD...
...AND HAS MOVED ON TO COMPLETE ANNIHILATION.
THE FINAL BATTLE FOR OUR VERY SURVIVAL IS AT HAND.
COMMANDER DASK?
KING ZENTER!
TAKE YOUR COMMANDO TEAM AND FIND HONEYCUTT, WHEREVER HE IS. ONCE YOU HAVE, DO WHATEVER IT TAKES TO BRING HIM HERE AS COVERTLY AS POSSIBLE. LET NOTHING STOP YOU.
YES, YOUR MAJESTY!
I FEAR THE PROFESSOR IS OUR LAST REMAINING HOPE. WITHOUT HIM, ALL THAT WE LOVE AND CHERISH...
"...MAY SOON BE LOST FOREVER."

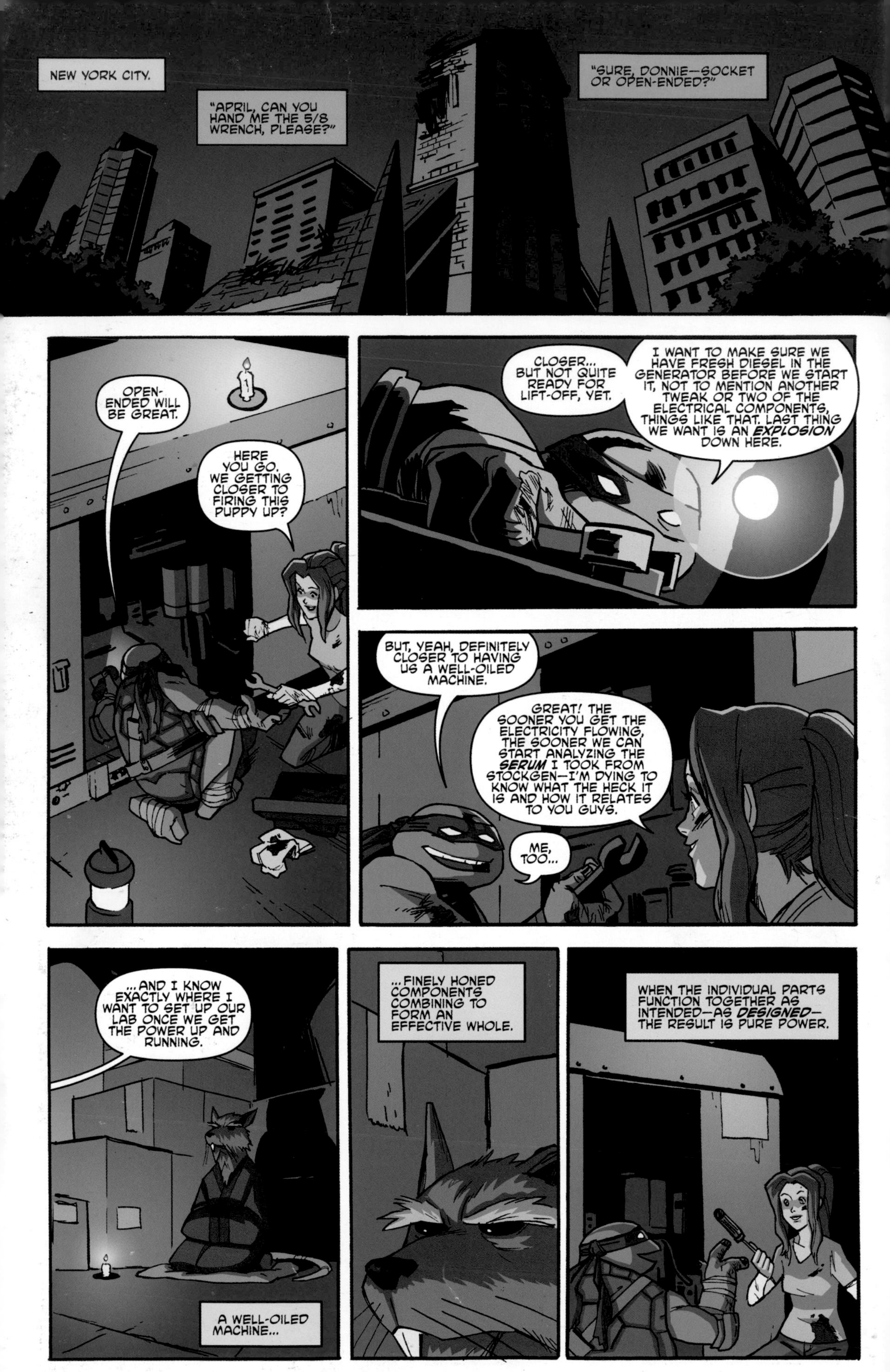
NEW YORK CITY.
"APRIL, CAN YOU HAND ME THE 5/8 WRENCH, PLEASE?"
"SURE, DONNIE—SOCKET OR OPEN-ENDED?"
OPEN-ENDED WILL BE GREAT.
HERE YOU GO. WE GETTING CLOSER TO FIRING THIS PUPPY UP?
CLOSER... BUT NOT QUITE READY FOR LIFT-OFF, YET.
I WANT TO MAKE SURE WE HAVE FRESH DIESEL IN THE GENERATOR BEFORE WE START IT, NOT TO MENTION ANOTHER TWEAK OR TWO OF THE ELECTRICAL COMPONENTS, THINGS LIKE THAT. LAST THING WE WANT IS AN EXPLOSION DOWN HERE.
BUT, YEAH, DEFINITELY CLOSER TO HAVING US A WELL-OILED MACHINE.
GREAT! THE SOONER YOU GET THE ELECTRICITY FLOWING, THE SOONER WE CAN START ANALYZING THE SERUM I TOOK FROM STOCKGEN—I'M DYING TO KNOW WHAT THE HECK IT IS AND HOW IT RELATES TO YOU GUYS.
ME, TOO...
...AND I KNOW EXACTLY WHERE I WANT TO SET UP OUR LAB ONCE WE GET THE POWER UP AND RUNNING.
A WELL-OILED MACHINE...
...FINELY HONED COMPONENTS COMBINING TO FORM AN EFFECTIVE WHOLE.
WHEN THE INDIVIDUAL PARTS FUNCTION TOGETHER AS INTENDED—AS DESIGNED—THE RESULT IS PURE POWER.

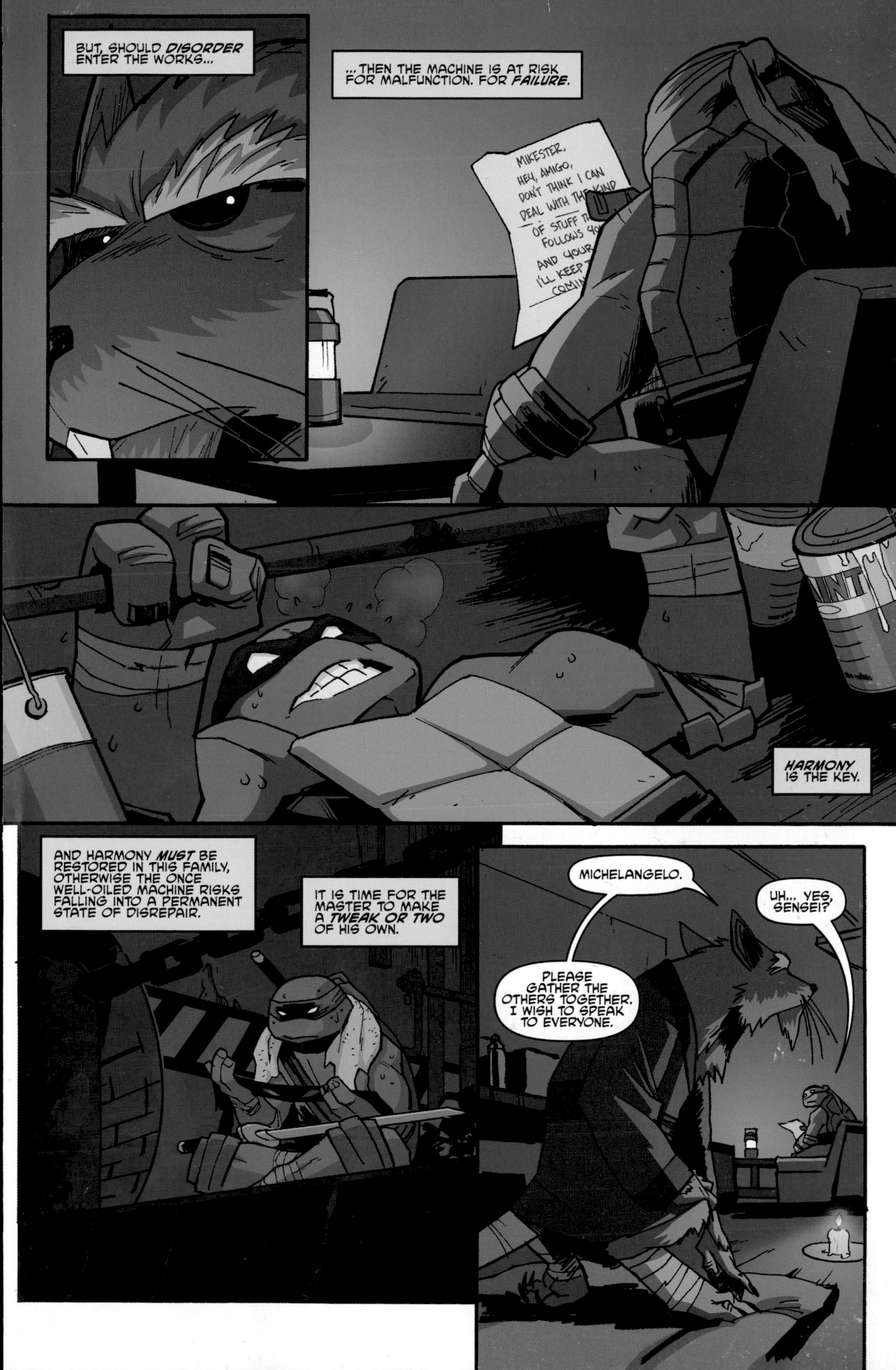
BUT, SHOULD *DISORDER* ENTER THE WORKS...
...THEN THE MACHINE IS AT RISK FOR MALFUNCTION. FOR *FAILURE*.
MIKESTER,
HEY, AMIGO,
DON'T THINK I CAN
HARMONY IS THE KEY.
AND HARMONY *MUST* BE RESTORED IN THIS FAMILY, OTHERWISE THE ONCE WELL-OILED MACHINE RISKS FALLING INTO A PERMANENT STATE OF DISREPAIR.
IT IS TIME FOR THE MASTER TO MAKE A *TWEAK OR TWO* OF HIS OWN.
MICHELANGELO.
UH... YES, SENSEI?
PLEASE GATHER THE OTHERS TOGETHER. I WISH TO SPEAK TO EVERYONE.

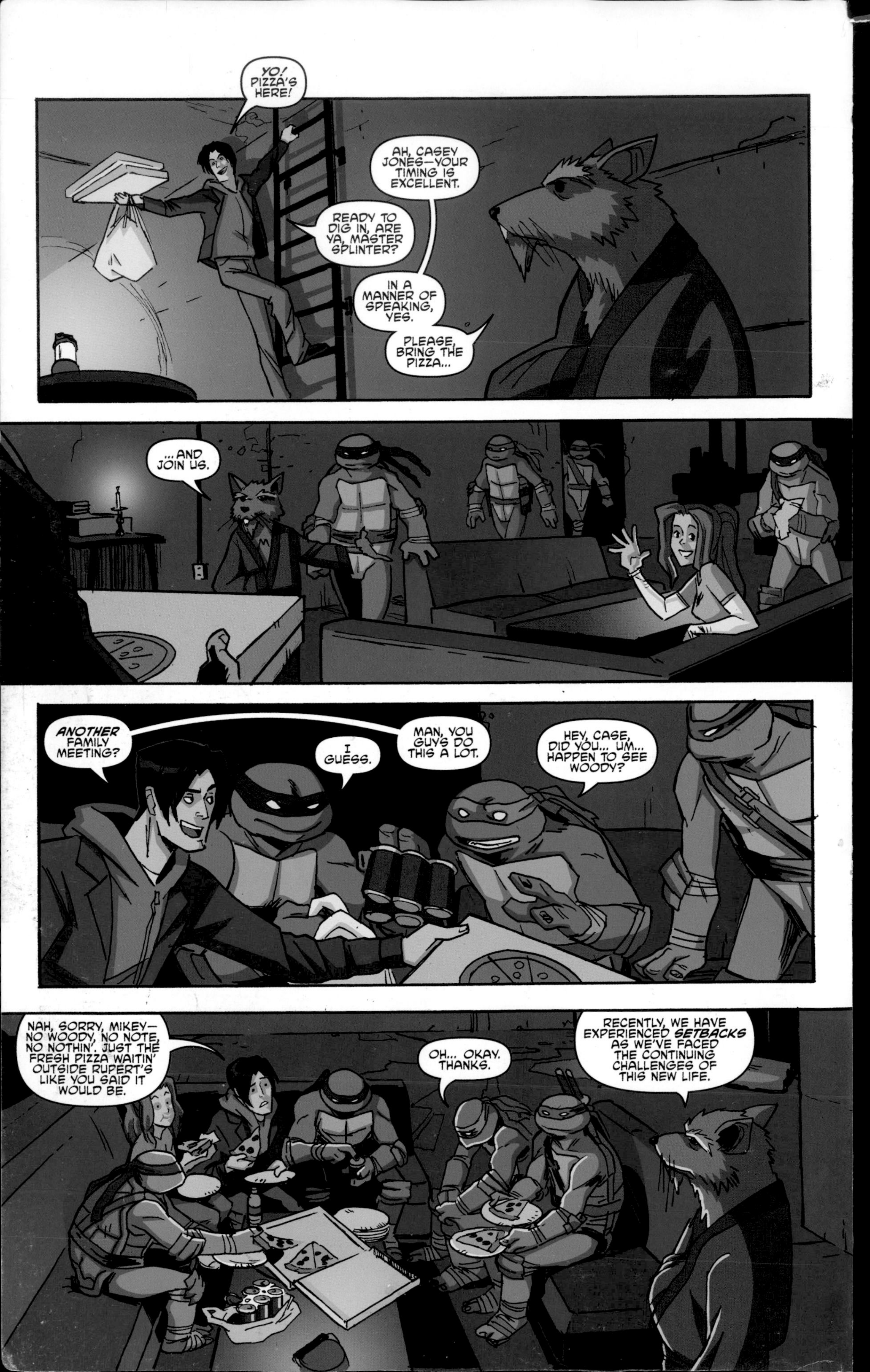
YO! PIZZA'S HERE!
AH, CASEY JONES—YOUR TIMING IS EXCELLENT.
READY TO DIG IN, ARE YA, MASTER SPLINTER?
IN A MANNER OF SPEAKING, YES.
PLEASE, BRING THE PIZZA...
...AND JOIN US.
ANOTHER FAMILY MEETING?
I GUESS.
MAN, YOU GUYS DO THIS A LOT.
HEY, CASE, DID YOU... UM... HAPPEN TO SEE WOODY?
NAH, SORRY, MIKEY—NO WOODY, NO NOTE, NO NOTHIN'. JUST THE FRESH PIZZA WAITIN' OUTSIDE RUPERT'S LIKE YOU SAID IT WOULD BE.
OH... OKAY. THANKS.
RECENTLY, WE HAVE EXPERIENCED SETBACKS AS WE'VE FACED THE CONTINUING CHALLENGES OF THIS NEW LIFE.

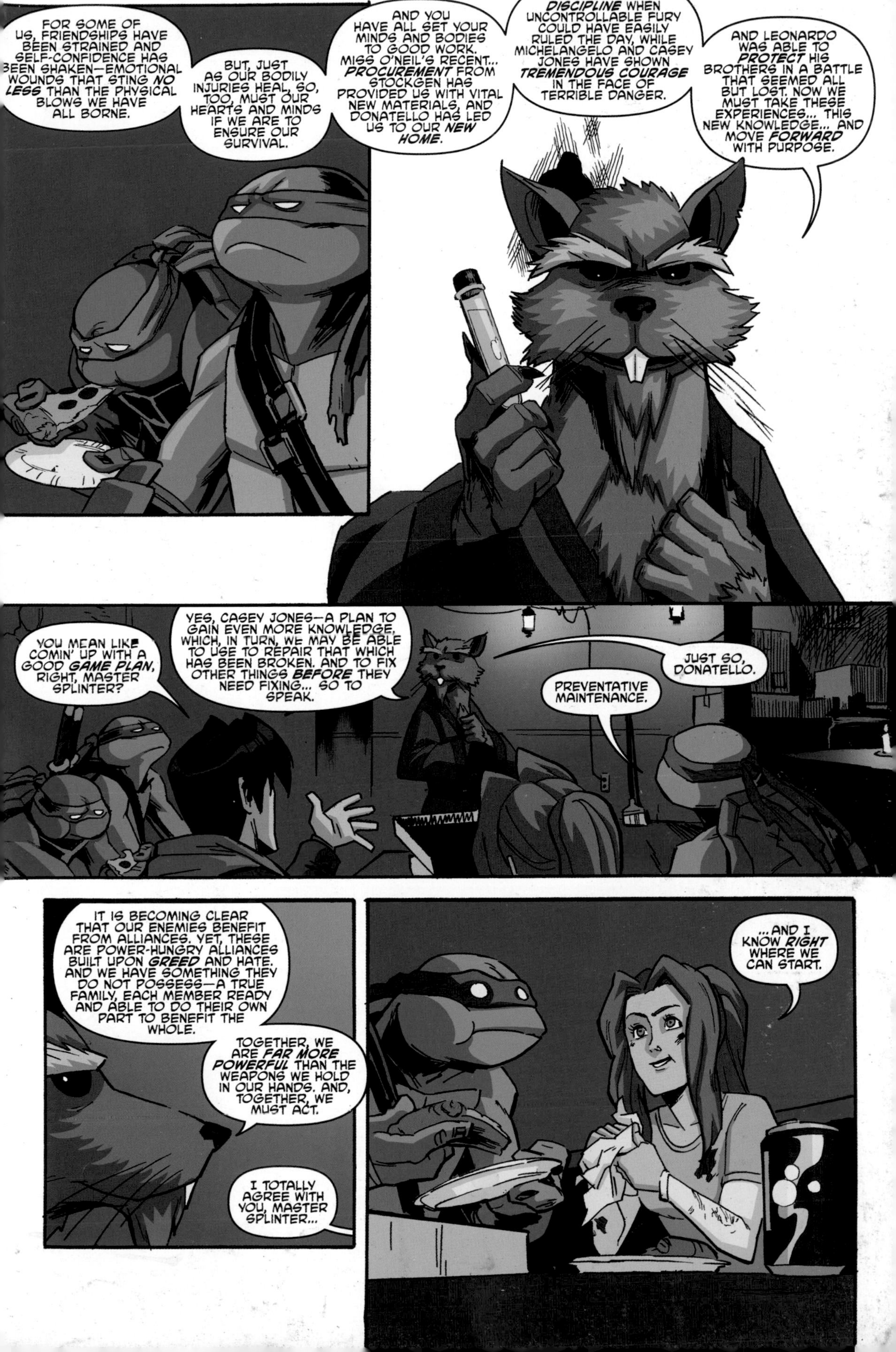
FOR SOME OF US, FRIENDSHIPS HAVE BEEN STRAINED AND SELF-CONFIDENCE HAS BEEN SHAKEN—EMOTIONAL WOUNDS THAT STING NO LESS THAN THE PHYSICAL BLOWS WE HAVE ALL BORNE.
BUT, JUST AS OUR BODILY INJURIES HEAL, SO, TOO, MUST OUR HEARTS AND MINDS IF WE ARE TO ENSURE OUR SURVIVAL.
AND YOU HAVE ALL SET YOUR MINDS AND BODIES TO GOOD WORK. MISS O'NEIL'S RECENT... PROCUREMENT FROM STOCKGEN HAS PROVIDED US WITH VITAL NEW MATERIALS, AND DONATELLO HAS LED US TO OUR NEW HOME.
RAPHAEL FOUND DISCIPLINE WHEN UNCONTROLLABLE FURY COULD HAVE EASILY RULED THE DAY, WHILE MICHELANGELO AND CASEY JONES HAVE SHOWN TREMENDOUS COURAGE IN THE FACE OF TERRIBLE DANGER.
AND LEONARDO WAS ABLE TO PROTECT HIS BROTHERS IN A BATTLE THAT SEEMED ALL BUT LOST. NOW WE MUST TAKE THESE EXPERIENCES... THIS NEW KNOWLEDGE... AND MOVE FORWARD WITH PURPOSE.
YOU MEAN LIKE COMIN' UP WITH A GOOD GAME PLAN, RIGHT, MASTER SPLINTER?
YES, CASEY JONES—A PLAN TO GAIN EVEN MORE KNOWLEDGE, WHICH, IN TURN, WE MAY BE ABLE TO USE TO REPAIR THAT WHICH HAS BEEN BROKEN. AND TO FIX OTHER THINGS BEFORE THEY NEED FIXING... SO TO SPEAK.
PREVENTATIVE MAINTENANCE.
JUST SO, DONATELLO.
IT IS BECOMING CLEAR THAT OUR ENEMIES BENEFIT FROM ALLIANCES. YET, THESE ARE POWER-HUNGRY ALLIANCES BUILT UPON GREED AND HATE. AND WE HAVE SOMETHING THEY DO NOT POSSESS—A TRUE FAMILY, EACH MEMBER READY AND ABLE TO DO THEIR OWN PART TO BENEFIT THE WHOLE.
TOGETHER, WE ARE FAR MORE POWERFUL THAN THE WEAPONS WE HOLD IN OUR HANDS. AND, TOGETHER, WE MUST ACT.
I TOTALLY AGREE WITH YOU, MASTER SPLINTER...
...AND I KNOW RIGHT WHERE WE CAN START.

HRRGGK!

THE PLANET NEUTRINO.

WELL... ≶KOFF≶... THAT WAS UNPLEASANT.

INDEED. YOUR OBVIOUS INDIVIDUAL WEAKNESSES ASIDE, WE HAVE FOUND IT TAKES HUMANS SOME TIME TO ADAPT TO INTER-DIMENSIONAL PORTAL TRAVEL.

YES, WELL, A BIT OF ADVANCE WARNING WOULD HAVE BEEN NICE.

I DON'T DO NICE, STOCKMAN.

REALLY? I HADN'T NOTICED.

THEN, DO YOU NOTICE THAT CITY ON FIRE IN THE DISTANCE? THAT IS SMADA CITY, CENTRAL CAPITOL OF THIS FETID DUNG HEAP.

OR, RATHER, THE SOON-TO-BE FORMER CAPITOL CITY, ONCE MY ARMY GRINDS IT INTO RUBBLE.

CHARMING. AND DID YOU BRING ME HERE JUST TO TELL ME THIS? SEEMS A BIT EXCESSIVE, DON'T YOU THINK?

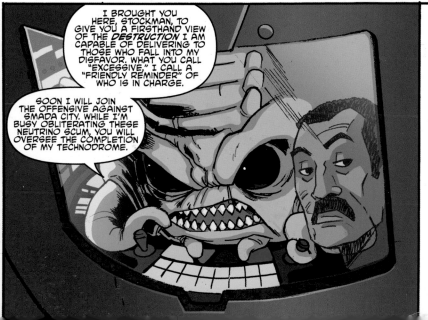

I BROUGHT YOU HERE, STOCKMAN, TO GIVE YOU A FIRSTHAND VIEW OF THE DESTRUCTION I AM CAPABLE OF DELIVERING TO THOSE WHO FALL INTO MY DISFAVOR. WHAT YOU CALL "EXCESSIVE," I CALL A "FRIENDLY REMINDER" OF WHO IS IN CHARGE.

SOON I WILL JOIN THE OFFENSIVE AGAINST SMADA CITY. WHILE I'M BUSY OBLITERATING THESE NEUTRINO SCUM, YOU WILL OVERSEE THE COMPLETION OF MY TECHNODROME.

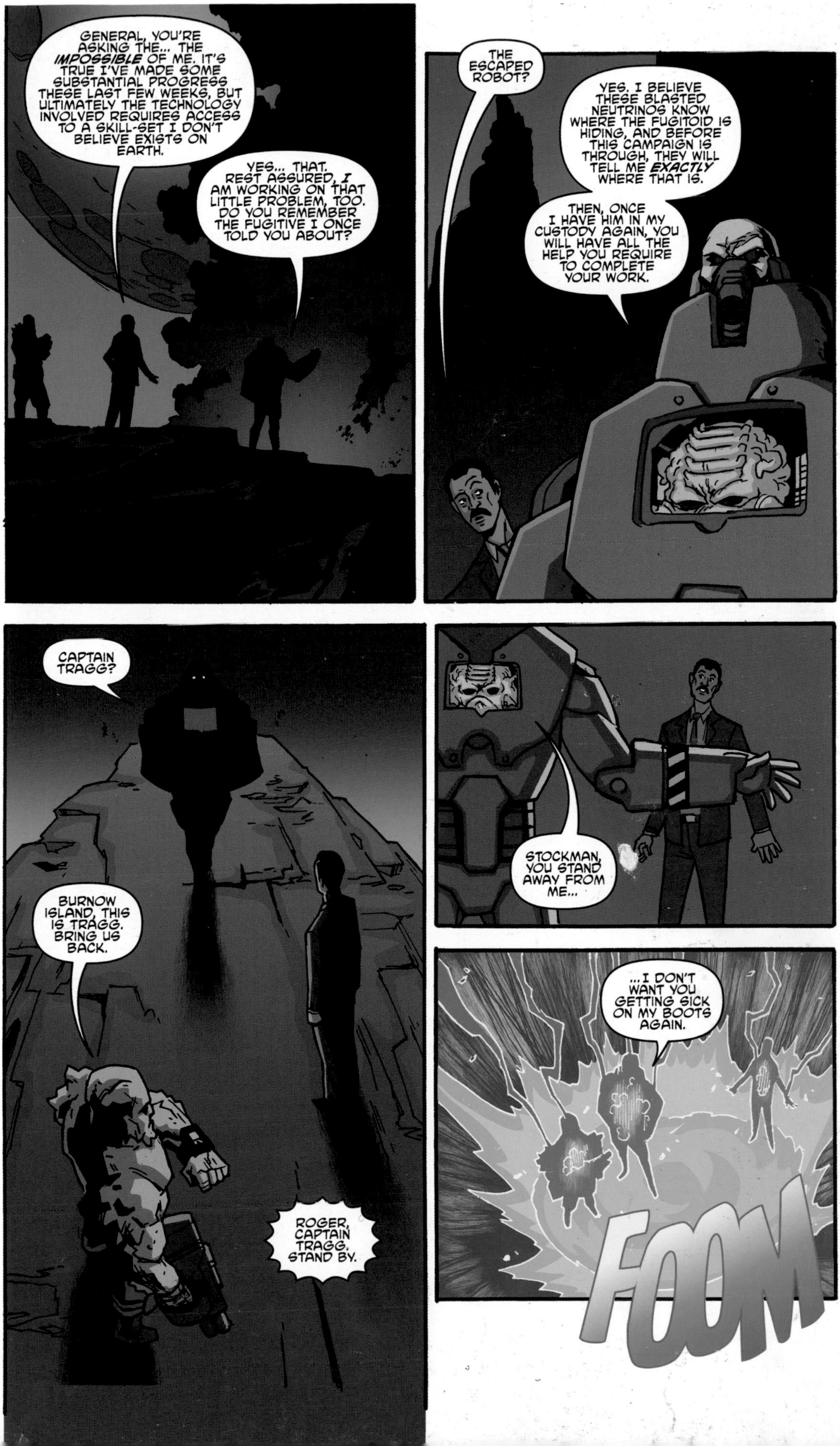
GENERAL, YOU'RE ASKING THE... THE *IMPOSSIBLE* OF ME. IT'S TRUE I'VE MADE SOME SUBSTANTIAL PROGRESS THESE LAST FEW WEEKS, BUT ULTIMATELY THE TECHNOLOGY INVOLVED REQUIRES ACCESS TO A SKILL-SET I DON'T BELIEVE EXISTS ON EARTH.
YES... THAT. REST ASSURED, *I* AM WORKING ON THAT LITTLE PROBLEM, TOO. DO YOU REMEMBER THE FUGITIVE I ONCE TOLD YOU ABOUT?
THE ESCAPED ROBOT?
YES. I BELIEVE THESE BLASTED NEUTRINOS KNOW WHERE THE FUGITOID IS HIDING, AND BEFORE THIS CAMPAIGN IS THROUGH, THEY WILL TELL ME *EXACTLY* WHERE THAT IS.
THEN, ONCE I HAVE HIM IN MY CUSTODY AGAIN, YOU WILL HAVE ALL THE HELP YOU REQUIRE TO COMPLETE YOUR WORK.
CAPTAIN TRAGG?
BURNOW ISLAND, THIS IS TRAGG. BRING US BACK.
ROGER, CAPTAIN TRAGG. STAND BY.
STOCKMAN, YOU STAND AWAY FROM ME...
...I DON'T WANT YOU GETTING SICK ON MY BOOTS AGAIN.
FOOM

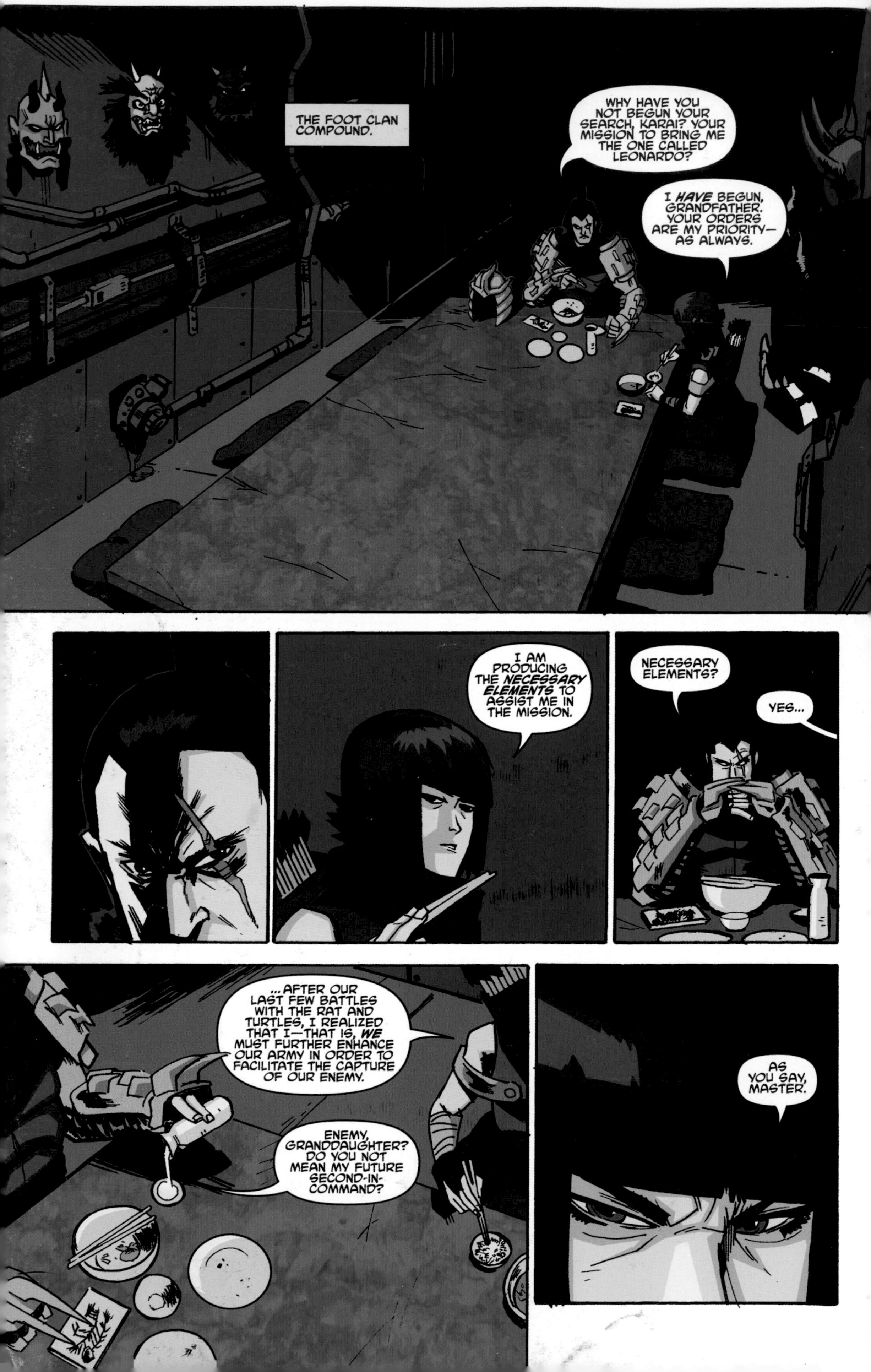
THE FOOT CLAN COMPOUND.
WHY HAVE YOU NOT BEGUN YOUR SEARCH, KARAI? YOUR MISSION TO BRING ME THE ONE CALLED LEONARDO?
I HAVE BEGUN, GRANDFATHER. YOUR ORDERS ARE MY PRIORITY— AS ALWAYS.
I AM PRODUCING THE NECESSARY ELEMENTS TO ASSIST ME IN THE MISSION.
NECESSARY ELEMENTS?
YES...
...AFTER OUR LAST FEW BATTLES WITH THE RAT AND TURTLES, I REALIZED THAT I—THAT IS, WE MUST FURTHER ENHANCE OUR ARMY IN ORDER TO FACILITATE THE CAPTURE OF OUR ENEMY.
ENEMY, GRANDDAUGHTER? DO YOU NOT MEAN MY FUTURE SECOND-IN-COMMAND?
AS YOU SAY, MASTER.

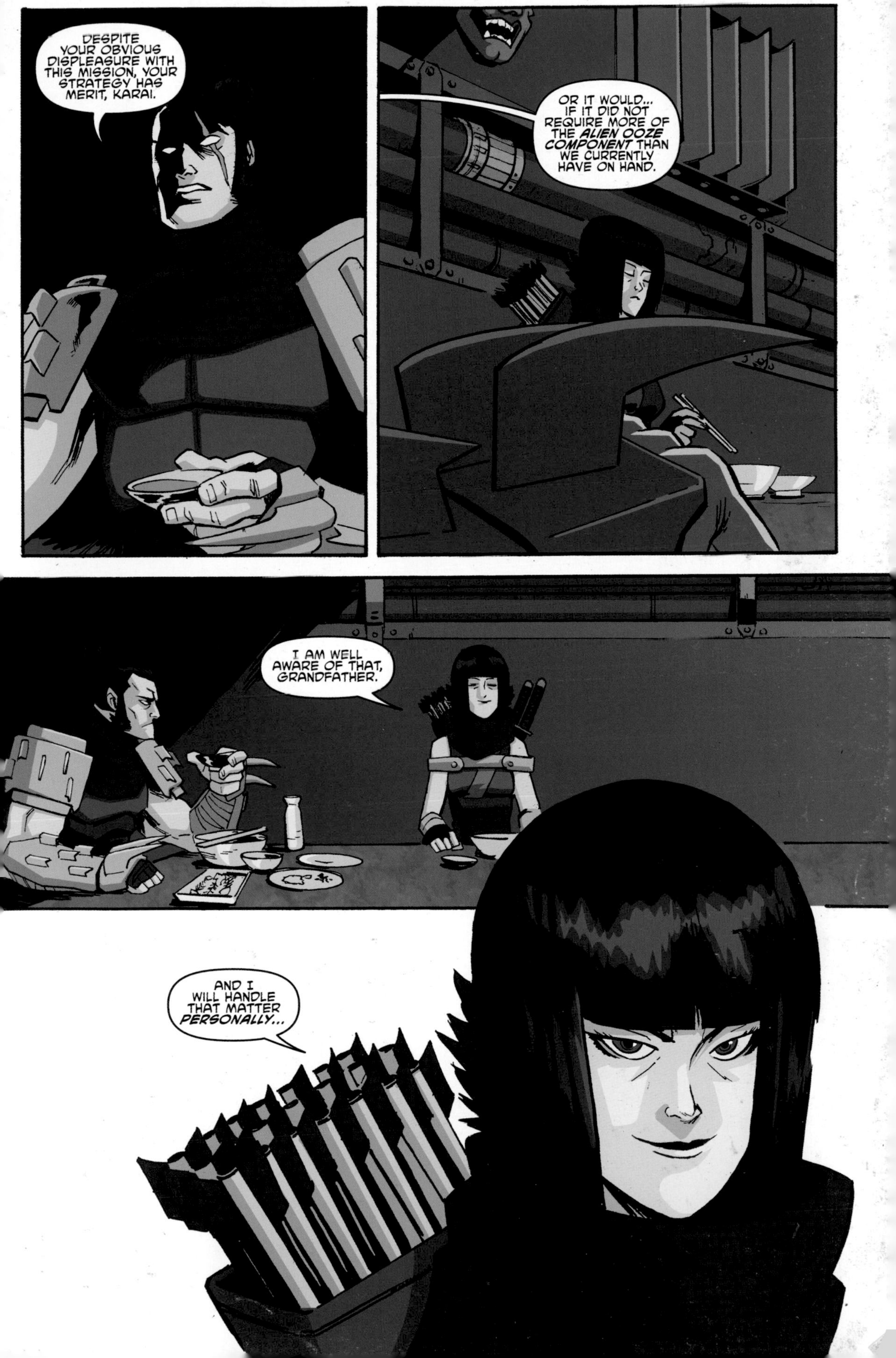
DESPITE YOUR OBVIOUS DISPLEASURE WITH THIS MISSION, YOUR STRATEGY HAS MERIT, KARAI.
OR IT WOULD... IF IT DID NOT REQUIRE MORE OF THE ALIEN OOZE COMPONENT THAN WE CURRENTLY HAVE ON HAND.
I AM WELL AWARE OF THAT, GRANDFATHER.
AND I WILL HANDLE THAT MATTER PERSONALLY...

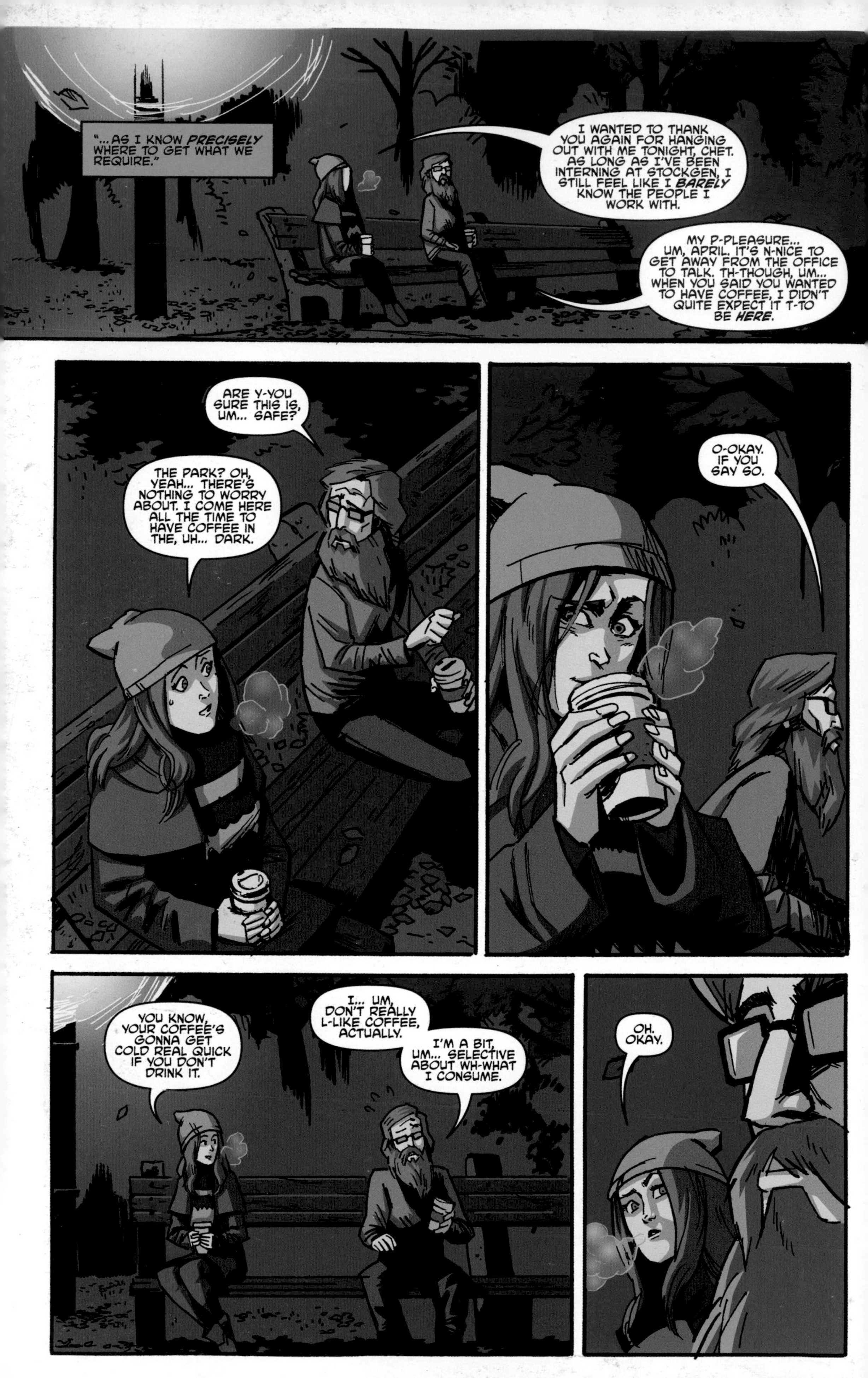
"...AS I KNOW PRECISELY WHERE TO GET WHAT WE REQUIRE."
I WANTED TO THANK YOU AGAIN FOR HANGING OUT WITH ME TONIGHT, CHET. AS LONG AS I'VE BEEN INTERNING AT STOCKGEN, I STILL FEEL LIKE I BARELY KNOW THE PEOPLE I WORK WITH.
MY P-PLEASURE... UM, APRIL. IT'S N-NICE TO GET AWAY FROM THE OFFICE TO TALK. TH-THOUGH, UM... WHEN YOU SAID YOU WANTED TO HAVE COFFEE, I DIDN'T QUITE EXPECT IT T-TO BE HERE.
ARE Y-YOU SURE THIS IS, UM... SAFE?
THE PARK? OH, YEAH... THERE'S NOTHING TO WORRY ABOUT. I COME HERE ALL THE TIME TO HAVE COFFEE IN THE, UH... DARK.
O-OKAY. IF YOU SAY SO.
YOU KNOW, YOUR COFFEE'S GONNA GET COLD REAL QUICK IF YOU DON'T DRINK IT.
I... UM, DON'T REALLY L-LIKE COFFEE, ACTUALLY.
I'M A BIT, UM... SELECTIVE ABOUT WH-WHAT I CONSUME.
OH. OKAY.

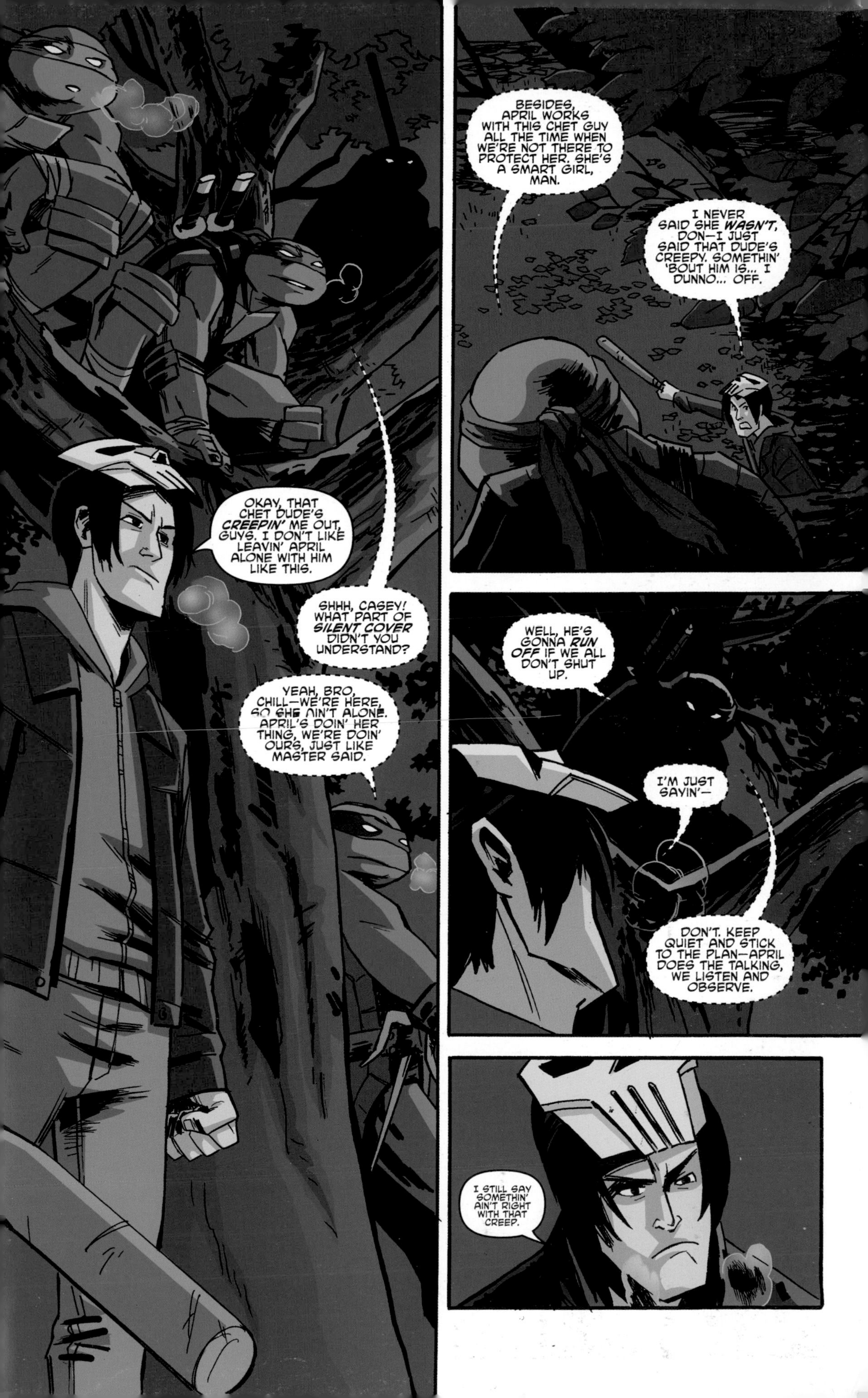
OKAY, THAT CHET DUDE'S *CREEPIN'* ME OUT, GUYS. I DON'T LIKE LEAVIN' APRIL ALONE WITH HIM LIKE THIS.
SHHH, CASEY! WHAT PART OF *SILENT COVER* DIDN'T YOU UNDERSTAND?
YEAH, BRO, CHILL—WE'RE HERE, SO SHE AIN'T ALONE. APRIL'S DOIN' HER THING, WE'RE DOIN' OURS, JUST LIKE MASTER SAID.
BESIDES, APRIL WORKS WITH THIS CHET GUY ALL THE TIME WHEN WE'RE NOT THERE TO PROTECT HER. SHE'S A SMART GIRL, MAN.
I NEVER SAID SHE *WASN'T*, DON—I JUST SAID THAT DUDE'S CREEPY. SOMETHIN' 'BOUT HIM IS... I DUNNO... OFF.
WELL, HE'S GONNA *RUN OFF* IF WE ALL DON'T SHUT UP.
I'M JUST SAYIN'—
DON'T. KEEP QUIET AND STICK TO THE PLAN—APRIL DOES THE TALKING, WE LISTEN AND OBSERVE.
I STILL SAY SOMETHIN' AIN'T RIGHT WITH THAT CREEP.

CHET, I HAVE TO ADMIT SOMETHING—I DIDN'T JUST INVITE YOU HERE FOR SMALL TALK. I'M WORRIED. I'VE BEEN NOTICING THINGS AT STOCKGEN... SOME REALLY *ODD STUFF* THAT, HONESTLY, DOESN'T SIT TOO WELL WITH ME.

ODD? H-HOW DO YOU MEAN?

I MEAN, ALL THAT ADVANCED TECHNOLOGY, THE SECRET TESTS, THE LOCKED DOORS AND ALL THAT HIGH SECURITY—

—YOU KNOW, IF A PERSON DIDN'T KNOW BETTER, THEY MIGHT THINK THERE WAS *A LOT MORE* GOING ON THERE THAN ADVERTISED.

MORE?

YEAH... MAYBE SOMETHING UNETHICAL OR ILLEGAL. OR BOTH.

WELL, I WOULDN'T S—

OF COURSE, THAT'S *SILLY*, RIGHT? I'M JUST AN INTERN, BUT EVEN I KNOW ABOUT CORPORATE ESPIONAGE. I'M SURE DOCTOR STOCKMAN'S JUST TRYING TO PROTECT THE COMPANY FROM ITS COMPETITORS.

I MEAN, WE'VE ALREADY SEEN HOW VICIOUS *THEY* CAN BE, RIGHT?

WHO?

STOCKGEN'S COMPETITORS.

WE H-HAVE?

SURE—WHEN THOSE NINJA GUYS ATTACKED ME THAT NIGHT IN THE LABS, REMEMBER? THEY STOLE A BUNCH OF STUFF AND NEARLY KILLED ME IN THE PROCESS.

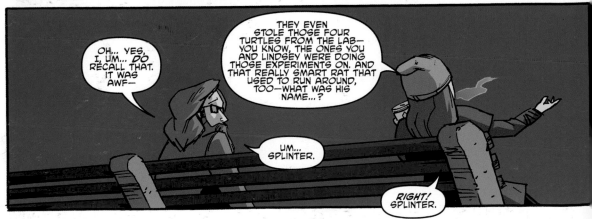

OH... YES, I, UM... *DO* RECALL THAT. IT WAS AWF—

THEY EVEN STOLE THOSE FOUR TURTLES FROM THE LAB— YOU KNOW, THE ONES YOU AND LINDSEY WERE DOING THOSE EXPERIMENTS ON. AND THAT REALLY SMART RAT THAT USED TO RUN AROUND, TOO—WHAT WAS HIS NAME...?

UM... SPLINTER.

RIGHT! SPLINTER.

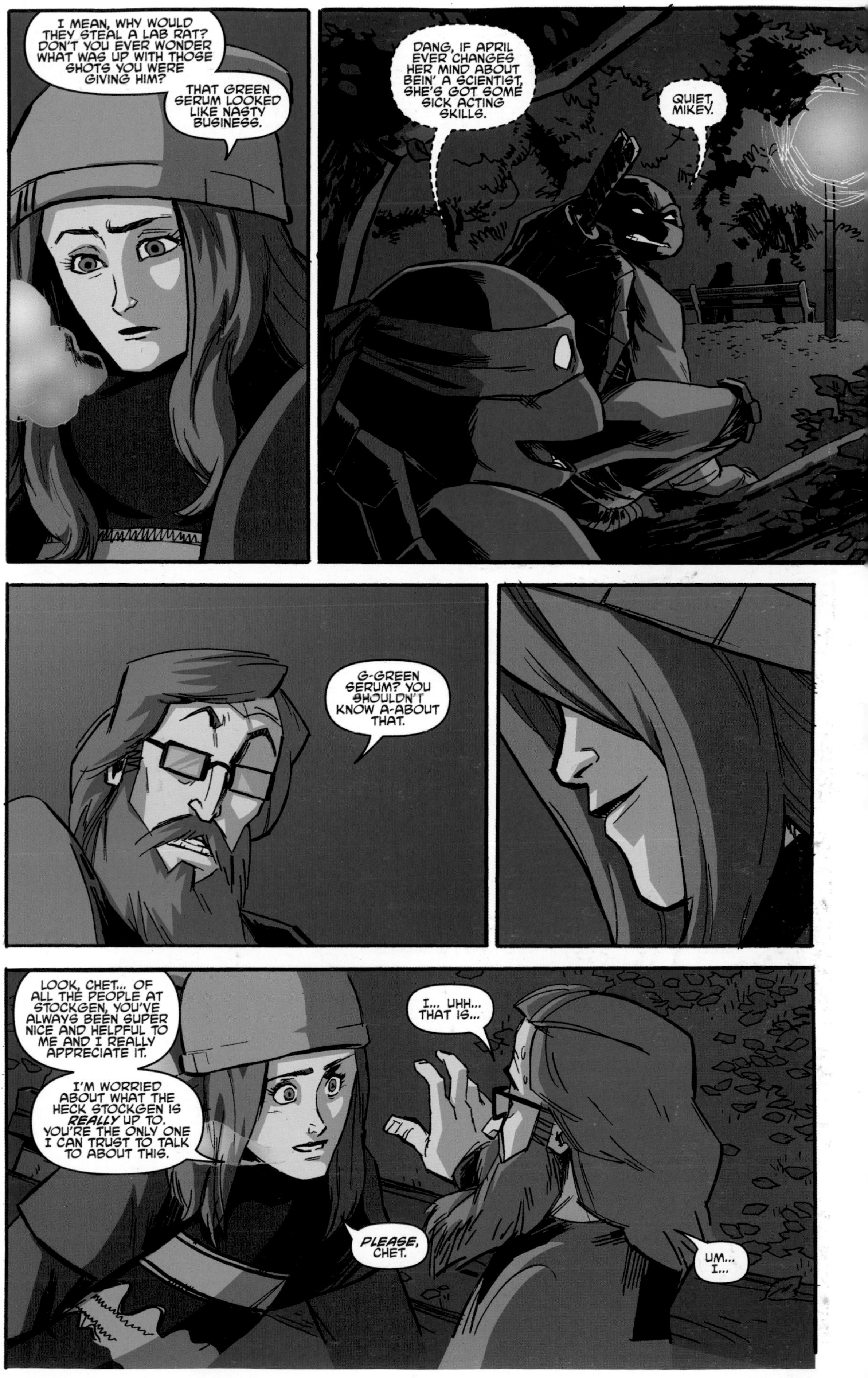
I MEAN, WHY WOULD THEY STEAL A LAB RAT? DON'T YOU EVER WONDER WHAT WAS UP WITH THOSE SHOTS YOU WERE GIVING HIM?
THAT GREEN SERUM LOOKED LIKE NASTY BUSINESS.
DANG, IF APRIL EVER CHANGES HER MIND ABOUT BEIN' A SCIENTIST, SHE'S GOT SOME SICK ACTING SKILLS.
QUIET, MIKEY.
G-GREEN SERUM? YOU SHOULDN'T KNOW A-ABOUT THAT.
LOOK, CHET... OF ALL THE PEOPLE AT STOCKGEN, YOU'VE ALWAYS BEEN SUPER NICE AND HELPFUL TO ME AND I REALLY APPRECIATE IT.
I'M WORRIED ABOUT WHAT THE HECK STOCKGEN IS *REALLY* UP TO. YOU'RE THE ONLY ONE I CAN TRUST TO TALK TO ABOUT THIS.
I... UHH... THAT IS...
PLEASE, CHET.
UM... I...

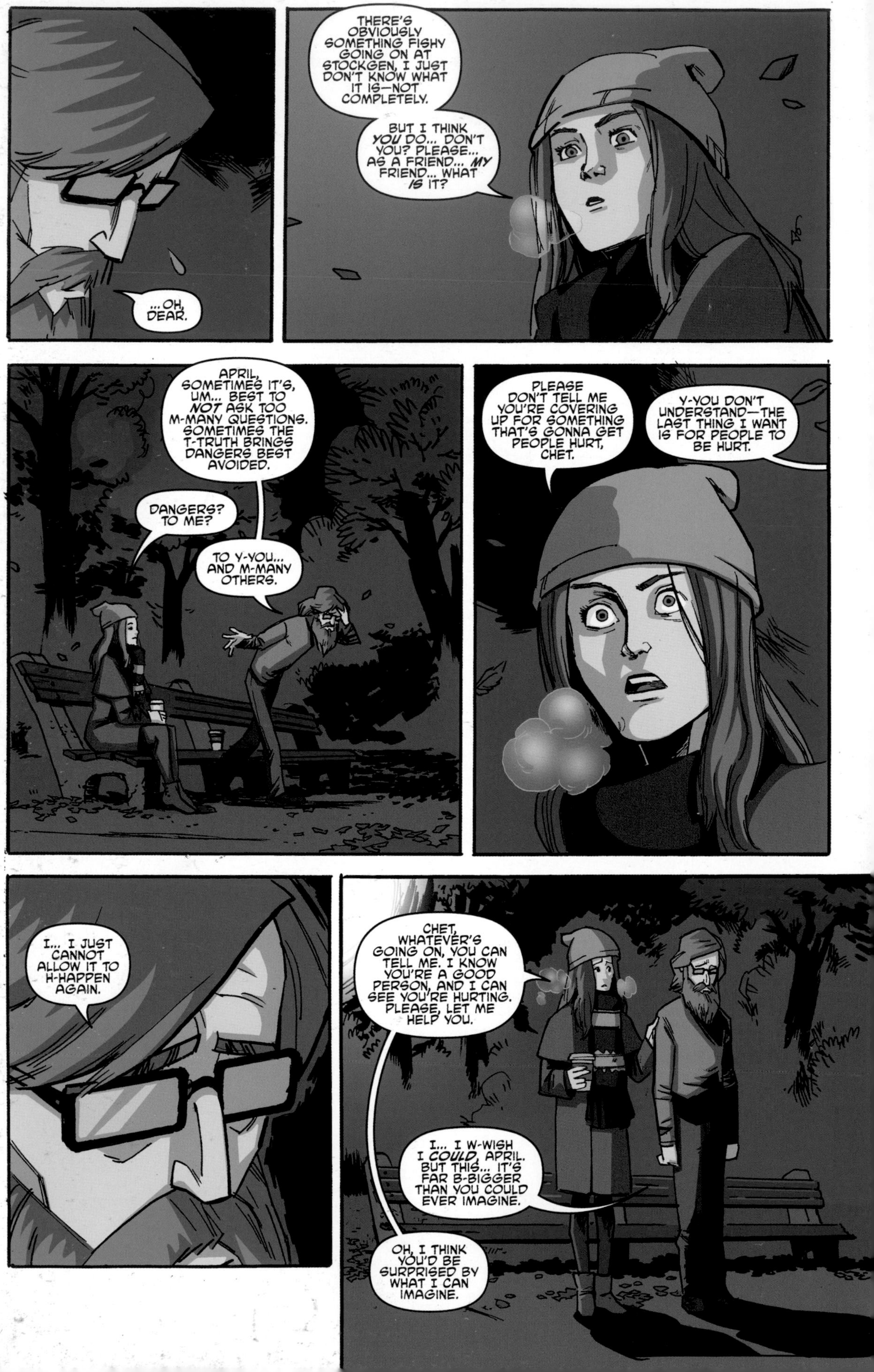
THERE'S OBVIOUSLY SOMETHING FISHY GOING ON AT STOCKGEN, I JUST DON'T KNOW WHAT IT IS—NOT COMPLETELY.
BUT I THINK YOU DO... DON'T YOU? PLEASE... AS A FRIEND... MY FRIEND... WHAT IS IT?
...OH, DEAR.
APRIL, SOMETIMES IT'S, UM... BEST TO NOT ASK TOO M-MANY QUESTIONS. SOMETIMES THE T-TRUTH BRINGS DANGERS BEST AVOIDED.
DANGERS? TO ME?
TO Y-YOU... AND M-MANY OTHERS.
PLEASE DON'T TELL ME YOU'RE COVERING UP FOR SOMETHING THAT'S GONNA GET PEOPLE HURT, CHET.
Y-YOU DON'T UNDERSTAND—THE LAST THING I WANT IS FOR PEOPLE TO BE HURT.
I... I JUST CANNOT ALLOW IT TO H-HAPPEN AGAIN.
CHET, WHATEVER'S GOING ON, YOU CAN TELL ME. I KNOW YOU'RE A GOOD PERSON, AND I CAN SEE YOU'RE HURTING. PLEASE, LET ME HELP YOU.
I... I W-WISH I COULD, APRIL. BUT THIS... IT'S FAR B-BIGGER THAN YOU COULD EVER IMAGINE.
OH, I THINK YOU'D BE SURPRISED BY WHAT I CAN IMAGINE.

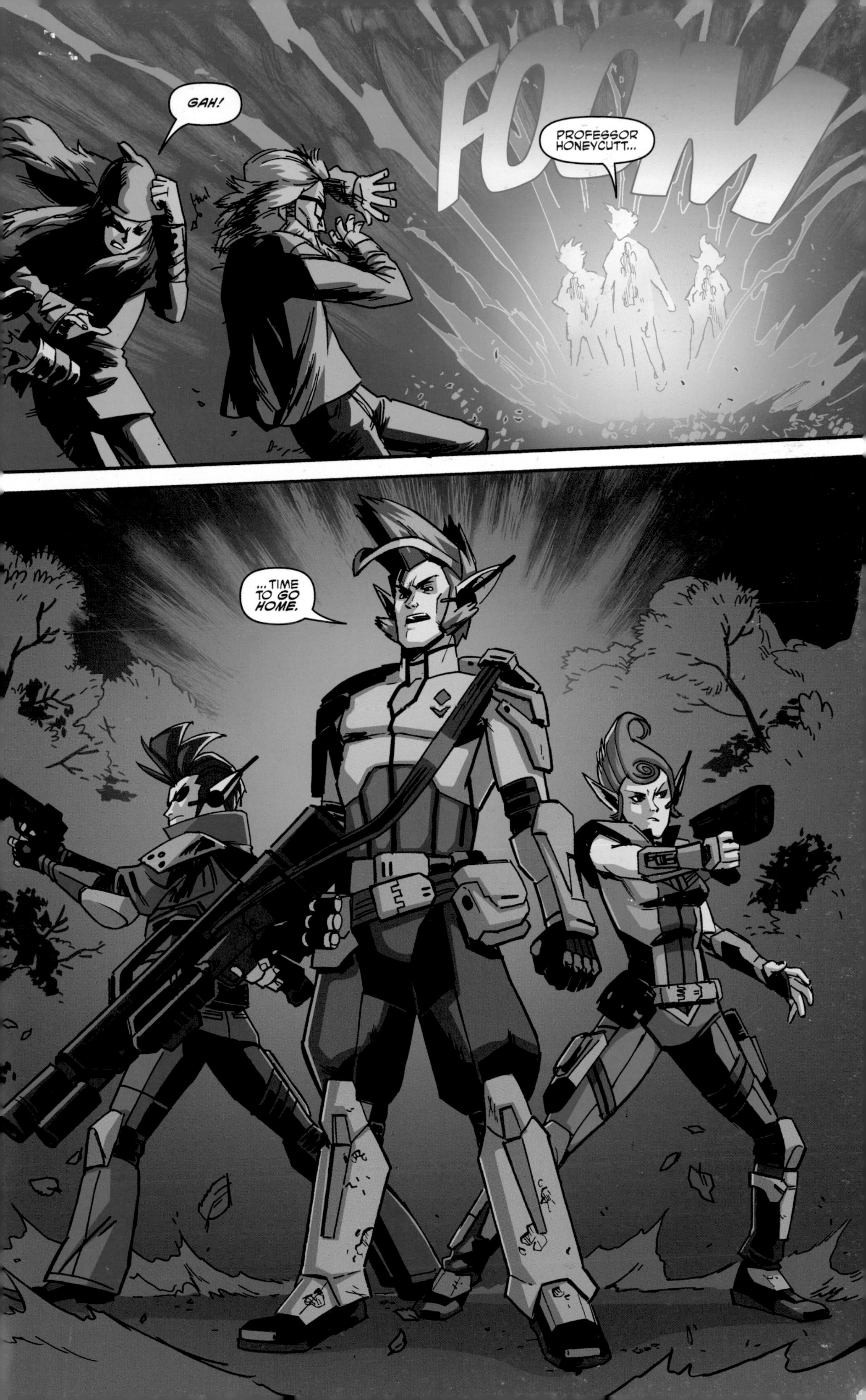
GAH!
FOOM
PROFESSOR HONEYCUTT...
...TIME TO GO HOME.

I *KNEW* SOMETHIN' WAS WRONG WITH THAT DUDE!

WHERE THE HELL DID *THEY* COME FROM?

WHO CARES?! WE GOTTA GET APRIL *OUTTA* THERE!

CRIPES, SO MUCH FOR OUR PLAN OF LAYING LOW.

IT WAS A BORING PLAN, ANYWAYS. *LET'S GO!*

COMMANDER DASK... H-HOW DID YOU FIND ME?

HONEYCUTT? PORTAL? CHET... WHAT THE HECK'S GOING ON? WHO *ARE* THESE PEOPLE?

NO TIME FOR THAT, HONEYCUTT—WE NEED TO GET YOU BACK THROUGH THE PORTAL NOW—BY ORDER OF KING ZENTER.

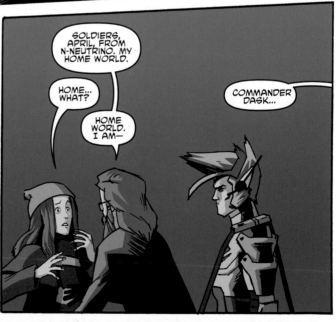

SOLDIERS, APRIL, FROM N-NEUTRINO. MY HOME WORLD.

HOME... WHAT?

HOME WORLD. I AM—

COMMANDER DASK...

...DON'T MEAN TO INTERRUPT, SIR, BUT...

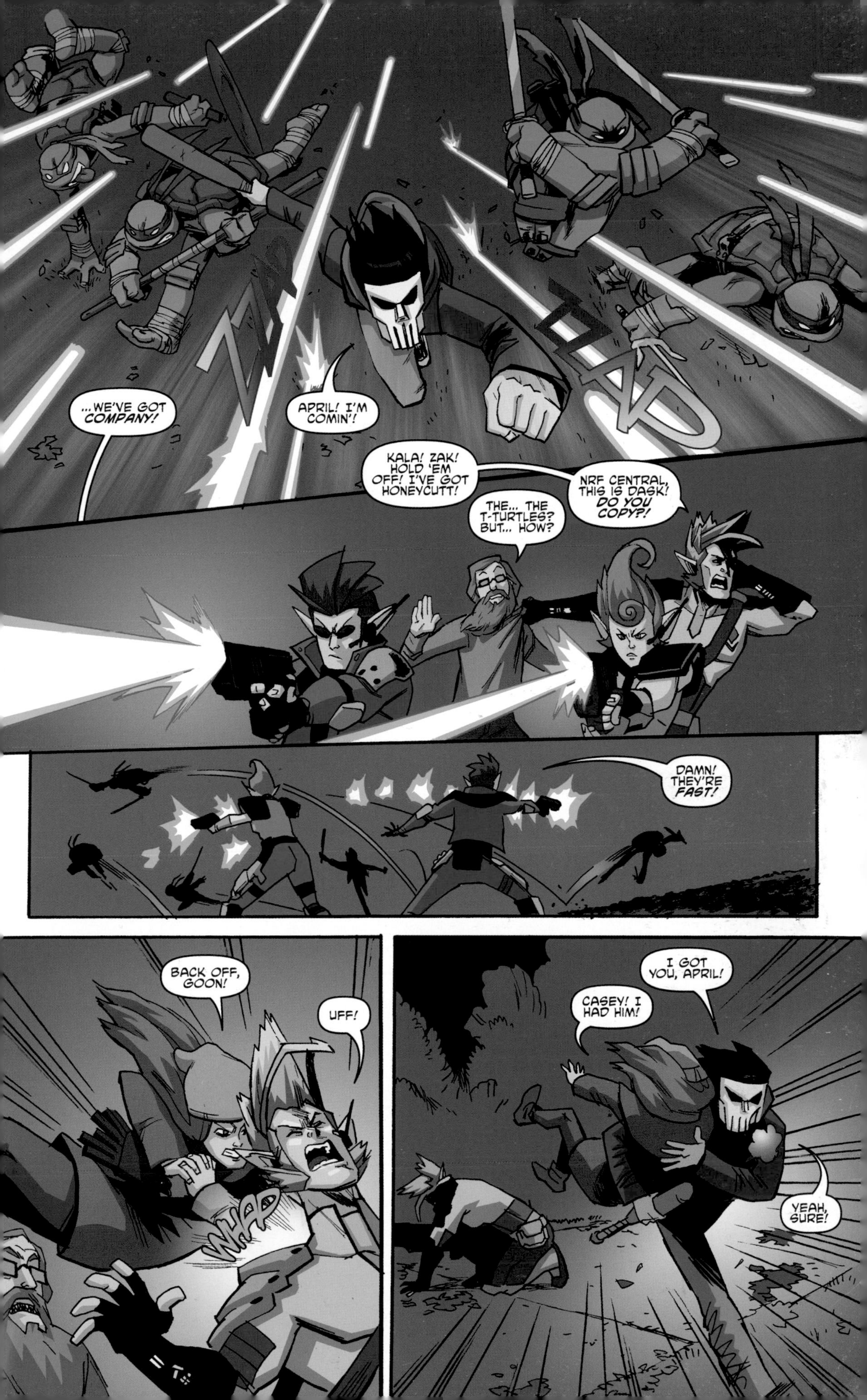
...WE'VE GOT COMPANY!
APRIL! I'M COMIN'!
KALA! ZAK! HOLD 'EM OFF! I'VE GOT HONEYCUTT!
NRF CENTRAL, THIS IS DASK! DO YOU COPY?!
THE... THE T-TURTLES? BUT... HOW?
DAMN! THEY'RE FAST!
BACK OFF, GOON!
UFF!
WHAP
I GOT YOU, APRIL!
CASEY! I HAD HIM!
YEAH, SURE!

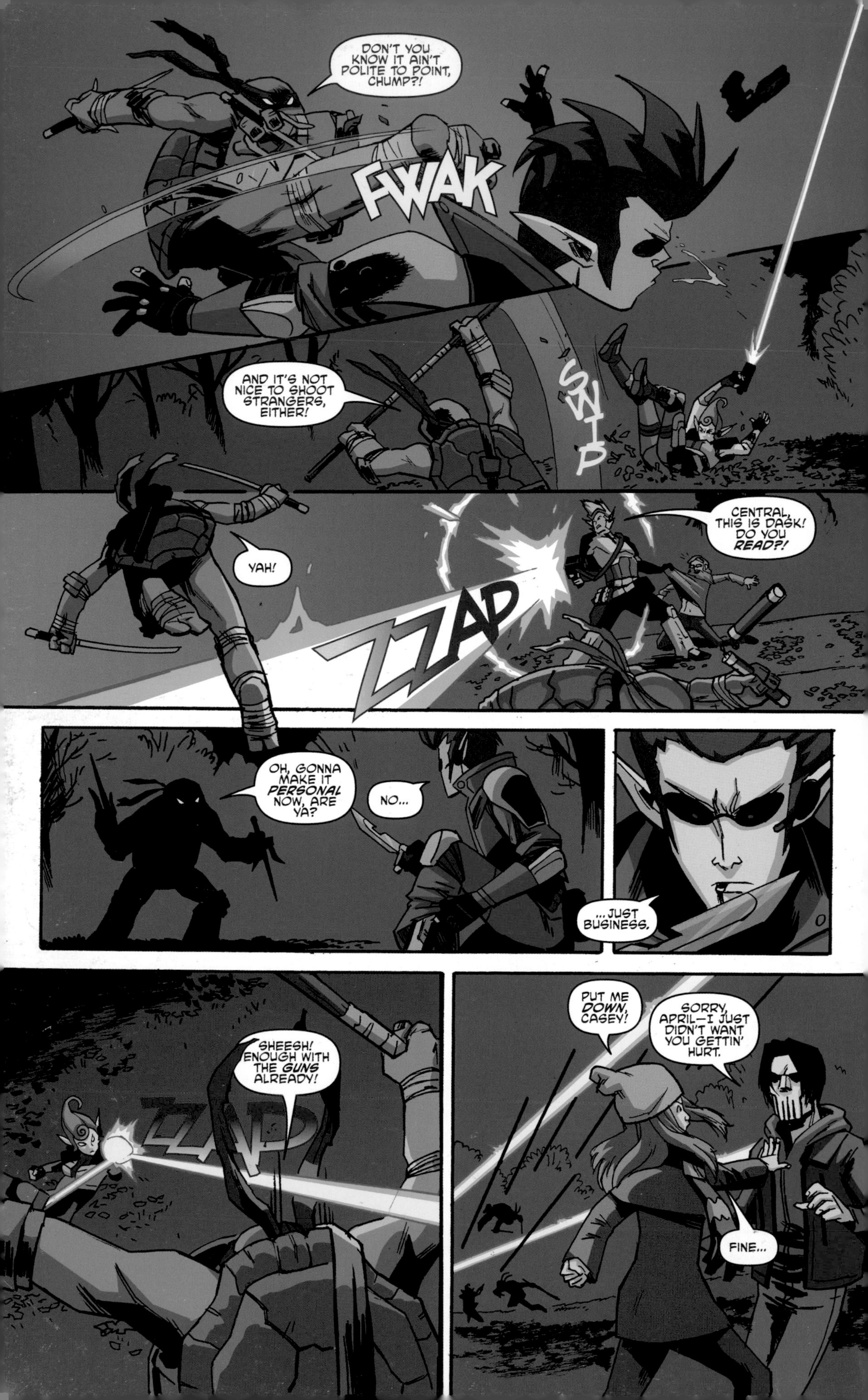
DON'T YOU KNOW IT AIN'T POLITE TO POINT, CHUMP?!
FWAK
AND IT'S NOT NICE TO SHOOT STRANGERS, EITHER!
SWIP
YAH!
CENTRAL, THIS IS DASK! DO YOU *READ?!*
ZZAP
OH, GONNA MAKE IT *PERSONAL* NOW, ARE YA?
NO...
...JUST BUSINESS.
SHEESH! ENOUGH WITH THE *GUNS* ALREADY!
ZZAP
PUT ME *DOWN*, CASEY!
SORRY, APRIL—I JUST DIDN'T WANT YOU GETTIN' HURT.
FINE...

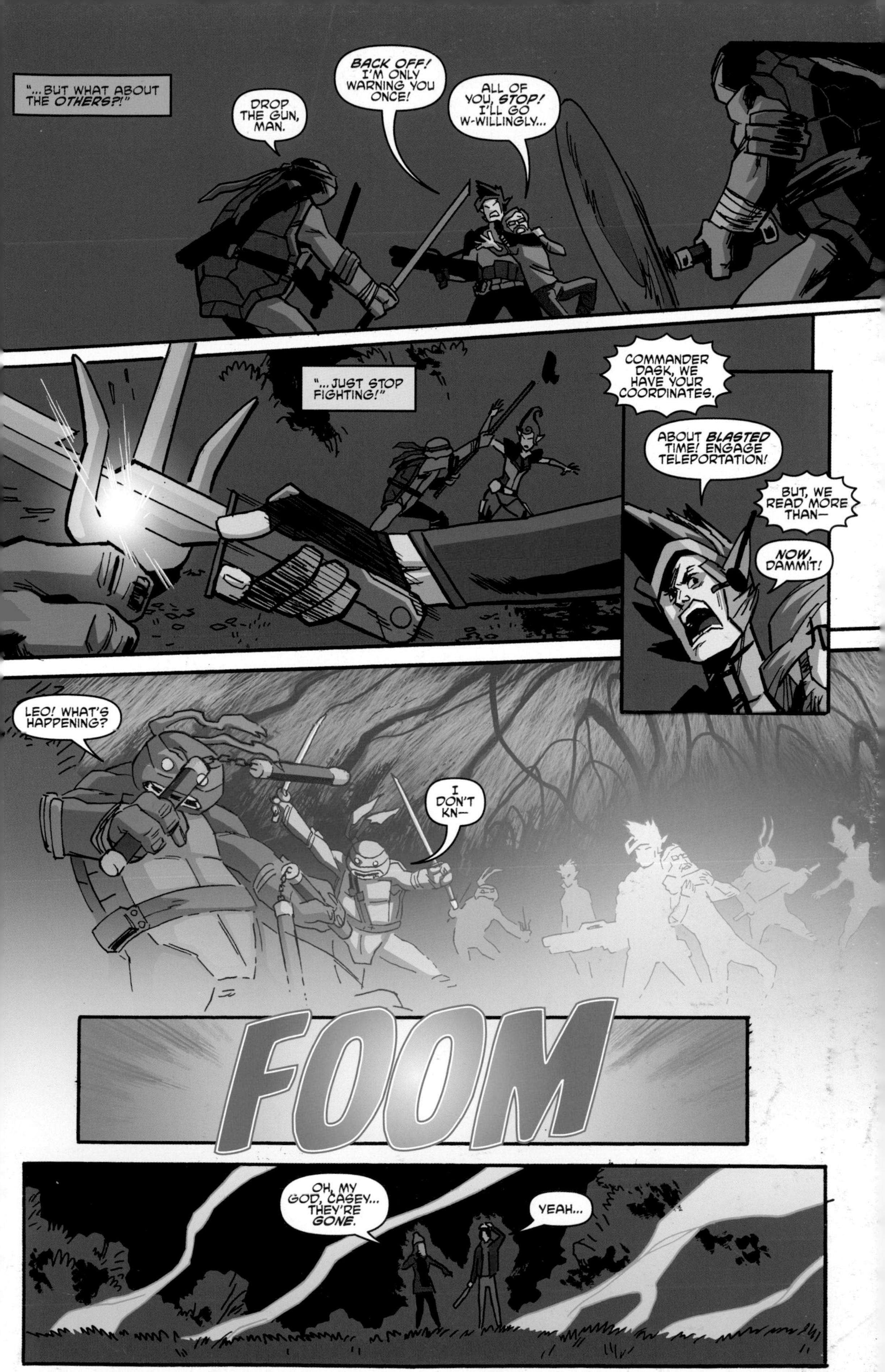
"...BUT WHAT ABOUT THE OTHERS?!"
DROP THE GUN, MAN.
BACK OFF! I'M ONLY WARNING YOU ONCE!
ALL OF YOU, STOP! I'LL GO W-WILLINGLY...
"...JUST STOP FIGHTING!"
COMMANDER DASK, WE HAVE YOUR COORDINATES.
ABOUT BLASTED TIME! ENGAGE TELEPORTATION!
BUT, WE READ MORE THAN—
NOW, DAMMIT!
LEO! WHAT'S HAPPENING?
I DON'T KN—
FOOM
OH, MY GOD, CASEY... THEY'RE GONE.
YEAH...

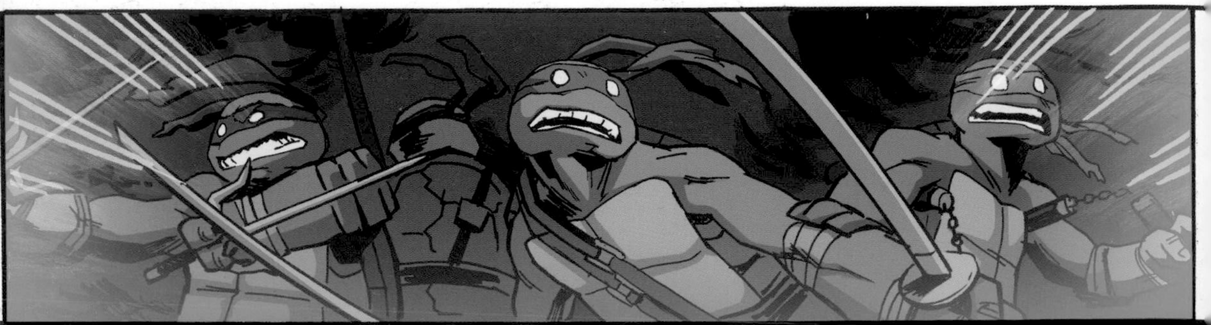

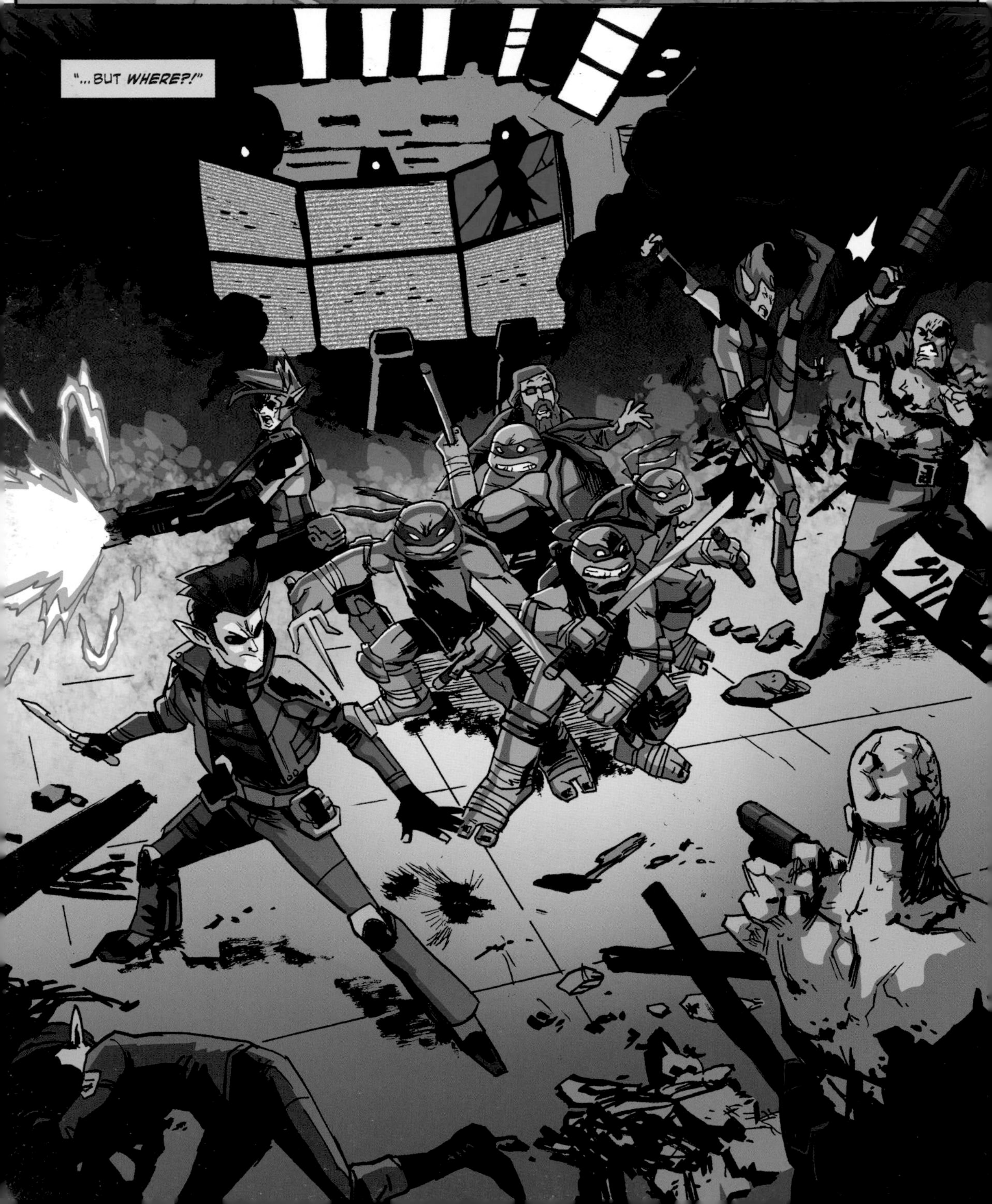
"...BUT WHERE?!"

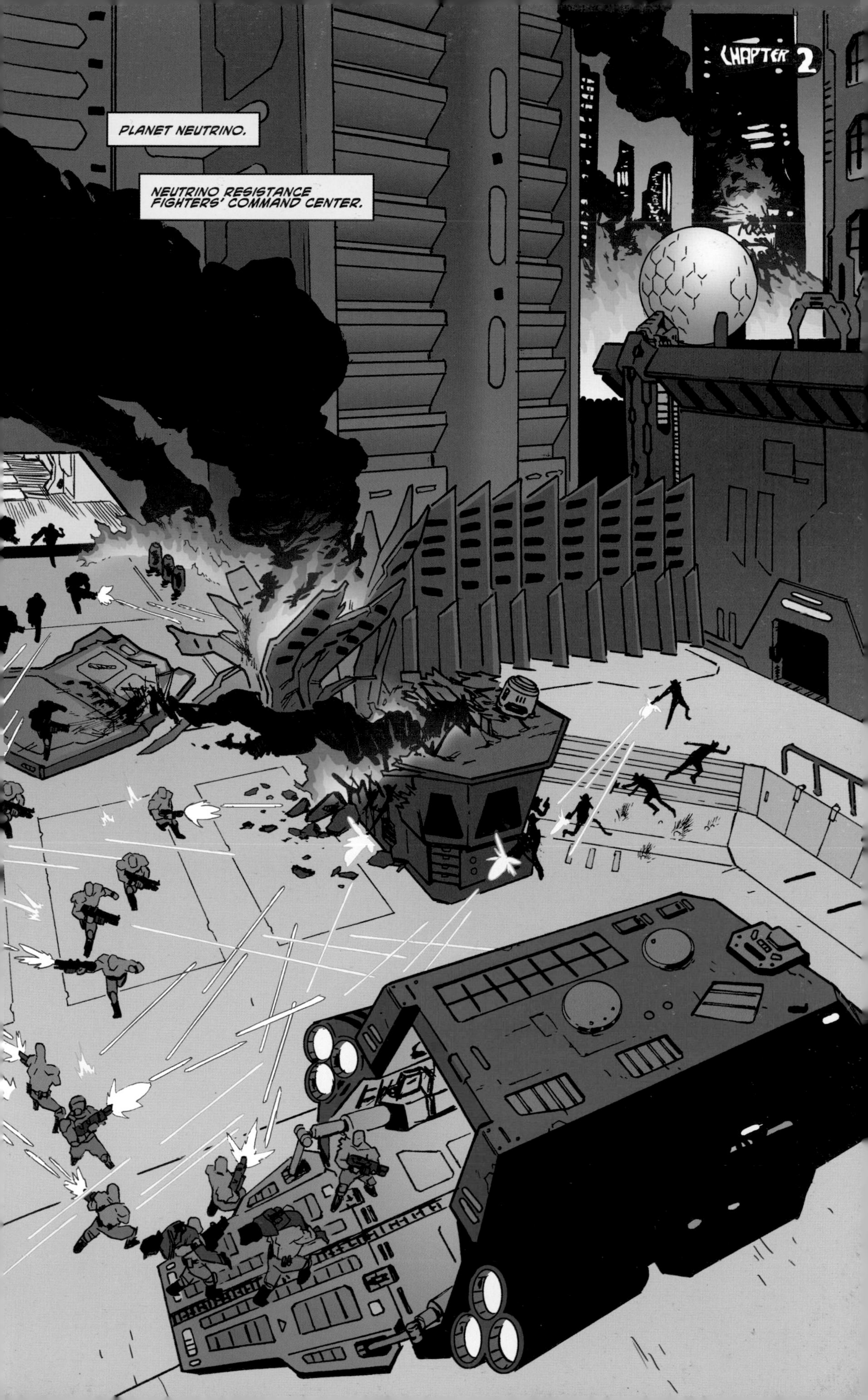
CHAPTER 2
PLANET NEUTRINO.
NEUTRINO RESISTANCE FIGHTERS' COMMAND CENTER.

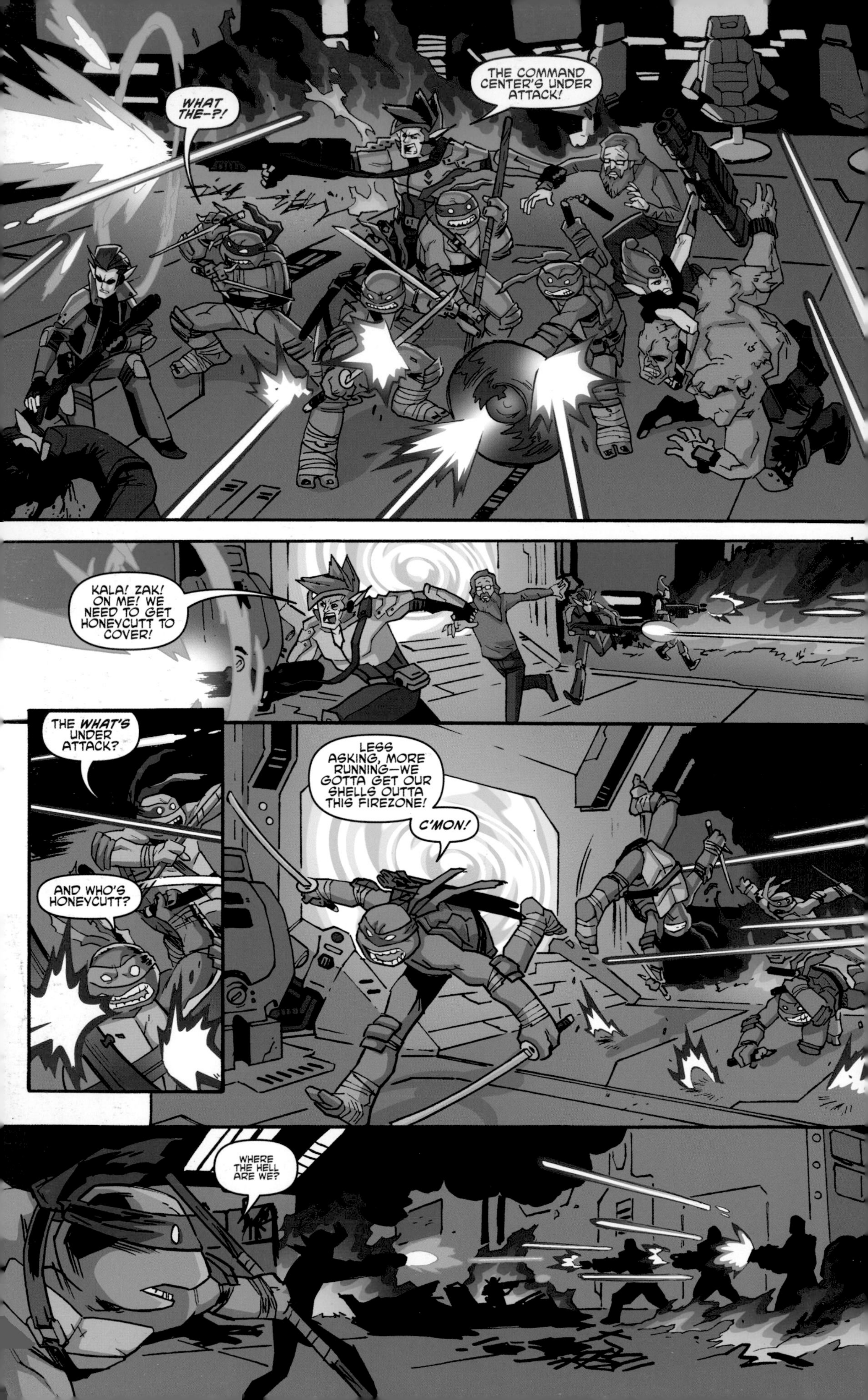
WHAT THE–?!
THE COMMAND CENTER'S UNDER ATTACK!
KALA! ZAK! ON ME! WE NEED TO GET HONEYCUTT TO COVER!
THE *WHAT'S* UNDER ATTACK?
AND WHO'S HONEYCUTT?
LESS ASKING, MORE RUNNING—WE GOTTA GET OUR SHELLS OUTTA THIS FIREZONE!
C'MON!
WHERE THE HELL ARE WE?

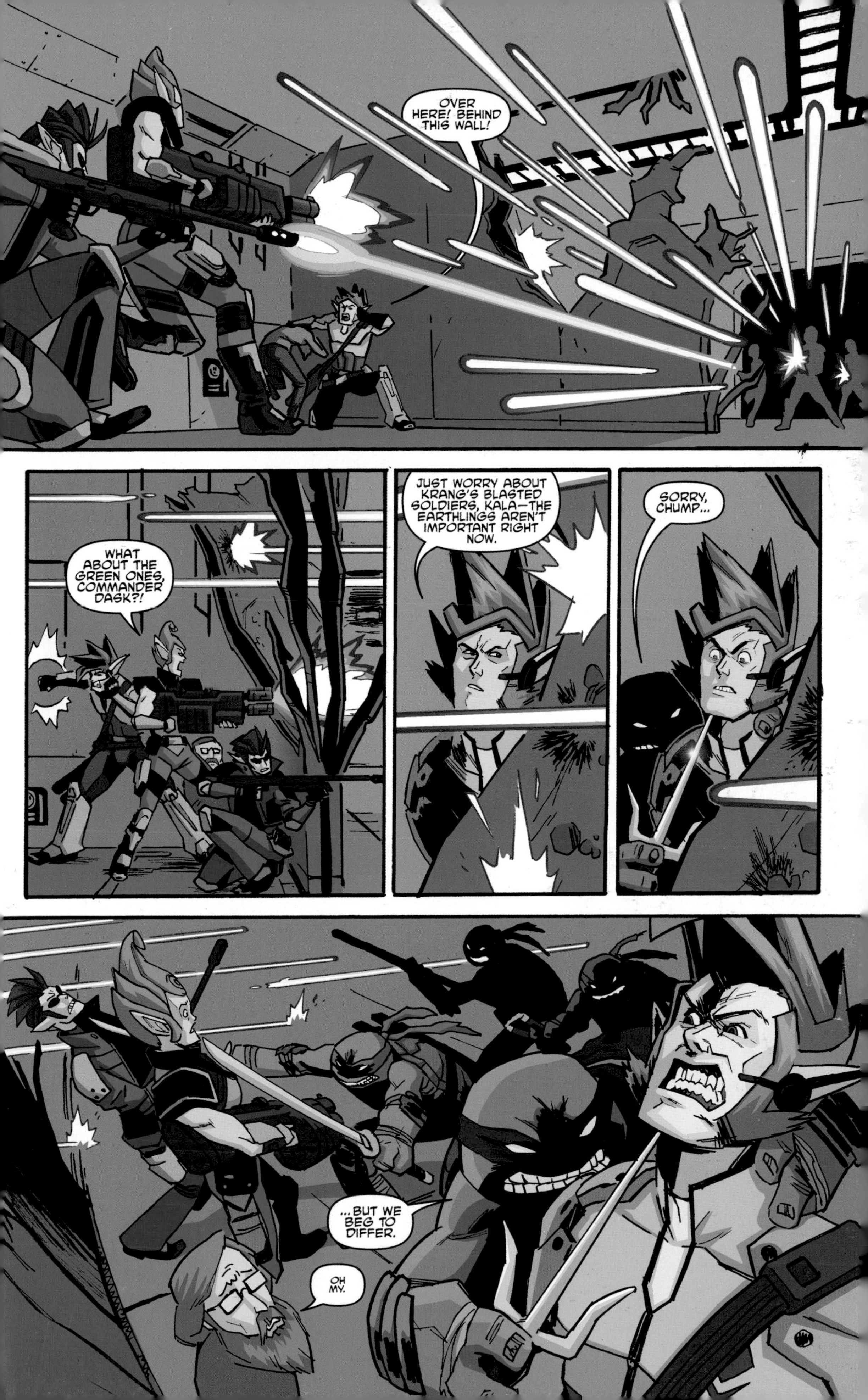

OVER HERE! BEHIND THIS WALL!
WHAT ABOUT THE GREEN ONES, COMMANDER DASK?!
JUST WORRY ABOUT KRANG'S BLASTED SOLDIERS, KALA—THE EARTHLINGS AREN'T IMPORTANT RIGHT NOW.
SORRY, CHUMP...
...BUT WE BEG TO DIFFER.
OH MY.

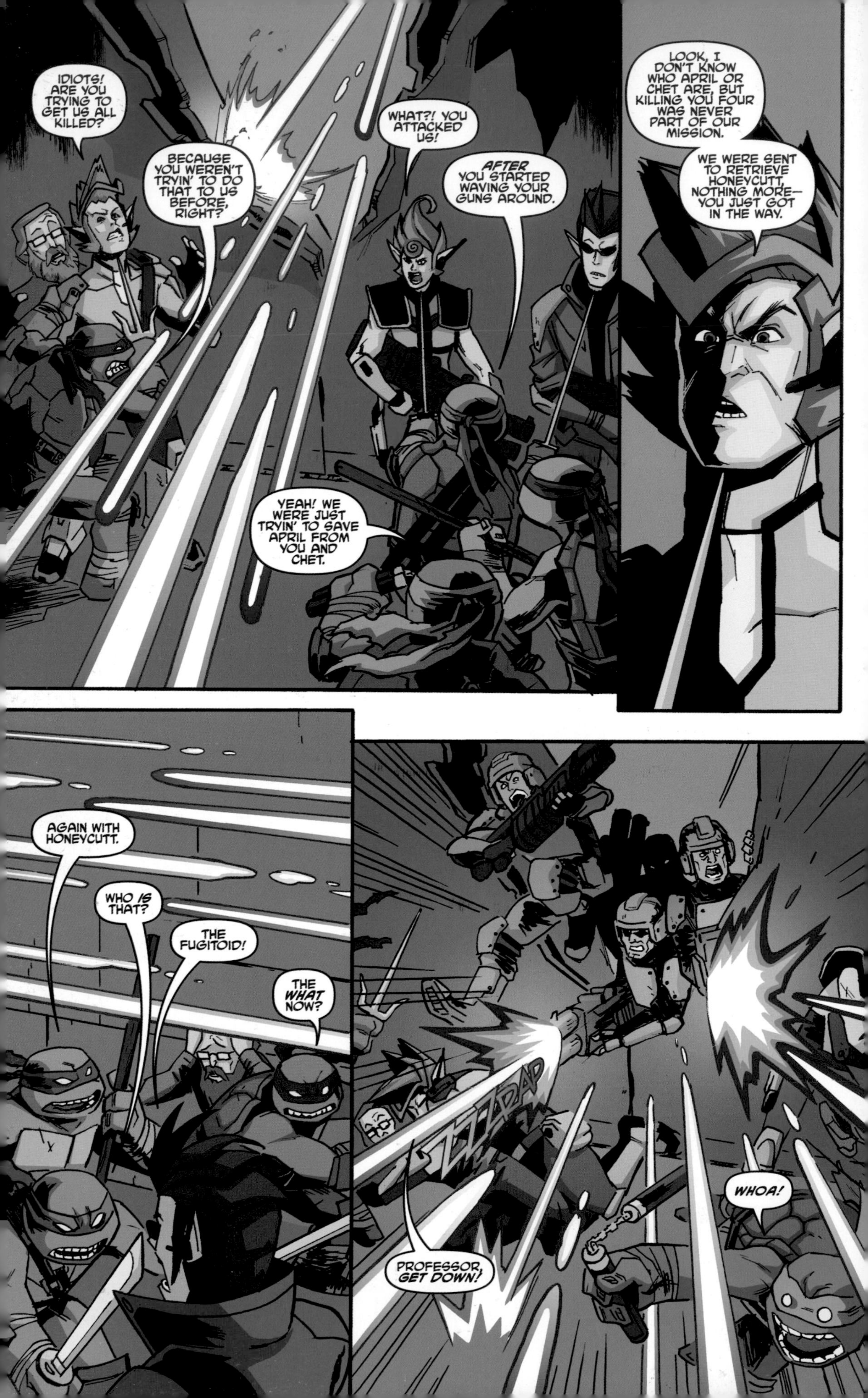
IDIOTS! ARE YOU TRYING TO GET US ALL KILLED?
BECAUSE YOU WEREN'T TRYIN' TO DO THAT TO US BEFORE, RIGHT?
WHAT?! YOU ATTACKED US!
AFTER YOU STARTED WAVING YOUR GUNS AROUND.
YEAH! WE WERE JUST TRYIN' TO SAVE APRIL FROM YOU AND CHET.
LOOK, I DON'T KNOW WHO APRIL OR CHET ARE, BUT KILLING YOU FOUR WAS NEVER PART OF OUR MISSION.
WE WERE SENT TO RETRIEVE HONEYCUTT, NOTHING MORE-- YOU JUST GOT IN THE WAY.
AGAIN WITH HONEYCUTT.
WHO IS THAT?
THE FUGITOID!
THE WHAT NOW?
ZZZZAP
PROFESSOR, GET DOWN!
WHOA!

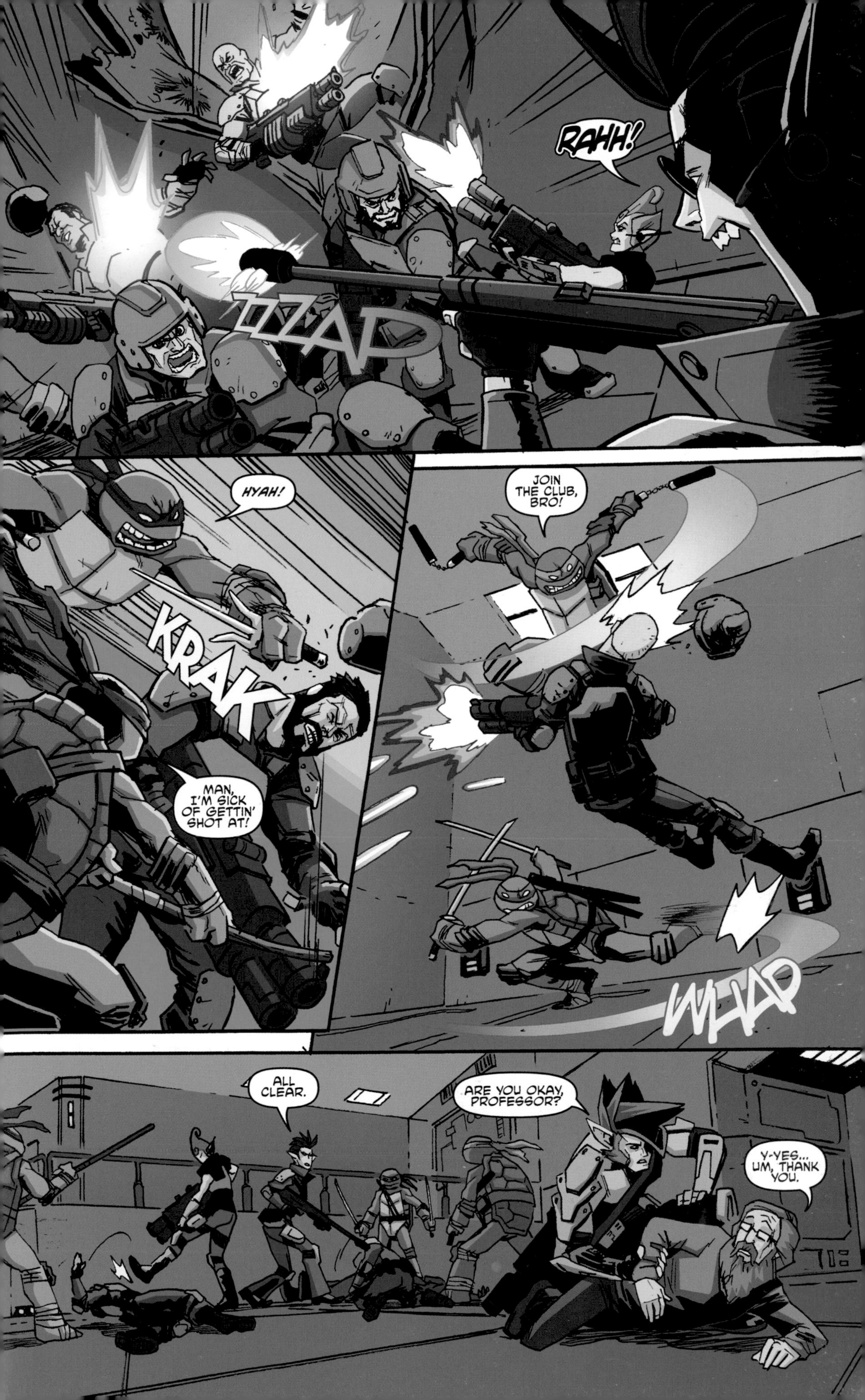
RAHH!
ZZZAP
HYAH!
KRAK
MAN, I'M SICK OF GETTIN' SHOT AT!
JOIN THE CLUB, BRO!
WHAP
ALL CLEAR.
ARE YOU OKAY, PROFESSOR?
Y-YES... UM, THANK YOU.

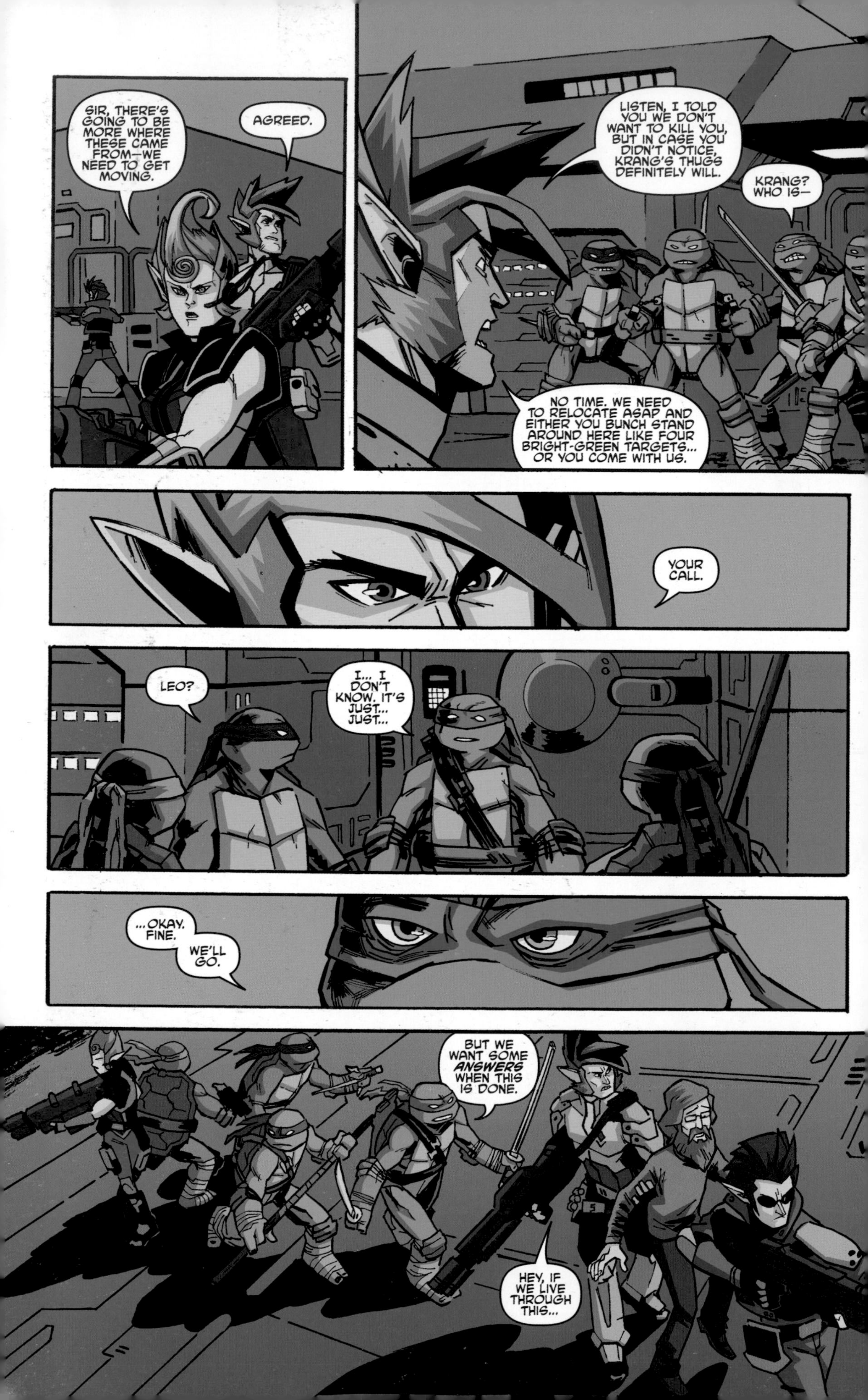
SIR, THERE'S GOING TO BE MORE WHERE THESE CAME FROM—WE NEED TO GET MOVING.
AGREED.
LISTEN, I TOLD YOU WE DON'T WANT TO KILL YOU, BUT IN CASE YOU DIDN'T NOTICE, KRANG'S THUGS DEFINITELY WILL.
KRANG? WHO IS—
NO TIME. WE NEED TO RELOCATE ASAP AND EITHER YOU BUNCH STAND AROUND HERE LIKE FOUR BRIGHT-GREEN TARGETS... OR YOU COME WITH US.
YOUR CALL.
LEO?
I... I DON'T KNOW. IT'S JUST... JUST...
...OKAY. FINE.
WE'LL GO.
BUT WE WANT SOME *ANSWERS* WHEN THIS IS DONE.
HEY, IF WE LIVE THROUGH THIS...

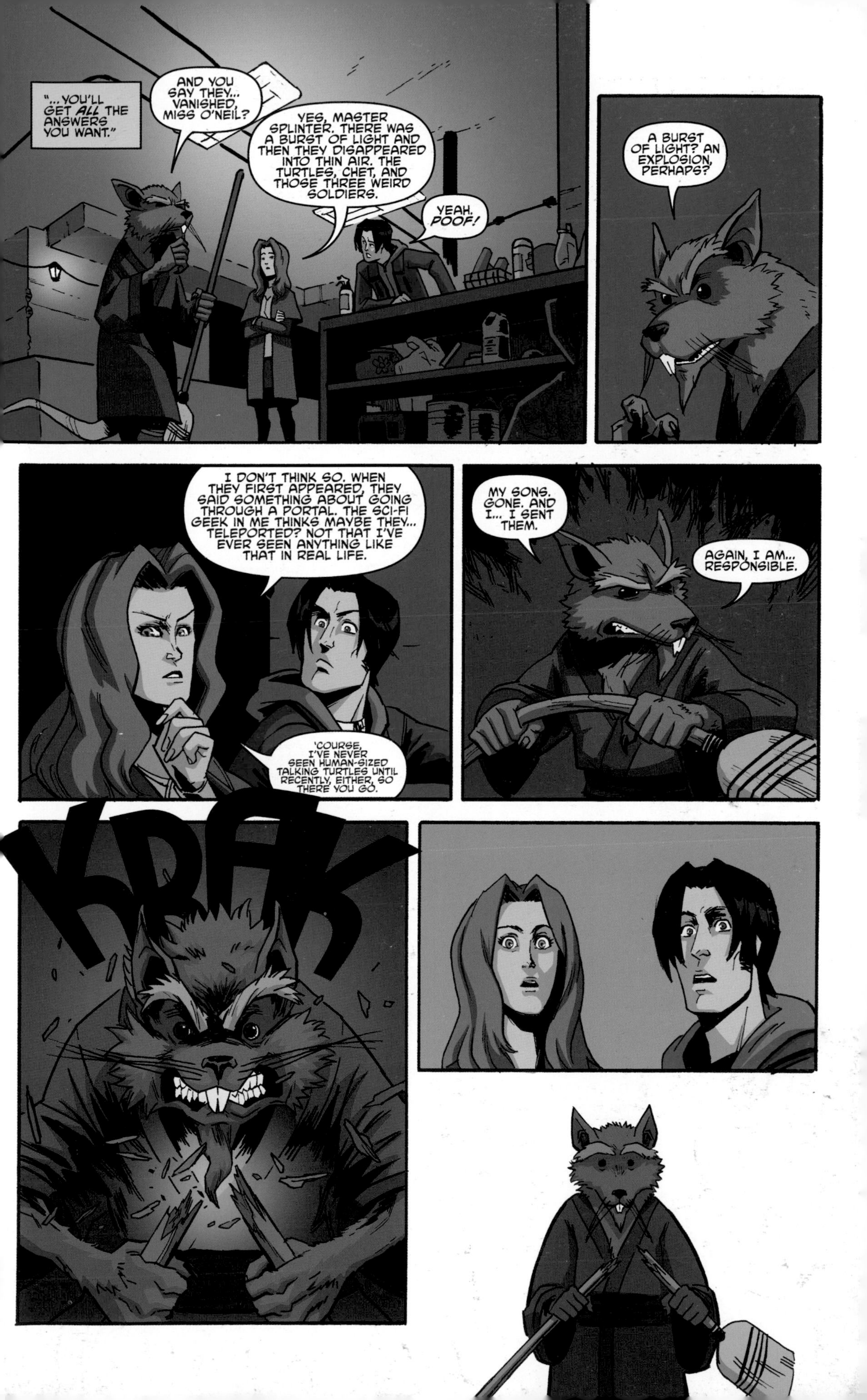
"...YOU'LL GET ALL THE ANSWERS YOU WANT."
AND YOU SAY THEY... VANISHED, MISS O'NEIL?
YES, MASTER SPLINTER. THERE WAS A BURST OF LIGHT AND THEN THEY DISAPPEARED INTO THIN AIR. THE TURTLES, CHET, AND THOSE THREE WEIRD SOLDIERS.
YEAH. POOF!
A BURST OF LIGHT? AN EXPLOSION, PERHAPS?
I DON'T THINK SO. WHEN THEY FIRST APPEARED, THEY SAID SOMETHING ABOUT GOING THROUGH A PORTAL. THE SCI-FI GEEK IN ME THINKS MAYBE THEY... TELEPORTED? NOT THAT I'VE EVER SEEN ANYTHING LIKE THAT IN REAL LIFE.
'COURSE, I'VE NEVER SEEN HUMAN-SIZED TALKING TURTLES UNTIL RECENTLY, EITHER, SO THERE YOU GO.
MY SONS. GONE. AND I... I SENT THEM.
AGAIN, I AM... RESPONSIBLE.
KRAK

THAT... ...THAT WAS UNNECESSARY.

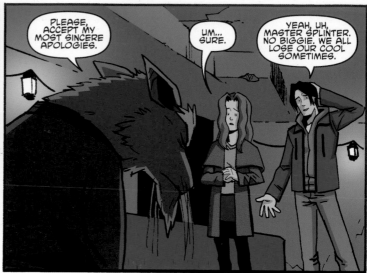

PLEASE, ACCEPT MY MOST SINCERE APOLOGIES.

UM... SURE.

YEAH, UH, MASTER SPLINTER. NO BIGGIE. WE ALL LOSE OUR COOL SOMETIMES.

PERHAPS, CASEY JONES, BUT THAT MAKES IT NO LESS POINTLESS OR WASTEFUL.

I—WE—MUST REMEMBER THAT MY SONS HAVE ALL BEEN WELL-TRAINED AND ARE MORE THAN CAPABLE OF PROTECTING EACH OTHER IN EVEN THE MOST DIRE CIRCUMSTANCES.

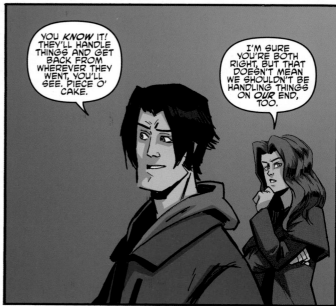

YOU *KNOW* IT! THEY'LL HANDLE THINGS AND GET BACK FROM WHEREVER THEY WENT, YOU'LL SEE. PIECE O' CAKE.

I'M SURE YOU'RE BOTH RIGHT, BUT THAT DOESN'T MEAN WE SHOULDN'T BE HANDLING THINGS ON *OUR* END, TOO.

I KEEP THINKING ABOUT THOSE SOLDIERS. THIS ISN'T THE FIRST TIME I'VE SEEN STRANGE-LOOKING SOLDIERS AROUND CHET—THERE WERE SOME BIG, MEAN ONES IN THE LABS THE NIGHT I SNAGGED THE TURTLE TRACKERS.

NO. BUT THEY DID HAVE SOME WEIRD SKIN—ALMOST LIKE ARMOR.

WITH POINTY EARS?

THIS ALL POINTS TO *STOCKGEN*, I JUST KNOW IT. BUT I NEED TO DIG A LITTLE DEEPER TO FIGURE OUT HOW. WANNA GO FOR A *RIDE*, CASEY?

LET'S GO. LIKE MY HOCKEY COACH ALWAYS SAYS, THE *BEST DEFENSE*...

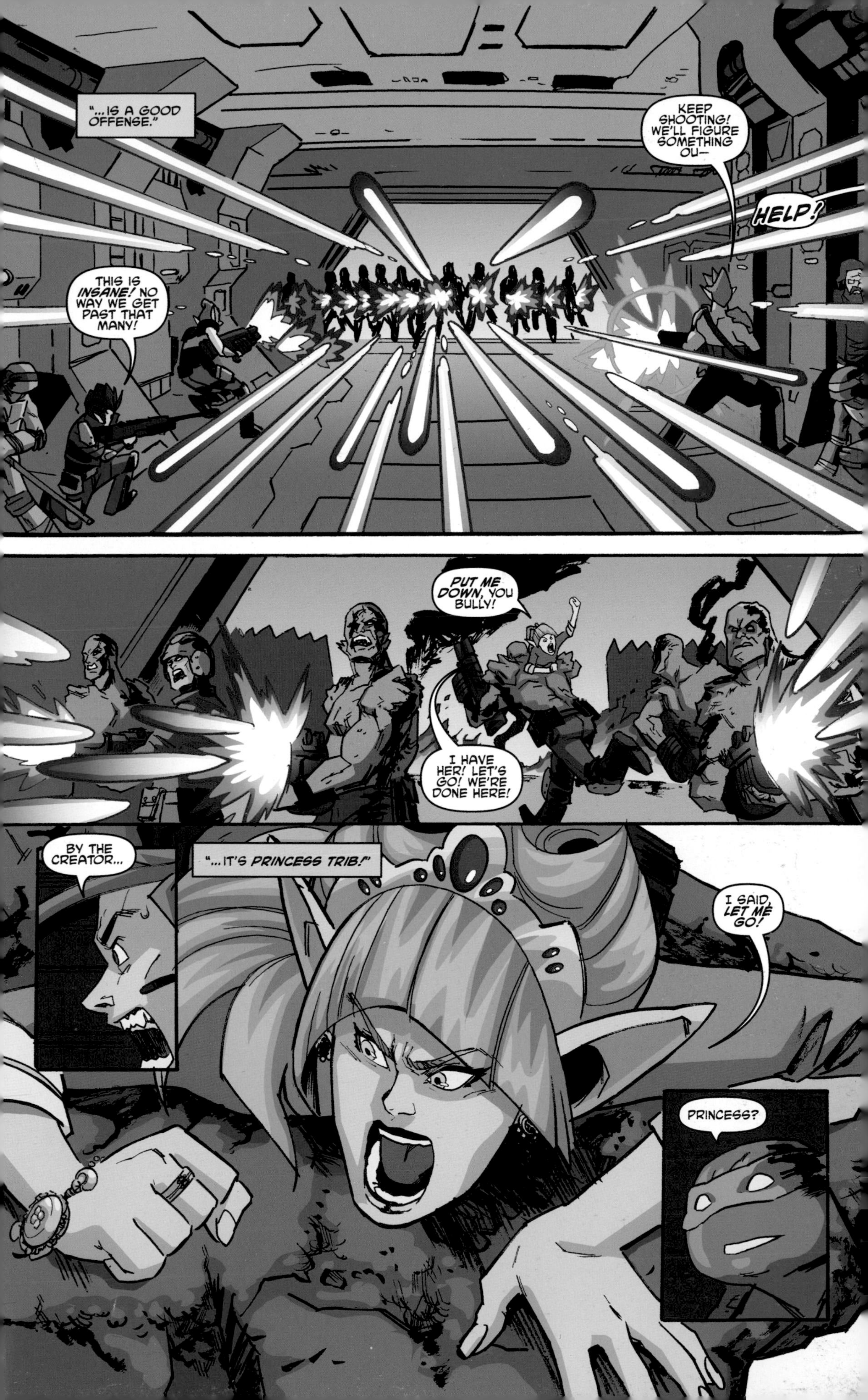
"...IS A GOOD OFFENSE."
KEEP SHOOTING! WE'LL FIGURE SOMETHING OU--
HELP!
THIS IS INSANE! NO WAY WE GET PAST THAT MANY!
PUT ME DOWN, YOU BULLY!
I HAVE HER! LET'S GO! WE'RE DONE HERE!
BY THE CREATOR...
"...IT'S PRINCESS TRIB!"
I SAID, LET ME GO!
PRINCESS?

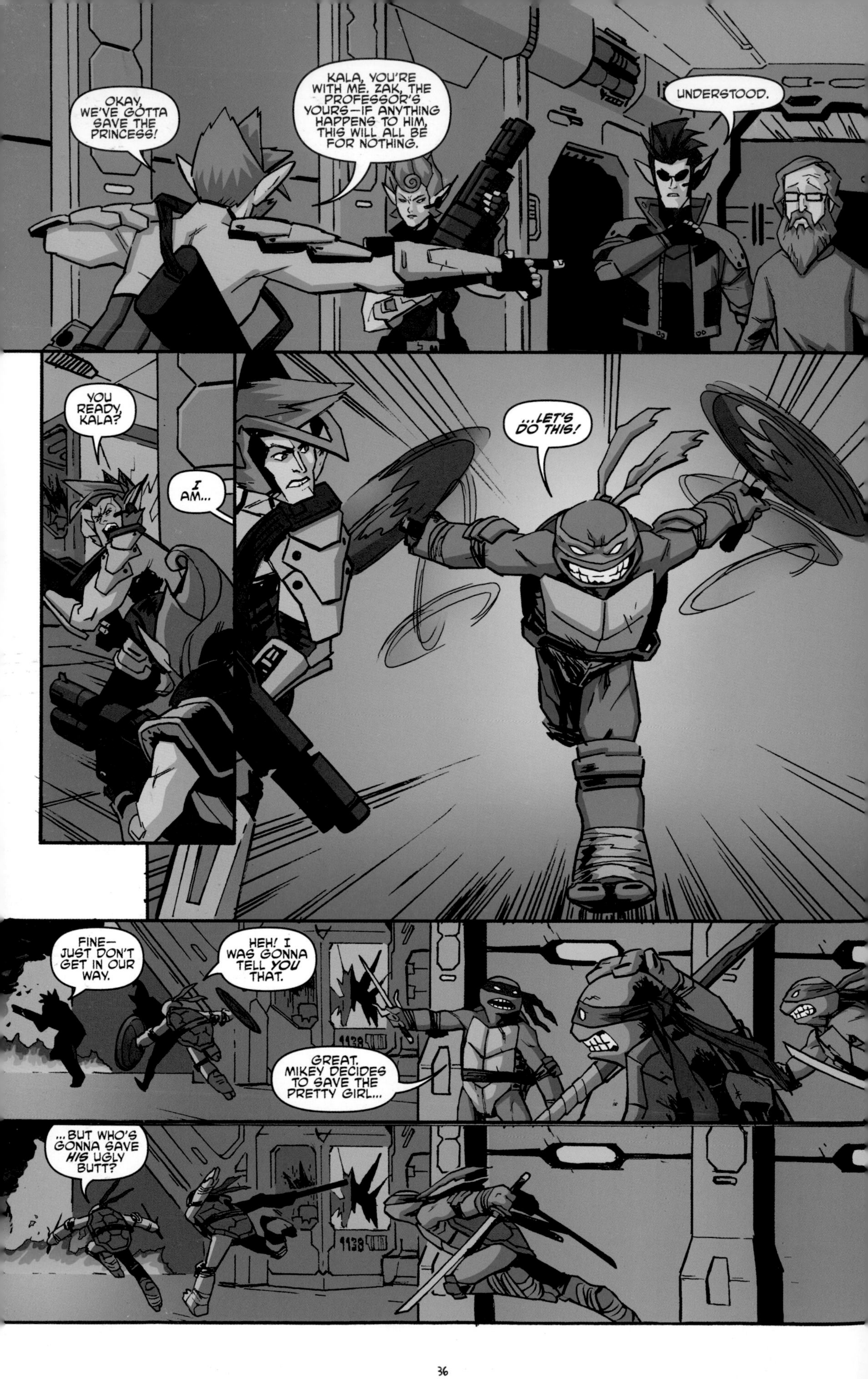
OKAY, WE'VE GOTTA SAVE THE PRINCESS!
KALA, YOU'RE WITH ME. ZAK, THE PROFESSOR'S YOURS—IF ANYTHING HAPPENS TO HIM, THIS WILL ALL BE FOR NOTHING.
UNDERSTOOD.
YOU READY, KALA?
I AM...
...LET'S DO THIS!
FINE—JUST DON'T GET IN OUR WAY.
HEH! I WAS GONNA TELL YOU THAT.
GREAT. MIKEY DECIDES TO SAVE THE PRETTY GIRL...
...BUT WHO'S GONNA SAVE HIS UGLY BUTT?

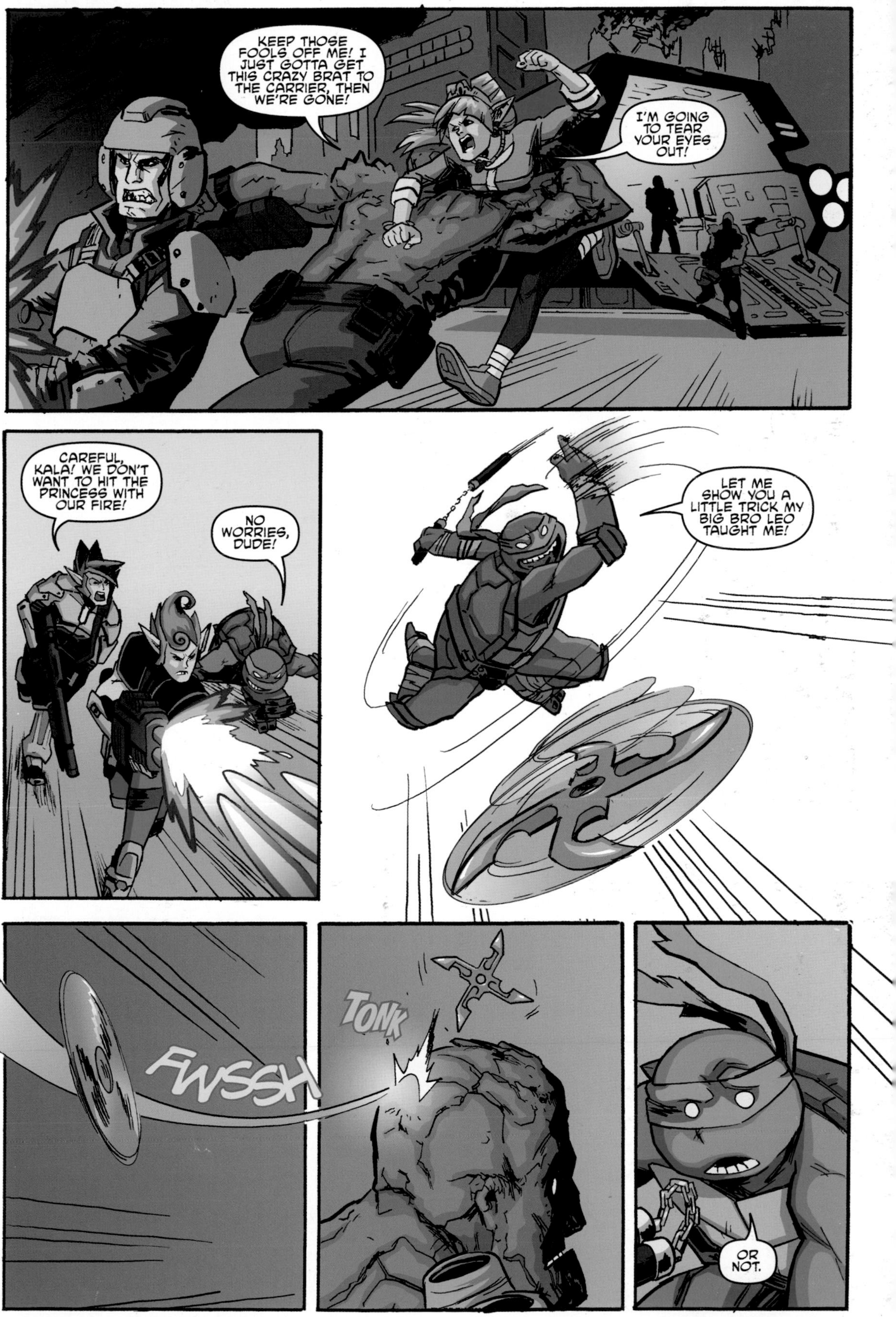
KEEP THOSE FOOLS OFF ME! I JUST GOTTA GET THIS CRAZY BRAT TO THE CARRIER, THEN WE'RE GONE!
I'M GOING TO TEAR YOUR EYES OUT!
CAREFUL, KALA! WE DON'T WANT TO HIT THE PRINCESS WITH OUR FIRE!
NO WORRIES, DUDE!
LET ME SHOW YOU A LITTLE TRICK MY BIG BRO LEO TAUGHT ME!
FWSSH
TONK
OR NOT.

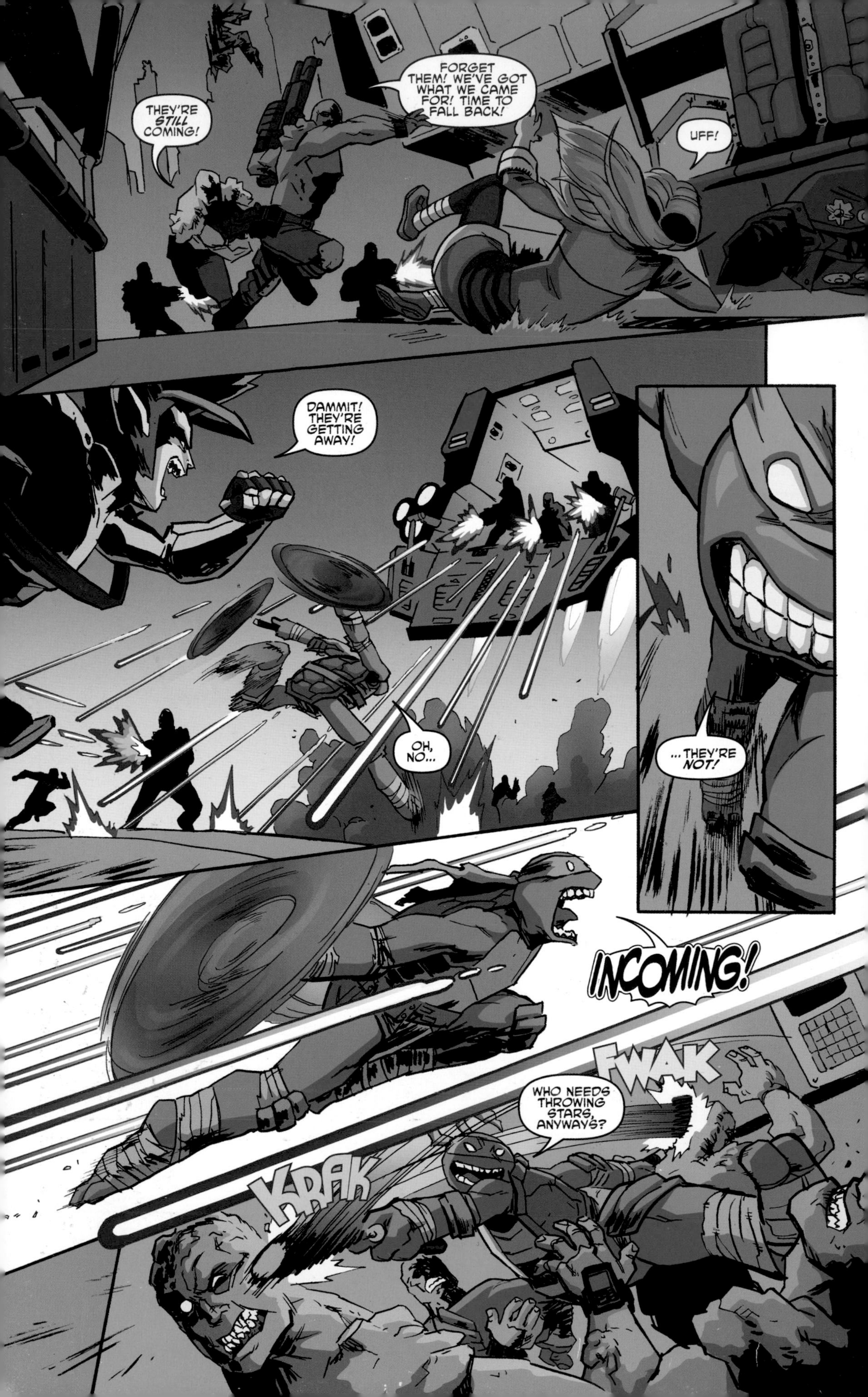
THEY'RE STILL COMING!
FORGET THEM! WE'VE GOT WHAT WE CAME FOR! TIME TO FALL BACK!
UFF!
DAMMIT! THEY'RE GETTING AWAY!
OH, NO...
...THEY'RE NOT!
INCOMING!
FWAK
WHO NEEDS THROWING STARS, ANYWAYS?
KRAK

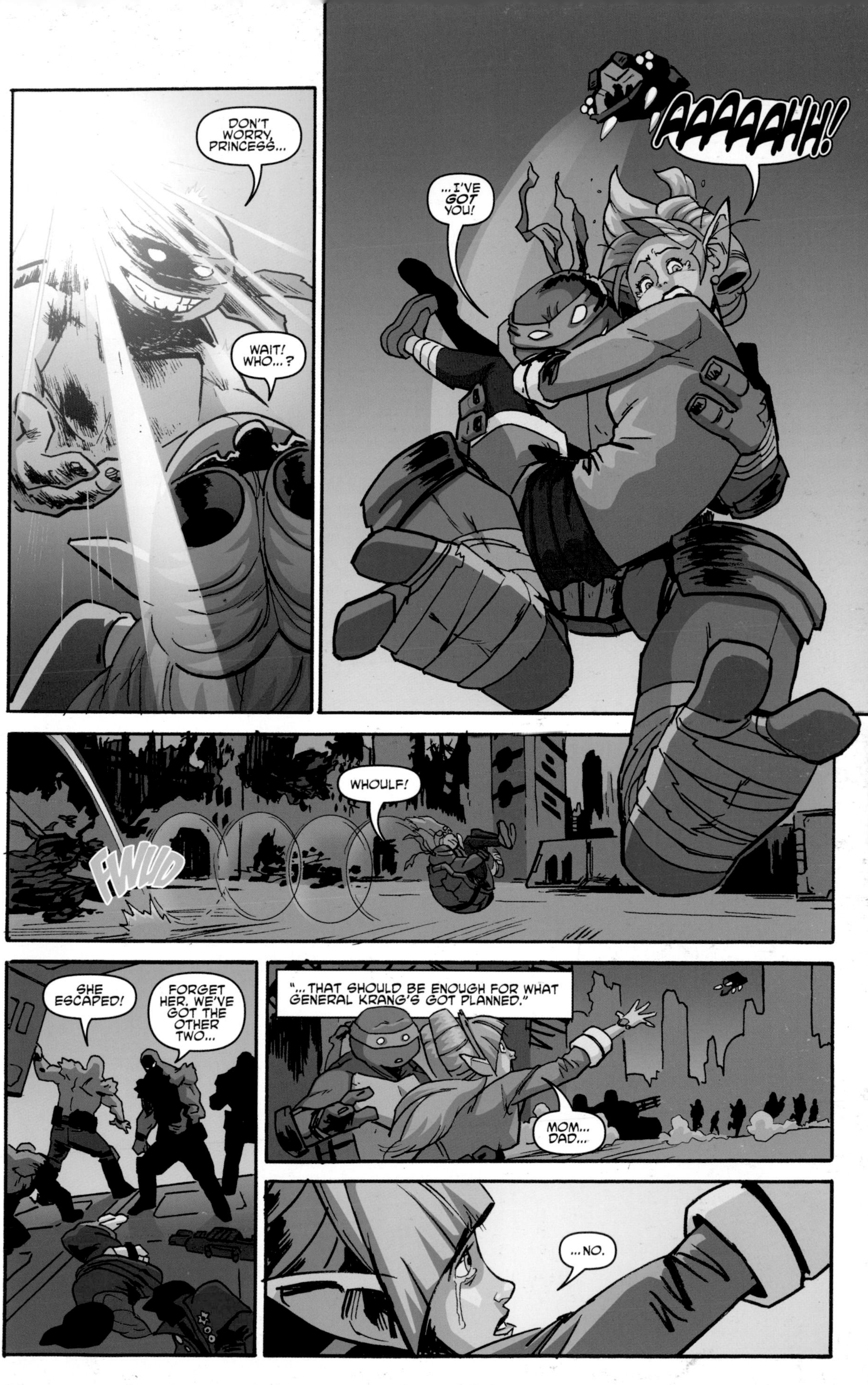
DON'T WORRY, PRINCESS...
WAIT! WHO...?
AAAAAAHH!
...I'VE GOT YOU!
WHOULF!
FWUD
SHE ESCAPED!
FORGET HER. WE'VE GOT THE OTHER TWO...
"...THAT SHOULD BE ENOUGH FOR WHAT GENERAL KRANG'S GOT PLANNED."
MOM... DAD...
...NO.

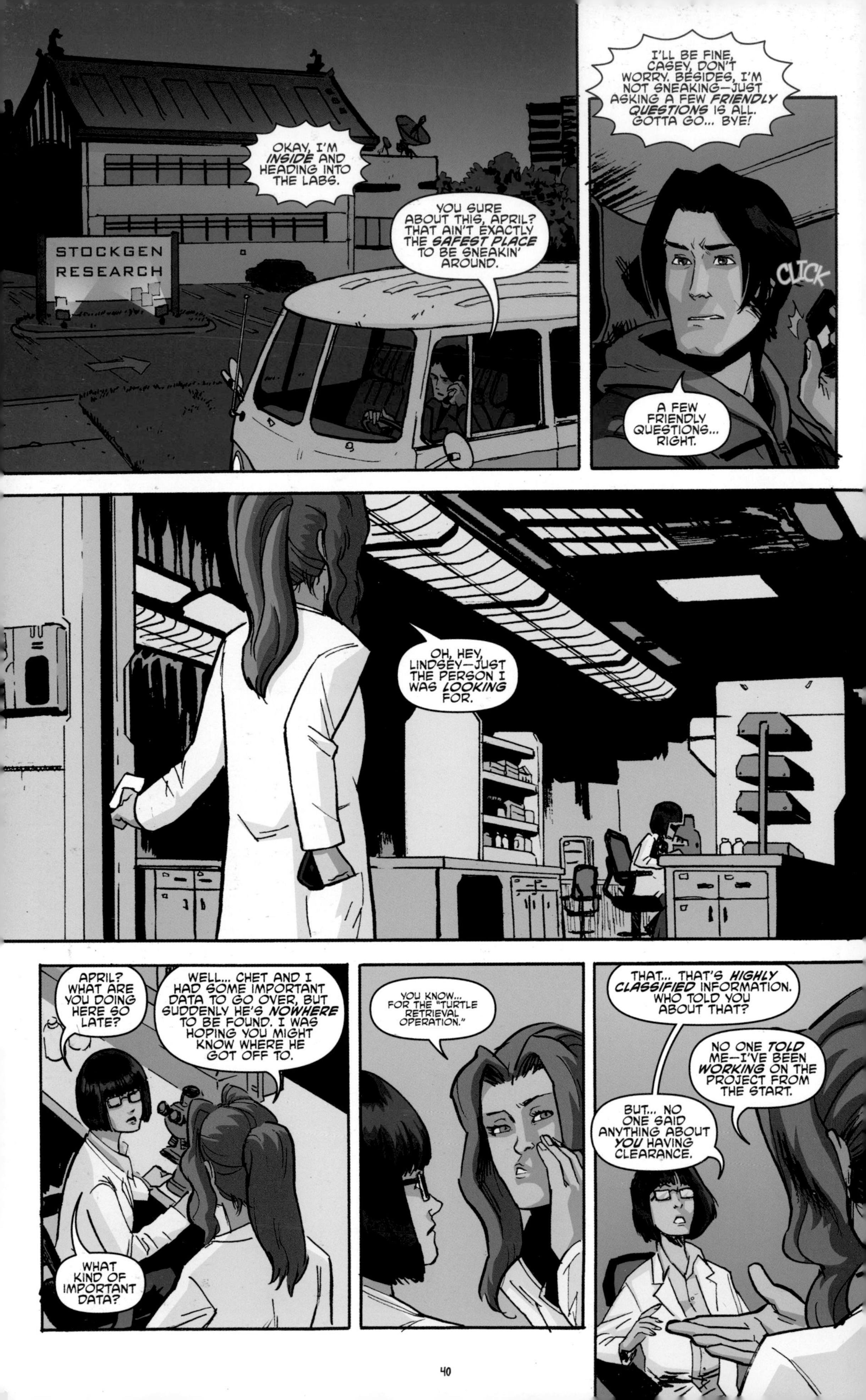
STOCKGEN RESEARCH
OKAY, I'M *INSIDE* AND HEADING INTO THE LABS.
YOU SURE ABOUT THIS, APRIL? THAT AIN'T EXACTLY THE *SAFEST PLACE* TO BE SNEAKIN' AROUND.
I'LL BE FINE, CASEY, DON'T WORRY. BESIDES, I'M NOT SNEAKING—JUST ASKING A FEW *FRIENDLY QUESTIONS* IS ALL. GOTTA GO... BYE!
CLICK
A FEW FRIENDLY QUESTIONS... RIGHT.
OH, HEY, LINDSEY—JUST THE PERSON I WAS *LOOKING* FOR.
APRIL? WHAT ARE YOU DOING HERE SO LATE?
WELL... CHET AND I HAD SOME IMPORTANT DATA TO GO OVER, BUT SUDDENLY HE'S *NOWHERE* TO BE FOUND. I WAS HOPING YOU MIGHT KNOW WHERE HE GOT OFF TO.
WHAT KIND OF IMPORTANT DATA?
YOU KNOW... FOR THE "TURTLE RETRIEVAL OPERATION."
THAT... THAT'S *HIGHLY CLASSIFIED* INFORMATION. WHO TOLD YOU ABOUT THAT?
NO ONE *TOLD* ME—I'VE BEEN *WORKING* ON THE PROJECT FROM THE START.
BUT... NO ONE SAID ANYTHING ABOUT *YOU* HAVING CLEARANCE.

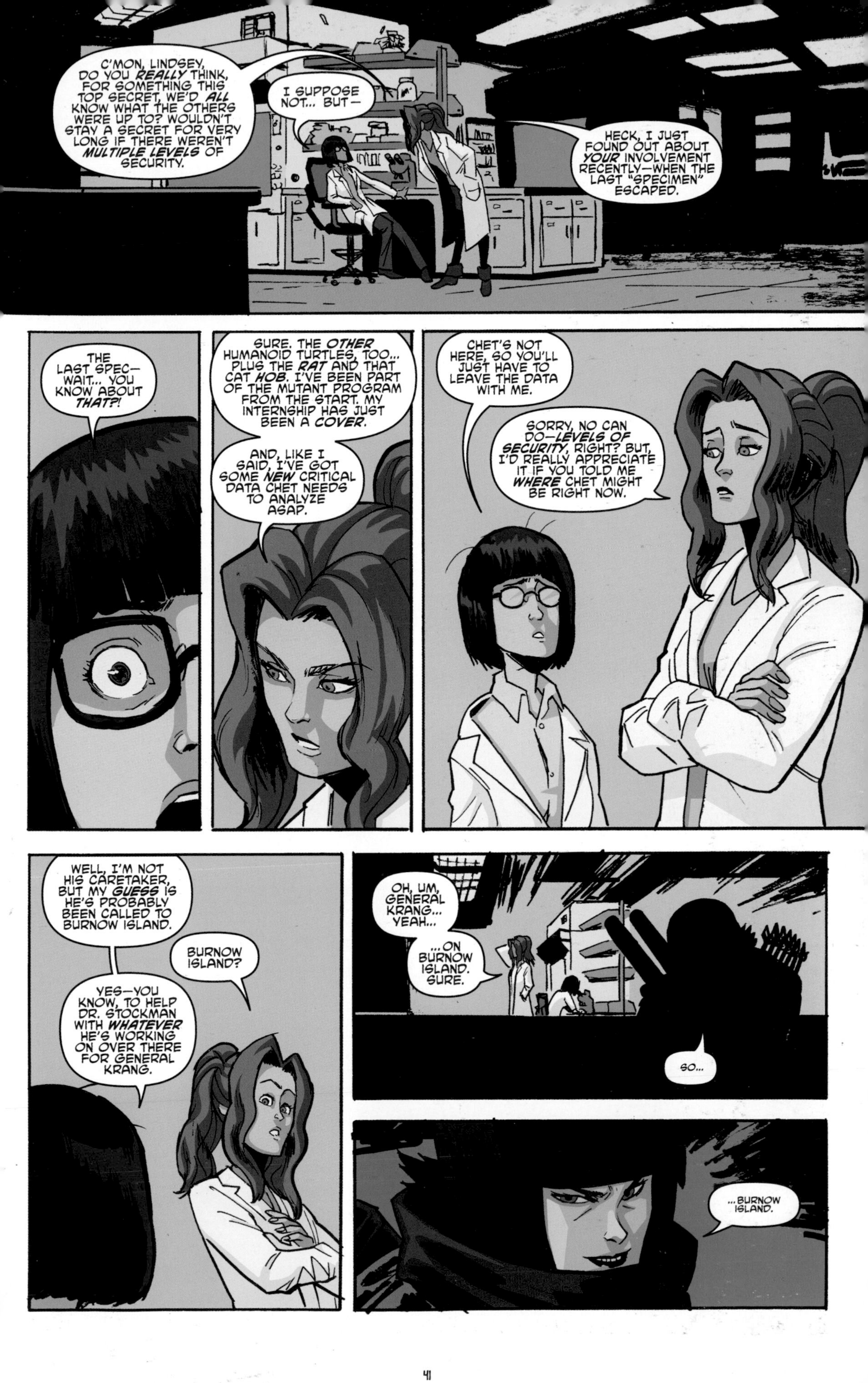
C'MON, LINDSEY, DO YOU REALLY THINK, FOR SOMETHING THIS TOP SECRET, WE'D ALL KNOW WHAT THE OTHERS WERE UP TO? WOULDN'T STAY A SECRET FOR VERY LONG IF THERE WEREN'T MULTIPLE LEVELS OF SECURITY.
I SUPPOSE NOT... BUT—
HECK, I JUST FOUND OUT ABOUT YOUR INVOLVEMENT RECENTLY—WHEN THE LAST "SPECIMEN" ESCAPED.
THE LAST SPEC— WAIT... YOU KNOW ABOUT THAT?!
SURE. THE OTHER HUMANOID TURTLES, TOO... PLUS THE RAT AND THAT CAT HOB. I'VE BEEN PART OF THE MUTANT PROGRAM FROM THE START. MY INTERNSHIP HAS JUST BEEN A COVER.
AND, LIKE I SAID, I'VE GOT SOME NEW CRITICAL DATA CHET NEEDS TO ANALYZE ASAP.
CHET'S NOT HERE, SO YOU'LL JUST HAVE TO LEAVE THE DATA WITH ME.
SORRY, NO CAN DO—LEVELS OF SECURITY, RIGHT? BUT, I'D REALLY APPRECIATE IT IF YOU TOLD ME WHERE CHET MIGHT BE RIGHT NOW.
WELL, I'M NOT HIS CARETAKER, BUT MY GUESS IS HE'S PROBABLY BEEN CALLED TO BURNOW ISLAND.
BURNOW ISLAND?
YES—YOU KNOW, TO HELP DR. STOCKMAN WITH WHATEVER HE'S WORKING ON OVER THERE FOR GENERAL KRANG.
OH, UM, GENERAL KRANG... YEAH...
...ON BURNOW ISLAND. SURE.
SO...
...BURNOW ISLAND.

SO, THEY'VE TAKEN THE KING AND QUEEN, YOUR HIGHNESS?

YES, COMMANDER DASK. WE ALL THOUGHT WE WERE DOOMED WHEN KRANG'S SOLDIERS BROKE THROUGH OUR INNER DEFENSES.

BUT INSTEAD OF KILLING US, THEY *GRABBED* MY MOTHER AND FATHER AND DRAGGED THEM AWAY. THEY WERE TRYING TO DO THE SAME TO ME WHEN YOU AND YOUR NEW FRIENDS ARRIVED AND SAVED ME.

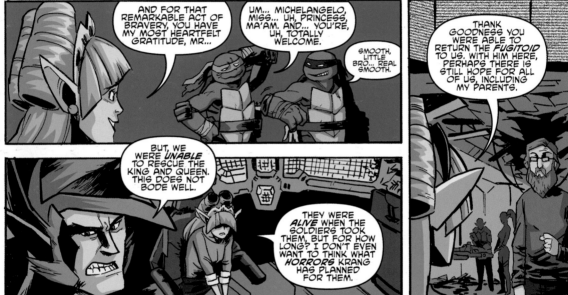

AND FOR THAT REMARKABLE ACT OF BRAVERY, YOU HAVE MY MOST HEARTFELT GRATITUDE, MR...

UM... MICHELANGELO, MISS... UH, PRINCESS, MA'AM. AND... YOU'RE, UH, TOTALLY WELCOME.

SMOOTH, LITTLE BRO... REAL SMOOTH.

THANK GOODNESS YOU WERE ABLE TO RETURN THE *FUGITOID* TO US. WITH HIM HERE, PERHAPS THERE IS STILL HOPE FOR ALL OF US, INCLUDING MY PARENTS.

BUT, WE WERE *UNABLE* TO RESCUE THE KING AND QUEEN. THIS DOES NOT BODE WELL.

THEY WERE *ALIVE* WHEN THE SOLDIERS TOOK THEM, BUT FOR HOW LONG? I DON'T EVEN WANT TO THINK WHAT *HORRORS* KRANG HAS PLANNED FOR THEM.

UM, NO DISRESPECT, PRINCESS, BUT WE HAVE NO IDEA *WHO* ANY OF YOU ARE OR *WHAT* THE HECK ALL THIS IS ABOUT, AND MY BROTHERS AND I JUST RISKED OUR NECKS TO HELP SAVE YOU.

YOUR GUY HERE PROMISED US *ANSWERS* WHEN THE FIGHTING STOPPED AND WE'D REALLY APPRECIATE THEM NOW.

STARTING WITH TELLING US WHO THIS *KRANG* GUY IS YOU KEEP MENTIONING.

YEAH... AND WHAT THE *HELL'S* A FUGITOID?

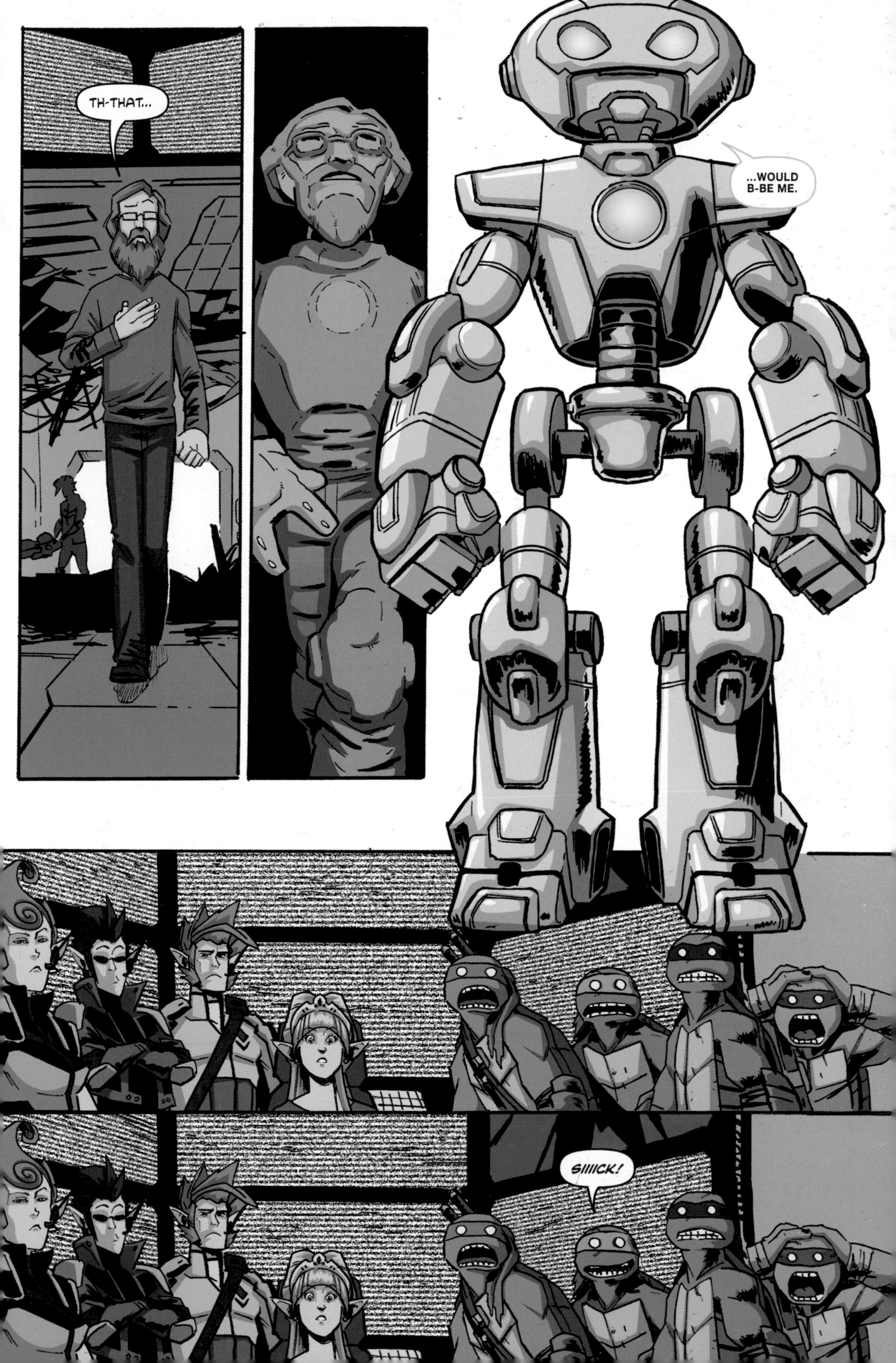
TH-THAT...
...WOULD B-BE ME.
SIIIICK!

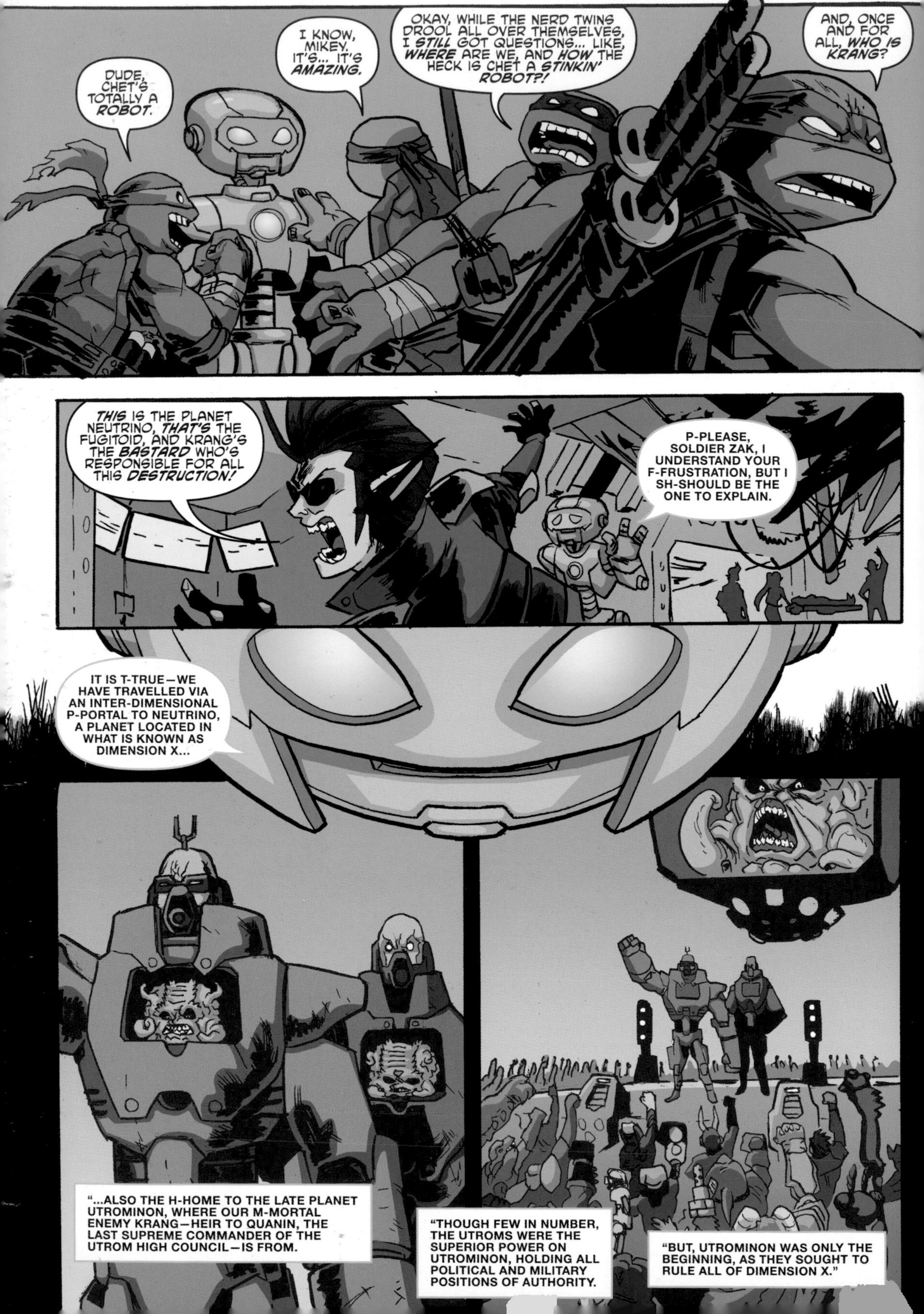
DUDE, CHET'S TOTALLY A *ROBOT*.
I KNOW, MIKEY. IT'S... IT'S *AMAZING*.
OKAY, WHILE THE NERD TWINS DROOL ALL OVER THEMSELVES, I *STILL* GOT QUESTIONS... LIKE, *WHERE* ARE WE, AND *HOW* THE HECK IS CHET A *STINKIN'* ROBOT?!
AND, ONCE AND FOR ALL, *WHO IS KRANG*?
THIS IS THE PLANET NEUTRINO, *THAT'S* THE FUGITOID, AND KRANG'S THE *BASTARD* WHO'S RESPONSIBLE FOR ALL THIS *DESTRUCTION!*
P-PLEASE, SOLDIER ZAK, I UNDERSTAND YOUR F-FRUSTRATION, BUT I SH-SHOULD BE THE ONE TO EXPLAIN.
IT IS T-TRUE—WE HAVE TRAVELLED VIA AN INTER-DIMENSIONAL P-PORTAL TO NEUTRINO, A PLANET LOCATED IN WHAT IS KNOWN AS DIMENSION X...
"...ALSO THE H-HOME TO THE LATE PLANET UTROMINON, WHERE OUR M-MORTAL ENEMY KRANG—HEIR TO QUANIN, THE LAST SUPREME COMMANDER OF THE UTROM HIGH COUNCIL—IS FROM.
"THOUGH FEW IN NUMBER, THE UTROMS WERE THE SUPERIOR POWER ON UTROMINON, HOLDING ALL POLITICAL AND MILITARY POSITIONS OF AUTHORITY.
"BUT, UTROMINON WAS ONLY THE BEGINNING, AS THEY SOUGHT TO RULE ALL OF DIMENSION X."

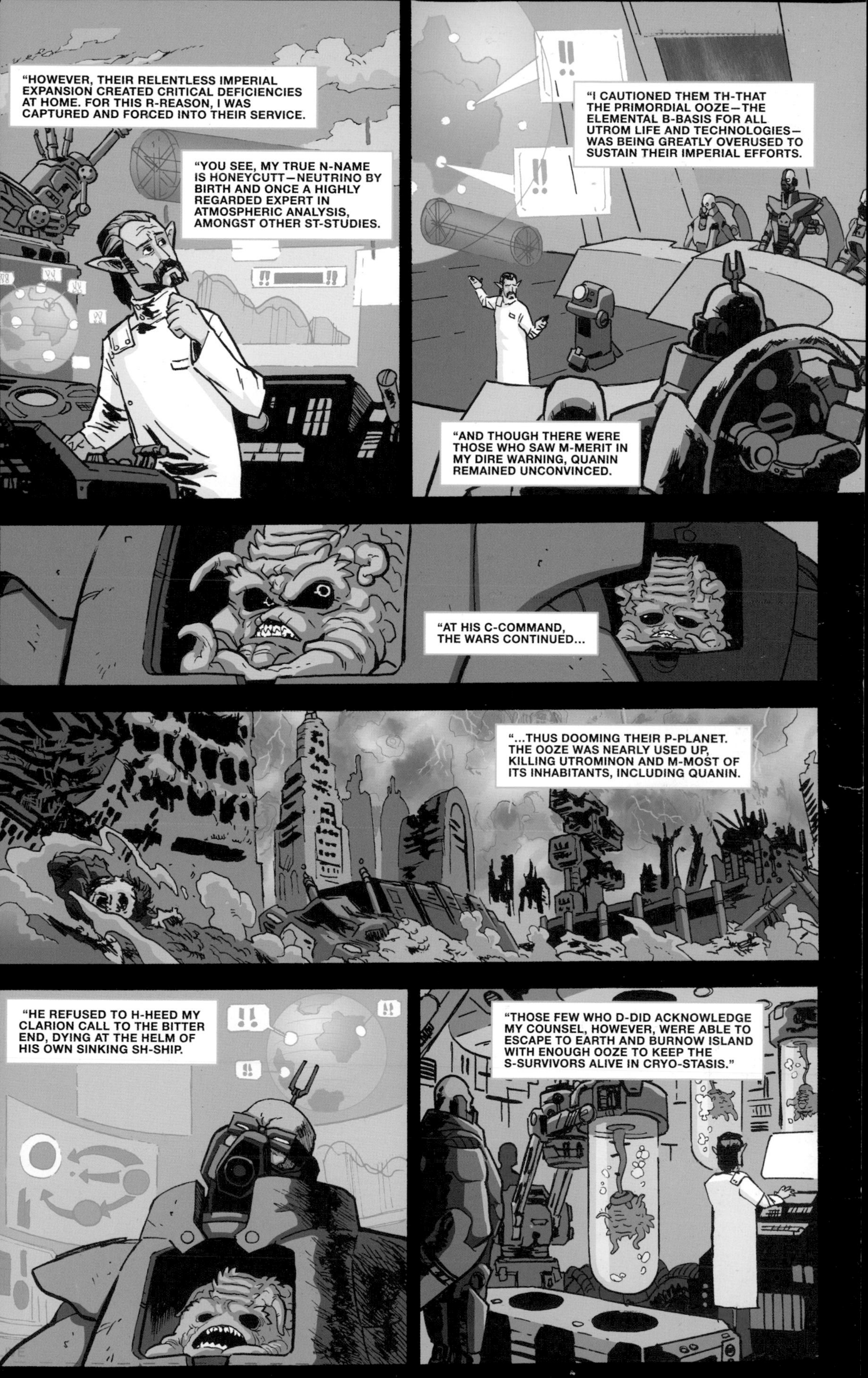
"HOWEVER, THEIR RELENTLESS IMPERIAL EXPANSION CREATED CRITICAL DEFICIENCIES AT HOME. FOR THIS R-REASON, I WAS CAPTURED AND FORCED INTO THEIR SERVICE.
"YOU SEE, MY TRUE N-NAME IS HONEYCUTT—NEUTRINO BY BIRTH AND ONCE A HIGHLY REGARDED EXPERT IN ATMOSPHERIC ANALYSIS, AMONGST OTHER ST-STUDIES.
"I CAUTIONED THEM TH-THAT THE PRIMORDIAL OOZE—THE ELEMENTAL B-BASIS FOR ALL UTROM LIFE AND TECHNOLOGIES—WAS BEING GREATLY OVERUSED TO SUSTAIN THEIR IMPERIAL EFFORTS.
"AND THOUGH THERE WERE THOSE WHO SAW M-MERIT IN MY DIRE WARNING, QUANIN REMAINED UNCONVINCED.
"AT HIS C-COMMAND, THE WARS CONTINUED...
"...THUS DOOMING THEIR P-PLANET. THE OOZE WAS NEARLY USED UP, KILLING UTROMINON AND M-MOST OF ITS INHABITANTS, INCLUDING QUANIN.
"HE REFUSED TO H-HEED MY CLARION CALL TO THE BITTER END, DYING AT THE HELM OF HIS OWN SINKING SH-SHIP.
"THOSE FEW WHO D-DID ACKNOWLEDGE MY COUNSEL, HOWEVER, WERE ABLE TO ESCAPE TO EARTH AND BURNOW ISLAND WITH ENOUGH OOZE TO KEEP THE S-SURVIVORS ALIVE IN CRYO-STASIS."

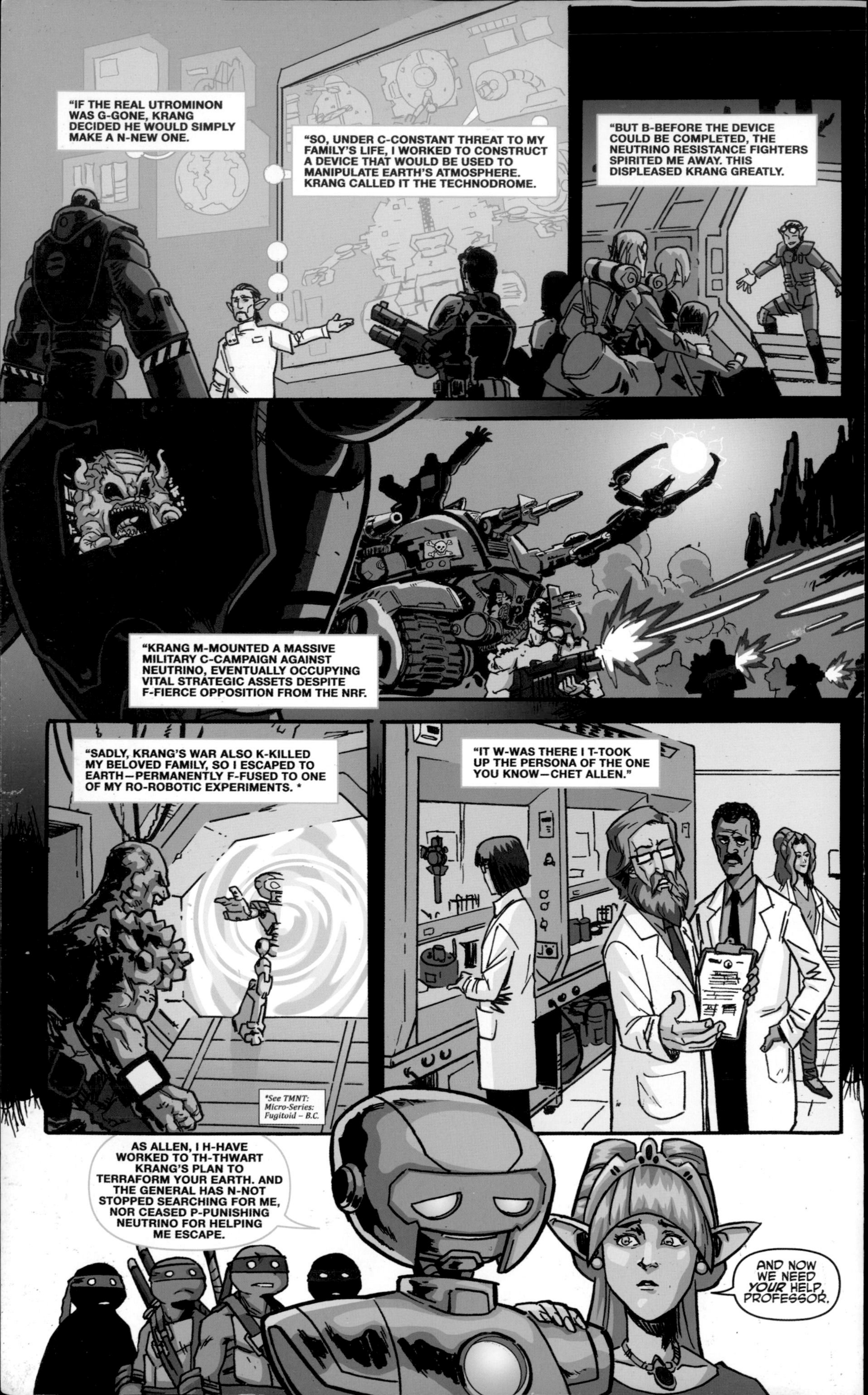
"IF THE REAL UTROMINON WAS G-GONE, KRANG DECIDED HE WOULD SIMPLY MAKE A N-NEW ONE.
"SO, UNDER C-CONSTANT THREAT TO MY FAMILY'S LIFE, I WORKED TO CONSTRUCT A DEVICE THAT WOULD BE USED TO MANIPULATE EARTH'S ATMOSPHERE. KRANG CALLED IT THE TECHNODROME.
"BUT B-BEFORE THE DEVICE COULD BE COMPLETED, THE NEUTRINO RESISTANCE FIGHTERS SPIRITED ME AWAY. THIS DISPLEASED KRANG GREATLY.
"KRANG M-MOUNTED A MASSIVE MILITARY C-CAMPAIGN AGAINST NEUTRINO, EVENTUALLY OCCUPYING VITAL STRATEGIC ASSETS DESPITE F-FIERCE OPPOSITION FROM THE NRF.
"SADLY, KRANG'S WAR ALSO K-KILLED MY BELOVED FAMILY, SO I ESCAPED TO EARTH—PERMANENTLY F-FUSED TO ONE OF MY RO-ROBOTIC EXPERIMENTS. *
*See TMNT: Micro-Series: Fugitoid – B.C.
"IT W-WAS THERE I T-TOOK UP THE PERSONA OF THE ONE YOU KNOW—CHET ALLEN."
AS ALLEN, I H-HAVE WORKED TO TH-THWART KRANG'S PLAN TO TERRAFORM YOUR EARTH. AND THE GENERAL HAS N-NOT STOPPED SEARCHING FOR ME, NOR CEASED P-PUNISHING NEUTRINO FOR HELPING ME ESCAPE.
AND NOW WE NEED YOUR HELP, PROFESSOR.

OUR NRF SCIENTISTS WERE NEARING COMPLETION OF A *WEAPON* THAT COULD TURN THIS WAR TO OUR FAVOR, BUT THEY REQUIRE YOUR *UNIQUE EXPERTISE* TO COMPLETE IT.

THAT IS WHY MY FATHER SENT COMMANDER DASK TO GET YOU. EITHER WE STOP KRANG *NOW*... OR *ALL* IS LOST.

SHE'S SO... *AWESOME.*

PUT YOUR TONGUE BACK IN YOUR MELON, MIKE—YOU'RE PRACTICALLY *LICKIN'* THE FLOOR.

YOUR H-HIGHNESS, I WILL DO WH-WHATEVER I CAN TO HELP WITH THIS NEW WEAPON. NO ONE W-WOULD BE HAPPIER TO SEE KRANG ST-STOPPED THAN M-ME.

THAT'S GREAT, BUT WE MIGHT HAVE A *PROBLEM*...

...I'M ALREADY GETTING REPORTS THAT THE WEAPON THE SCIENTISTS WERE WORKING ON WAS *DAMAGED* IN THIS ATTACK—AND SOME OF THE SCIENTISTS KILLED.

NOT TO MENTION, WE HAVE *NO CLUE* WHAT KRANG HAS PLANNED FOR THE KING AND QUEEN.

UH, BOSS... I THINK WE'RE ABOUT TO *FIND OUT.* LOOK.

GREETINGS, *CRETINS* OF NEUTRINO!

KRANG.

THAT'S KRANG?

HE LOOKS SO...

...*PINK* AND SQUISHY. GROSS.

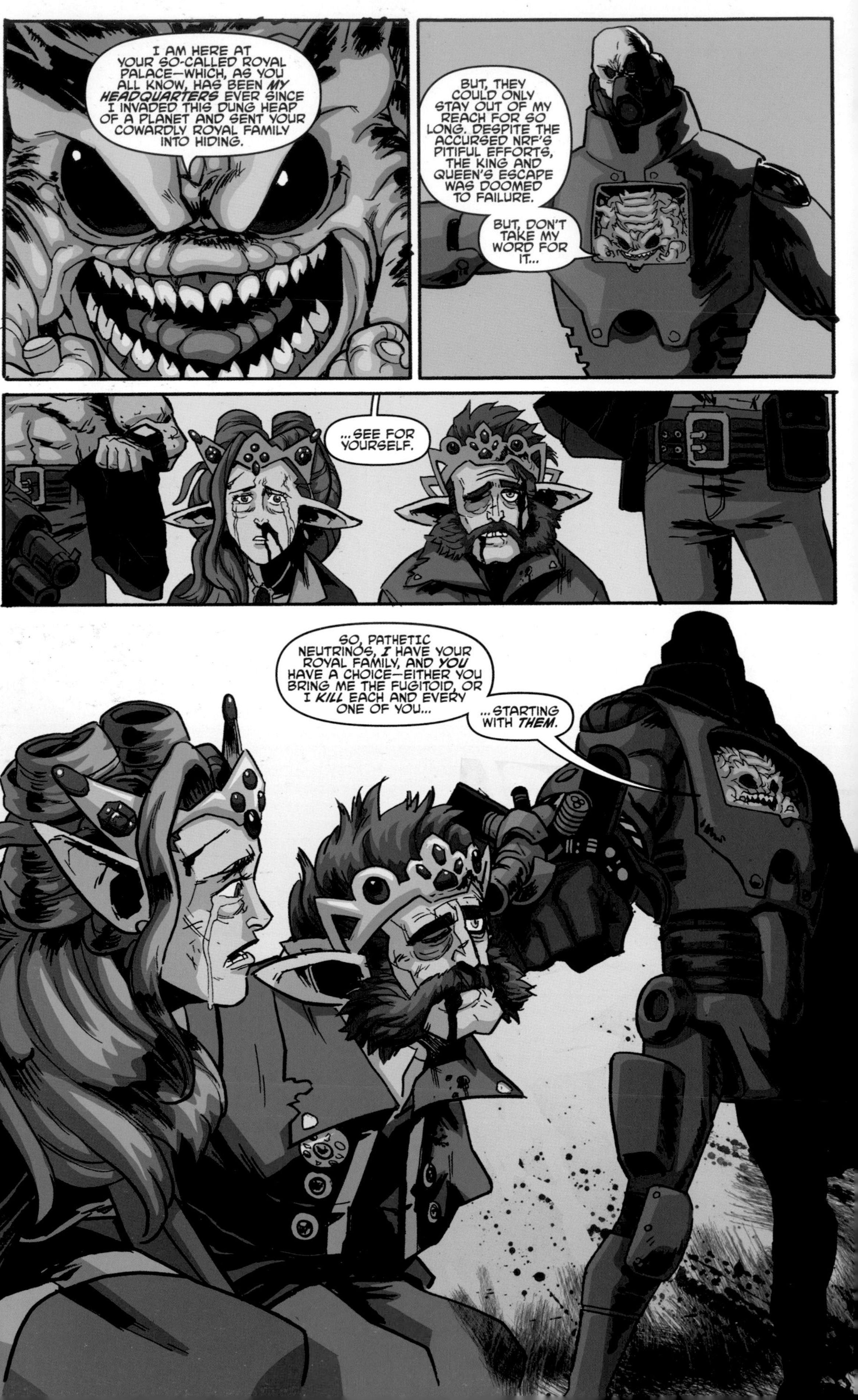
I AM HERE AT YOUR SO-CALLED ROYAL PALACE—WHICH, AS YOU ALL KNOW, HAS BEEN *MY HEADQUARTERS* EVER SINCE I INVADED THIS DUNG HEAP OF A PLANET AND SENT YOUR COWARDLY ROYAL FAMILY INTO HIDING.
BUT, THEY COULD ONLY STAY OUT OF MY REACH FOR SO LONG. DESPITE THE ACCURSED NRF'S PITIFUL EFFORTS, THE KING AND QUEEN'S ESCAPE WAS DOOMED TO FAILURE.
BUT, DON'T TAKE MY WORD FOR IT...
...SEE FOR YOURSELF.
SO, PATHETIC NEUTRINOS, *I* HAVE YOUR ROYAL FAMILY, AND *YOU* HAVE A CHOICE—EITHER YOU BRING ME THE FUGITOID, OR I *KILL* EACH AND EVERY ONE OF YOU...
...STARTING WITH *THEM*.

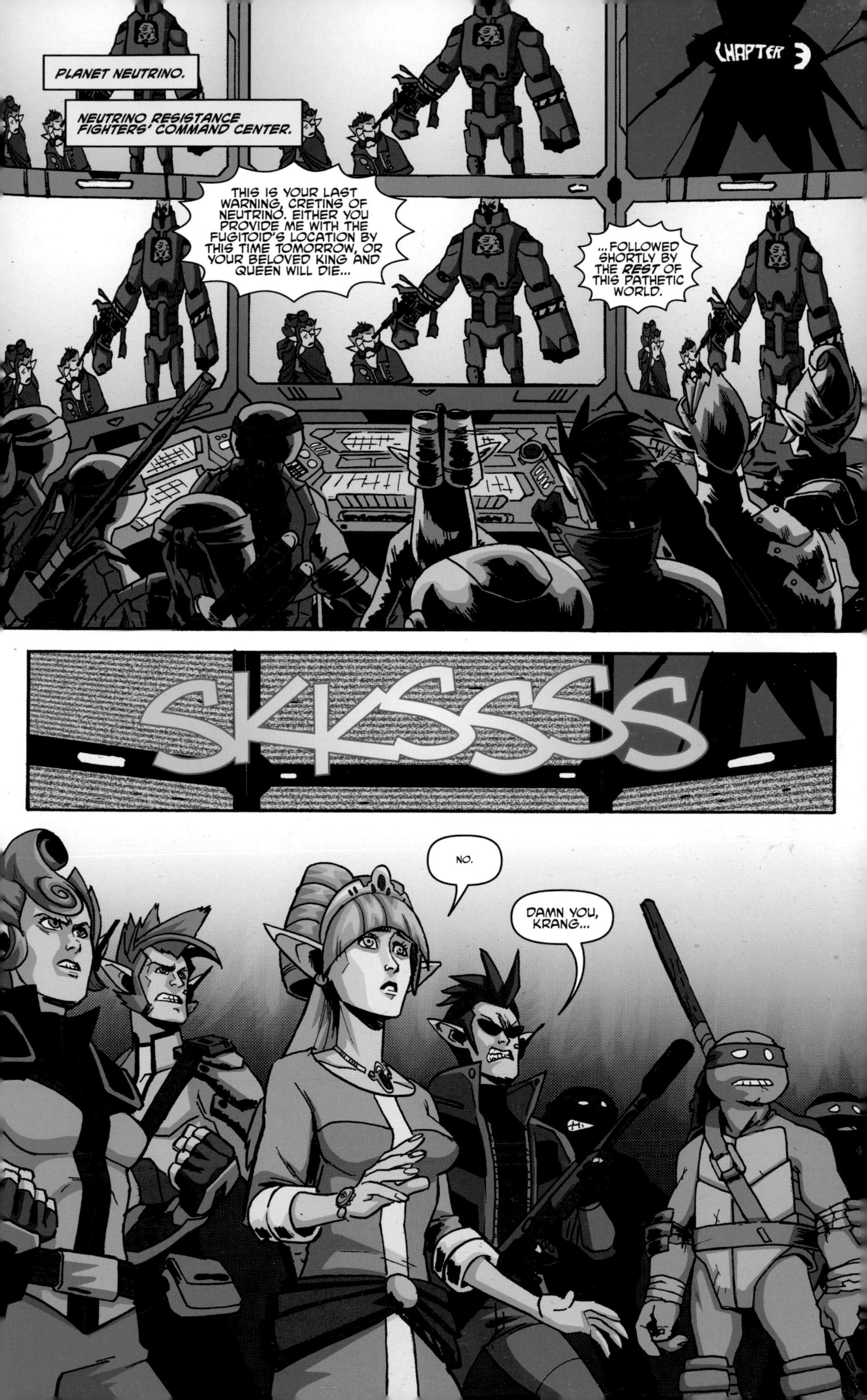
CHAPTER 3
PLANET NEUTRINO.
NEUTRINO RESISTANCE FIGHTERS' COMMAND CENTER.
THIS IS YOUR LAST WARNING, CRETINS OF NEUTRINO. EITHER YOU PROVIDE ME WITH THE FUGITOID'S LOCATION BY THIS TIME TOMORROW, OR YOUR BELOVED KING AND QUEEN WILL DIE...
...FOLLOWED SHORTLY BY THE REST OF THIS PATHETIC WORLD.
SKSSSS
NO.
DAMN YOU, KRANG...

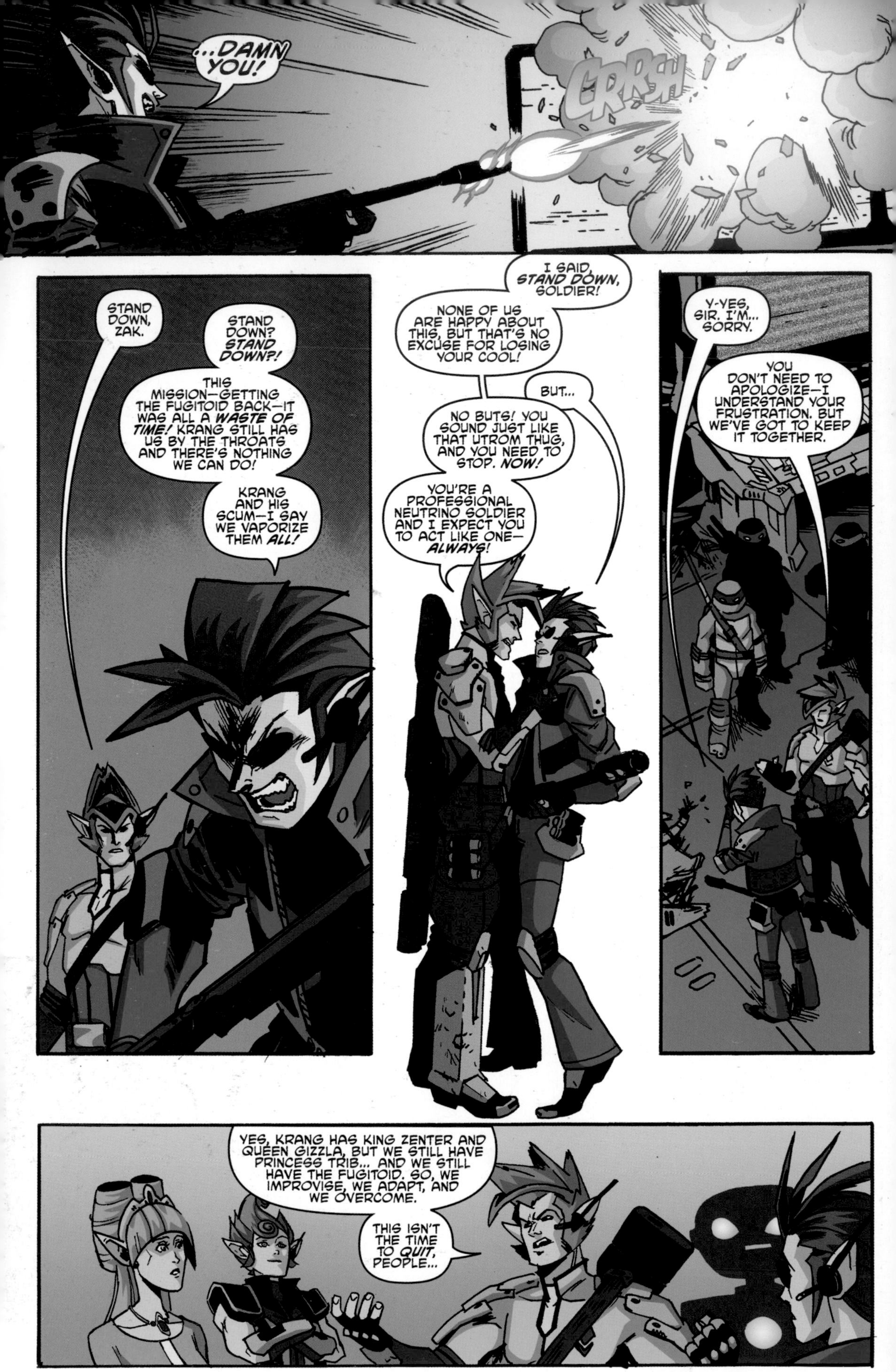
...DAMN YOU!
CRRSH
STAND DOWN, ZAK.
STAND DOWN? STAND DOWN?!
THIS MISSION—GETTING THE FUGITOID BACK—IT WAS ALL A WASTE OF TIME! KRANG STILL HAS US BY THE THROATS AND THERE'S NOTHING WE CAN DO!
KRANG AND HIS SCUM—I SAY WE VAPORIZE THEM ALL!
I SAID, STAND DOWN, SOLDIER!
NONE OF US ARE HAPPY ABOUT THIS, BUT THAT'S NO EXCUSE FOR LOSING YOUR COOL!
BUT...
NO BUTS! YOU SOUND JUST LIKE THAT UTROM THUG, AND YOU NEED TO STOP. NOW!
YOU'RE A PROFESSIONAL NEUTRINO SOLDIER AND I EXPECT YOU TO ACT LIKE ONE—ALWAYS!
Y-YES, SIR. I'M... SORRY.
YOU DON'T NEED TO APOLOGIZE—I UNDERSTAND YOUR FRUSTRATION. BUT WE'VE GOT TO KEEP IT TOGETHER.
YES, KRANG HAS KING ZENTER AND QUEEN GIZZLA, BUT WE STILL HAVE PRINCESS TRIB... AND WE STILL HAVE THE FUGITOID. SO, WE IMPROVISE, WE ADAPT, AND WE OVERCOME.
THIS ISN'T THE TIME TO QUIT, PEOPLE...

...IT'S THE TIME FOR A *NEW PLAN*.

AND I TH-THINK I KNOW WHAT THAT SHOULD B-BE, COMMANDER DASK.

I WILL SURRENDER M-MYSELF TO KRANG.

SURRENDER? YOU *CAN'T* BE SERIOUS.

YES, I AM. I H-HAVE ALREADY BEEN THE CAUSE OF F-FAR TOO MANY DEATHS. IF GIVING MYSELF OVER TO KRANG S-SAVES THE LIVES OF THE KING AND QUEEN, THEN IT'S WHAT I M-MUST DO.

NO, PROFESSOR, YOU ARE WRONG...

...*THAT* IS WHAT YOU ABSOLUTELY MUST *NOT* DO.

I AM TERRIFIED FOR MY PARENTS' LIVES, BUT ALLOWING YOU TO SURRENDER YOURSELF WOULD BE THE *LAST THING* THE KING AND QUEEN WOULD WANT YOU TO DO.

YOU WERE BROUGHT BACK HERE TO HELP US WIN THIS WAR...

...AND *THAT* IS WHAT WE NEED FROM YOU NOW.

I.... UM...

...Y-YES, YOUR HIGHNESS.

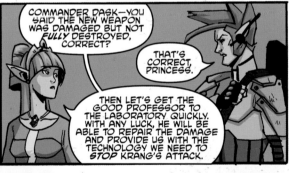

COMMANDER DASK—YOU SAID THE NEW WEAPON WAS DAMAGED BUT NOT *FULLY* DESTROYED, CORRECT?

THAT'S CORRECT, PRINCESS.

THEN LET'S GET THE *GOOD* PROFESSOR TO THE LABORATORY QUICKLY. WITH ANY LUCK, HE WILL BE ABLE TO REPAIR THE DAMAGE AND PROVIDE US WITH THE TECHNOLOGY WE NEED TO *STOP* KRANG'S ATTACK.

YOU:... AND YOU! ESCORT PROFESSOR HONEYCUTT TO THE LABS. MAKE SURE HE GETS THERE FAST AND IN ONE PIECE, UNDERSTOOD?

YES SIR!

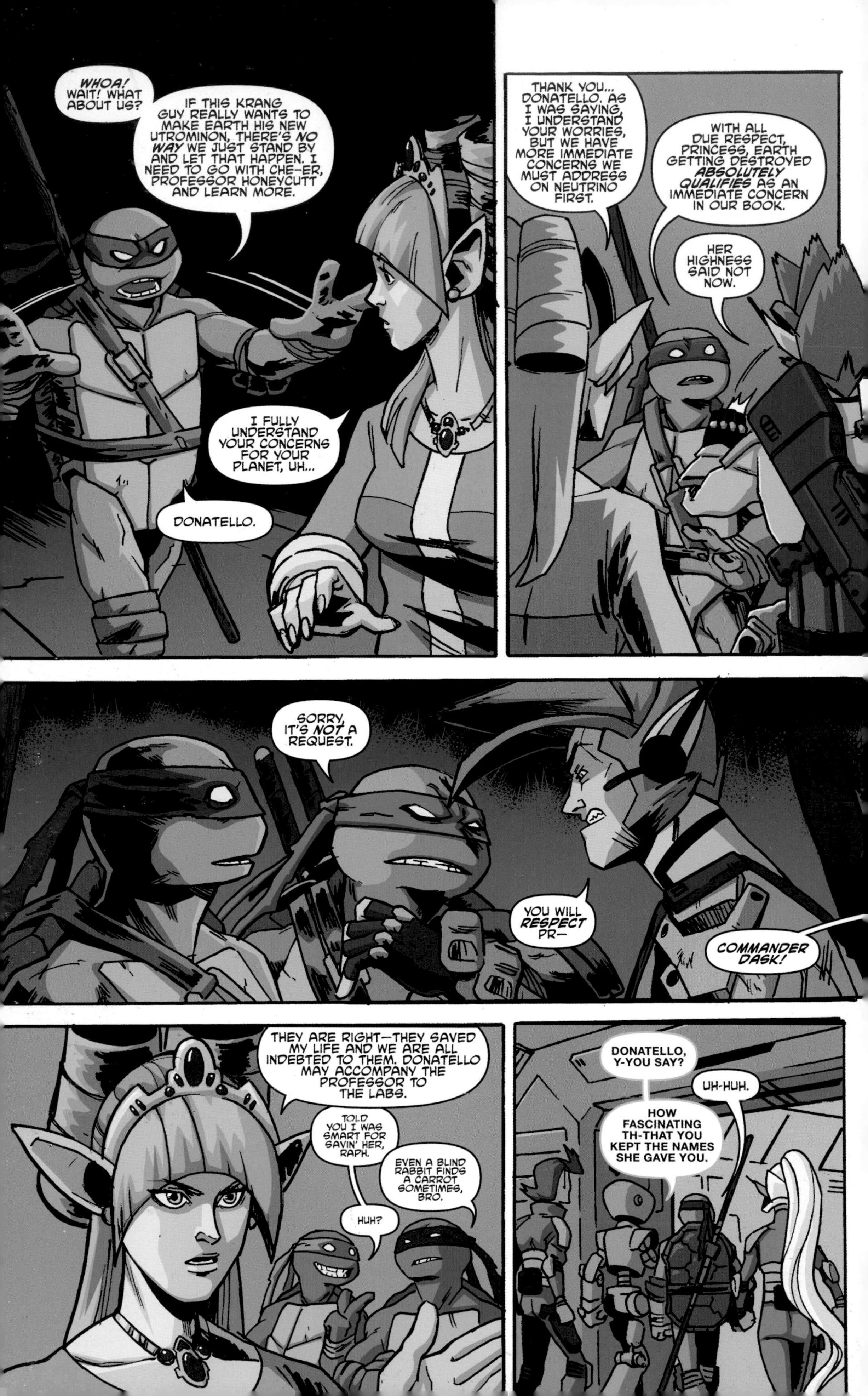
WHOA! WAIT! WHAT ABOUT US?
IF THIS KRANG GUY REALLY WANTS TO MAKE EARTH HIS NEW UTROMINON, THERE'S NO WAY WE JUST STAND BY AND LET THAT HAPPEN. I NEED TO GO WITH CHE—ER, PROFESSOR HONEYCUTT AND LEARN MORE.
I FULLY UNDERSTAND YOUR CONCERNS FOR YOUR PLANET, UH...
DONATELLO.
THANK YOU... DONATELLO. AS I WAS SAYING, I UNDERSTAND YOUR WORRIES, BUT WE HAVE MORE IMMEDIATE CONCERNS WE MUST ADDRESS ON NEUTRINO FIRST.
WITH ALL DUE RESPECT, PRINCESS, EARTH GETTING DESTROYED ABSOLUTELY QUALIFIES AS AN IMMEDIATE CONCERN IN OUR BOOK.
HER HIGHNESS SAID NOT NOW.
SORRY, IT'S NOT A REQUEST.
YOU WILL RESPECT PR—
COMMANDER DASK!
THEY ARE RIGHT—THEY SAVED MY LIFE AND WE ARE ALL INDEBTED TO THEM. DONATELLO MAY ACCOMPANY THE PROFESSOR TO THE LABS.
TOLD YOU I WAS SMART FOR SAVIN' HER, RAPH.
EVEN A BLIND RABBIT FINDS A CARROT SOMETIMES, BRO.
HUH?
DONATELLO, Y-YOU SAY?
UH-HUH.
HOW FASCINATING TH-THAT YOU KEPT THE NAMES SHE GAVE YOU.

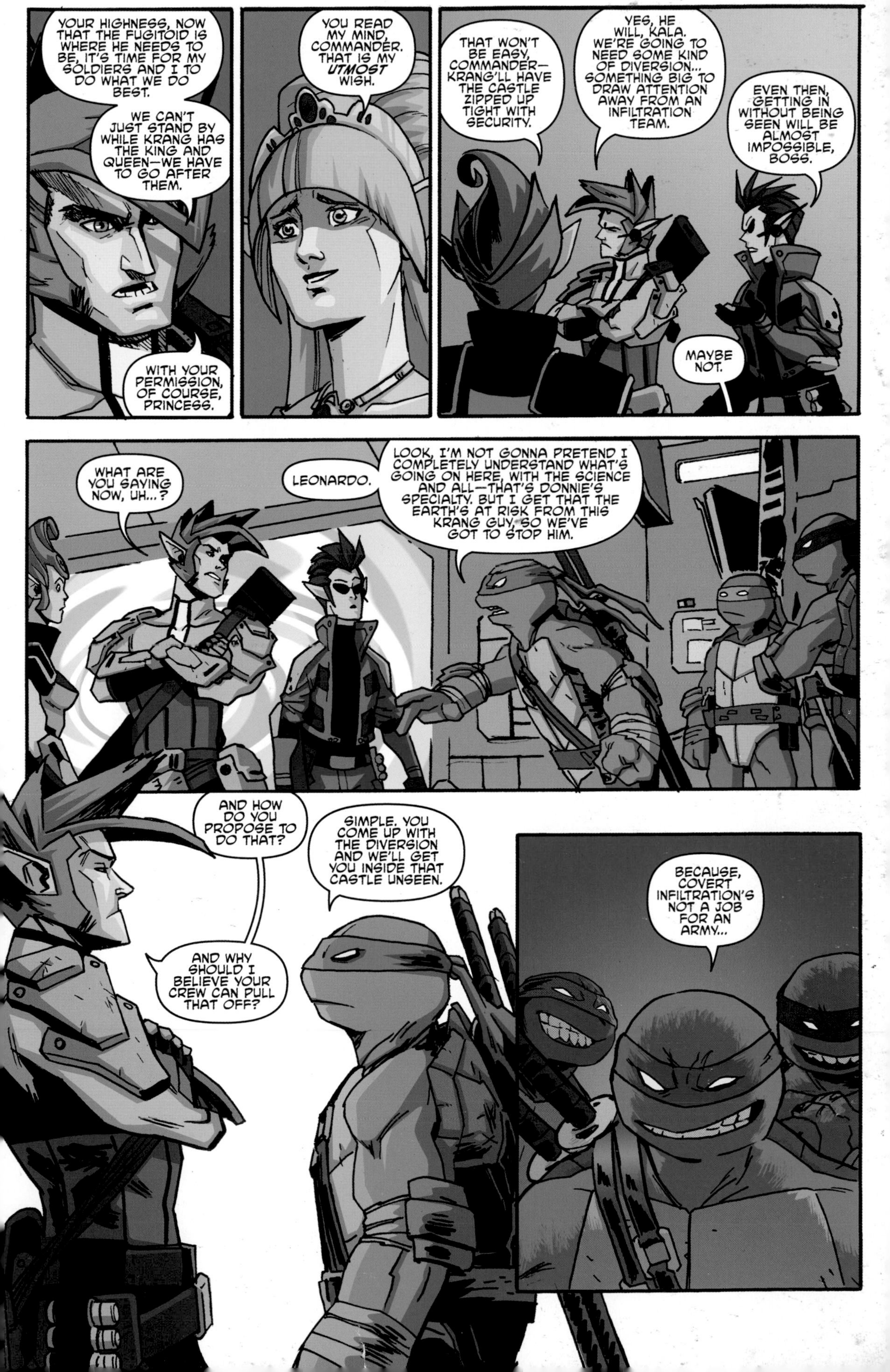
YOUR HIGHNESS, NOW THAT THE FUGITOID IS WHERE HE NEEDS TO BE, IT'S TIME FOR MY SOLDIERS AND I TO DO WHAT WE DO BEST.
WE CAN'T JUST STAND BY WHILE KRANG HAS THE KING AND QUEEN—WE HAVE TO GO AFTER THEM.
WITH YOUR PERMISSION, OF COURSE, PRINCESS.
YOU READ MY MIND, COMMANDER. THAT IS MY *UTMOST* WISH.
THAT WON'T BE EASY, COMMANDER— KRANG'LL HAVE THE CASTLE ZIPPED UP TIGHT WITH SECURITY.
YES, HE WILL, KALA. WE'RE GOING TO NEED SOME KIND OF DIVERSION... SOMETHING BIG TO DRAW ATTENTION AWAY FROM AN INFILTRATION TEAM.
EVEN THEN, GETTING IN WITHOUT BEING SEEN WILL BE ALMOST IMPOSSIBLE, BOSS.
MAYBE NOT.
WHAT ARE YOU SAYING NOW, UH...?
LEONARDO.
LOOK, I'M NOT GONNA PRETEND I COMPLETELY UNDERSTAND WHAT'S GOING ON HERE, WITH THE SCIENCE AND ALL—THAT'S DONNIE'S SPECIALTY. BUT I GET THAT THE EARTH'S AT RISK FROM THIS KRANG GUY, SO WE'VE GOT TO STOP HIM.
AND HOW DO YOU PROPOSE TO DO THAT?
AND WHY SHOULD I BELIEVE YOUR CREW CAN PULL THAT OFF?
SIMPLE. YOU COME UP WITH THE DIVERSION AND WE'LL GET YOU INSIDE THAT CASTLE UNSEEN.
BECAUSE, COVERT INFILTRATION'S NOT A JOB FOR AN ARMY...

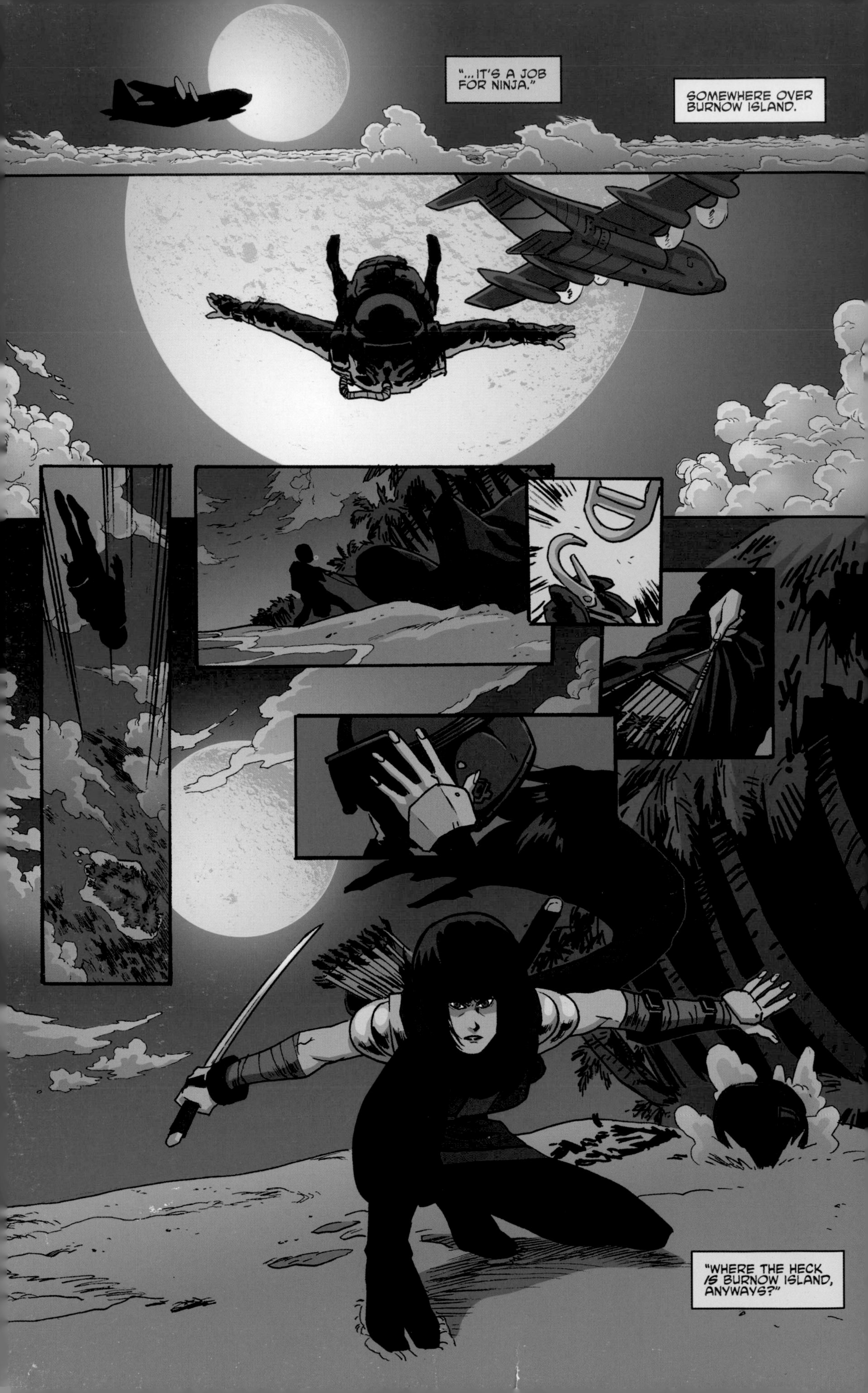
"...IT'S A JOB FOR NINJA."
SOMEWHERE OVER BURNOW ISLAND.
"WHERE THE HECK IS BURNOW ISLAND, ANYWAYS?"

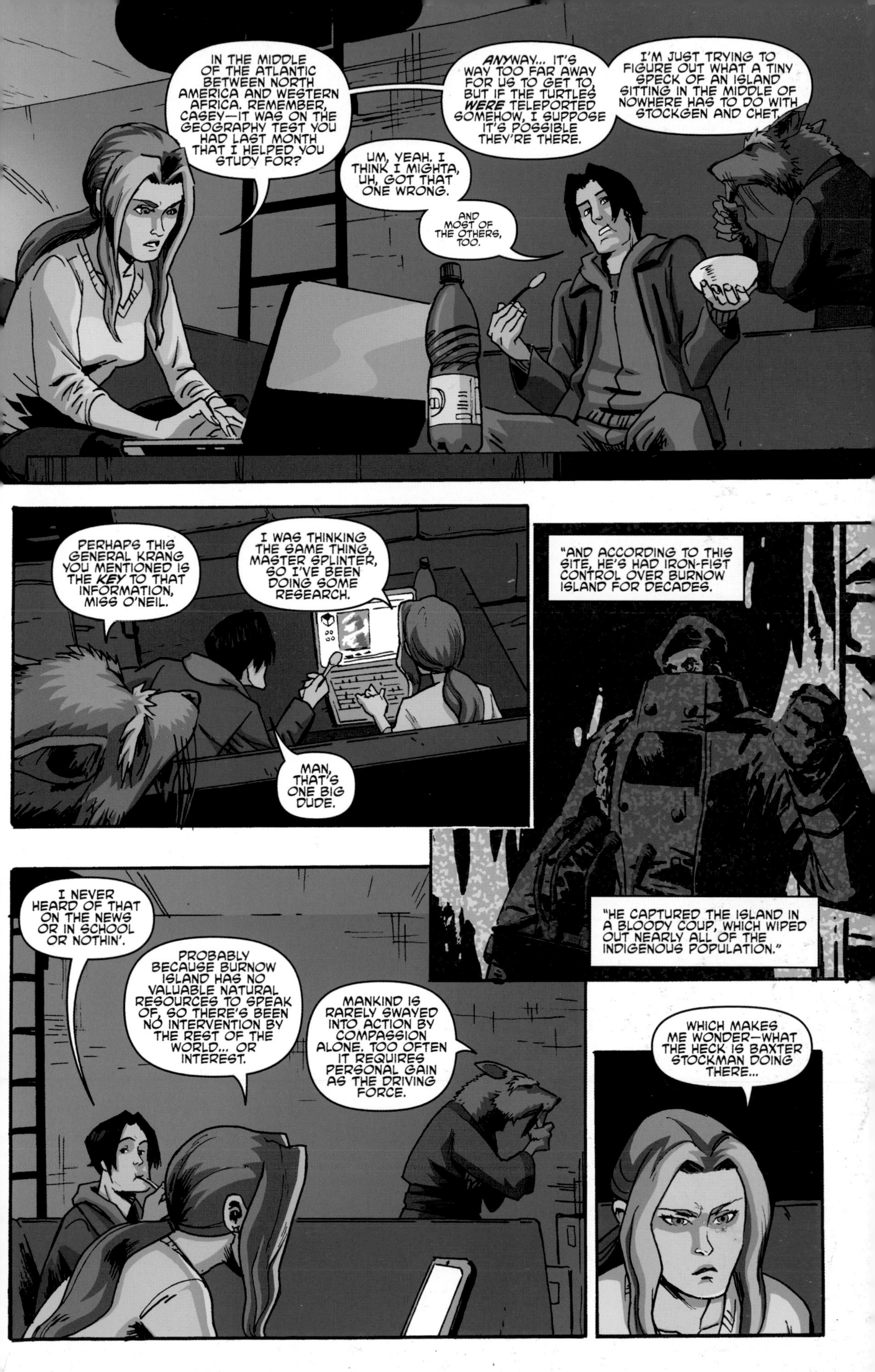

IN THE MIDDLE OF THE ATLANTIC BETWEEN NORTH AMERICA AND WESTERN AFRICA. REMEMBER, CASEY—IT WAS ON THE GEOGRAPHY TEST YOU HAD LAST MONTH THAT I HELPED YOU STUDY FOR?
UM, YEAH. I THINK I MIGHTA, UH, GOT THAT ONE WRONG.
AND MOST OF THE OTHERS, TOO.
ANYWAY... IT'S WAY TOO FAR AWAY FOR US TO GET TO, BUT IF THE TURTLES WERE TELEPORTED SOMEHOW, I SUPPOSE IT'S POSSIBLE THEY'RE THERE.
I'M JUST TRYING TO FIGURE OUT WHAT A TINY SPECK OF AN ISLAND SITTING IN THE MIDDLE OF NOWHERE HAS TO DO WITH STOCKGEN AND CHET.
PERHAPS THIS GENERAL KRANG YOU MENTIONED IS THE KEY TO THAT INFORMATION, MISS O'NEIL.
I WAS THINKING THE SAME THING, MASTER SPLINTER, SO I'VE BEEN DOING SOME RESEARCH.
MAN, THAT'S ONE BIG DUDE.
"AND ACCORDING TO THIS SITE, HE'S HAD IRON-FIST CONTROL OVER BURNOW ISLAND FOR DECADES.
"HE CAPTURED THE ISLAND IN A BLOODY COUP, WHICH WIPED OUT NEARLY ALL OF THE INDIGENOUS POPULATION."
I NEVER HEARD OF THAT ON THE NEWS OR IN SCHOOL OR NOTHIN'.
PROBABLY BECAUSE BURNOW ISLAND HAS NO VALUABLE NATURAL RESOURCES TO SPEAK OF, SO THERE'S BEEN NO INTERVENTION BY THE REST OF THE WORLD... OR INTEREST.
MANKIND IS RARELY SWAYED INTO ACTION BY COMPASSION ALONE. TOO OFTEN IT REQUIRES PERSONAL GAIN AS THE DRIVING FORCE.
WHICH MAKES ME WONDER—WHAT THE HECK IS BAXTER STOCKMAN DOING THERE...

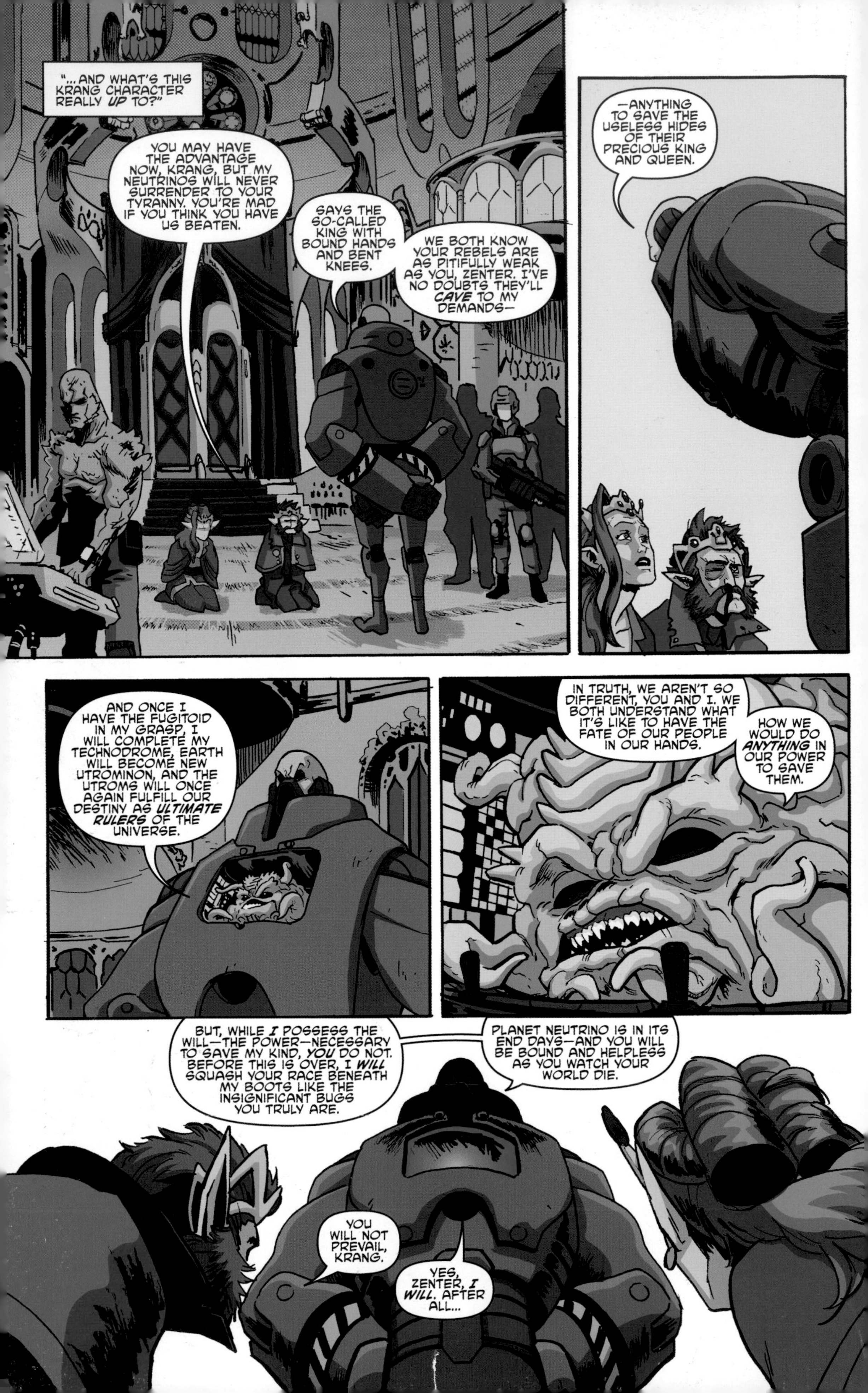
"...AND WHAT'S THIS KRANG CHARACTER REALLY UP TO?"
YOU MAY HAVE THE ADVANTAGE NOW, KRANG, BUT MY NEUTRINOS WILL NEVER SURRENDER TO YOUR TYRANNY. YOU'RE MAD IF YOU THINK YOU HAVE US BEATEN.
SAYS THE SO-CALLED KING WITH BOUND HANDS AND BENT KNEES.
WE BOTH KNOW YOUR REBELS ARE AS PITIFULLY WEAK AS YOU, ZENTER. I'VE NO DOUBTS THEY'LL CAVE TO MY DEMANDS—
—ANYTHING TO SAVE THE USELESS HIDES OF THEIR PRECIOUS KING AND QUEEN.
AND ONCE I HAVE THE FUGITOID IN MY GRASP, I WILL COMPLETE MY TECHNODROME, EARTH WILL BECOME NEW UTROMINON, AND THE UTROMS WILL ONCE AGAIN FULFILL OUR DESTINY AS ULTIMATE RULERS OF THE UNIVERSE.
IN TRUTH, WE AREN'T SO DIFFERENT, YOU AND I. WE BOTH UNDERSTAND WHAT IT'S LIKE TO HAVE THE FATE OF OUR PEOPLE IN OUR HANDS.
HOW WE WOULD DO ANYTHING IN OUR POWER TO SAVE THEM.
BUT, WHILE I POSSESS THE WILL—THE POWER—NECESSARY TO SAVE MY KIND, YOU DO NOT. BEFORE THIS IS OVER, I WILL SQUASH YOUR RACE BENEATH MY BOOTS LIKE THE INSIGNIFICANT BUGS YOU TRULY ARE.
PLANET NEUTRINO IS IN ITS END DAYS—AND YOU WILL BE BOUND AND HELPLESS AS YOU WATCH YOUR WORLD DIE.
YOU WILL NOT PREVAIL, KRANG.
YES, ZENTER, I WILL. AFTER ALL...

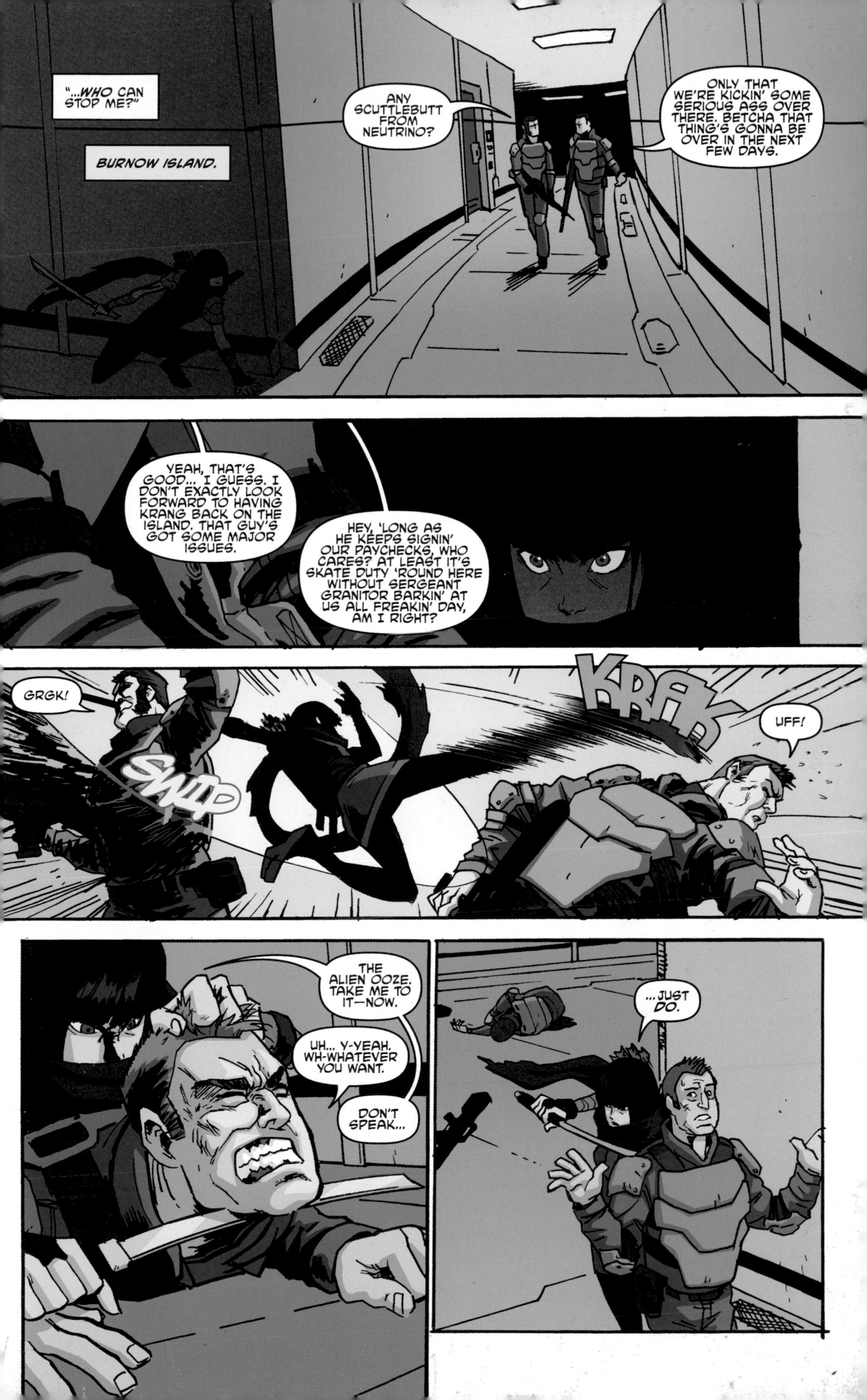
"...WHO CAN STOP ME?"
BURNOW ISLAND.
ANY SCUTTLEBUTT FROM NEUTRINO?
ONLY THAT WE'RE KICKIN' SOME SERIOUS ASS OVER THERE. BETCHA THAT THING'S GONNA BE OVER IN THE NEXT FEW DAYS.
YEAH, THAT'S GOOD... I GUESS. I DON'T EXACTLY LOOK FORWARD TO HAVING KRANG BACK ON THE ISLAND. THAT GUY'S GOT SOME MAJOR ISSUES.
HEY, 'LONG AS HE KEEPS SIGNIN' OUR PAYCHECKS, WHO CARES? AT LEAST IT'S SKATE DUTY 'ROUND HERE WITHOUT SERGEANT GRANITOR BARKIN' AT US ALL FREAKIN' DAY, AM I RIGHT?
GRGK!
SWIP
KRAK
UFF!
THE ALIEN OOZE. TAKE ME TO IT—NOW.
UH... Y-YEAH. WH-WHATEVER YOU WANT.
DON'T SPEAK...
...JUST DO.

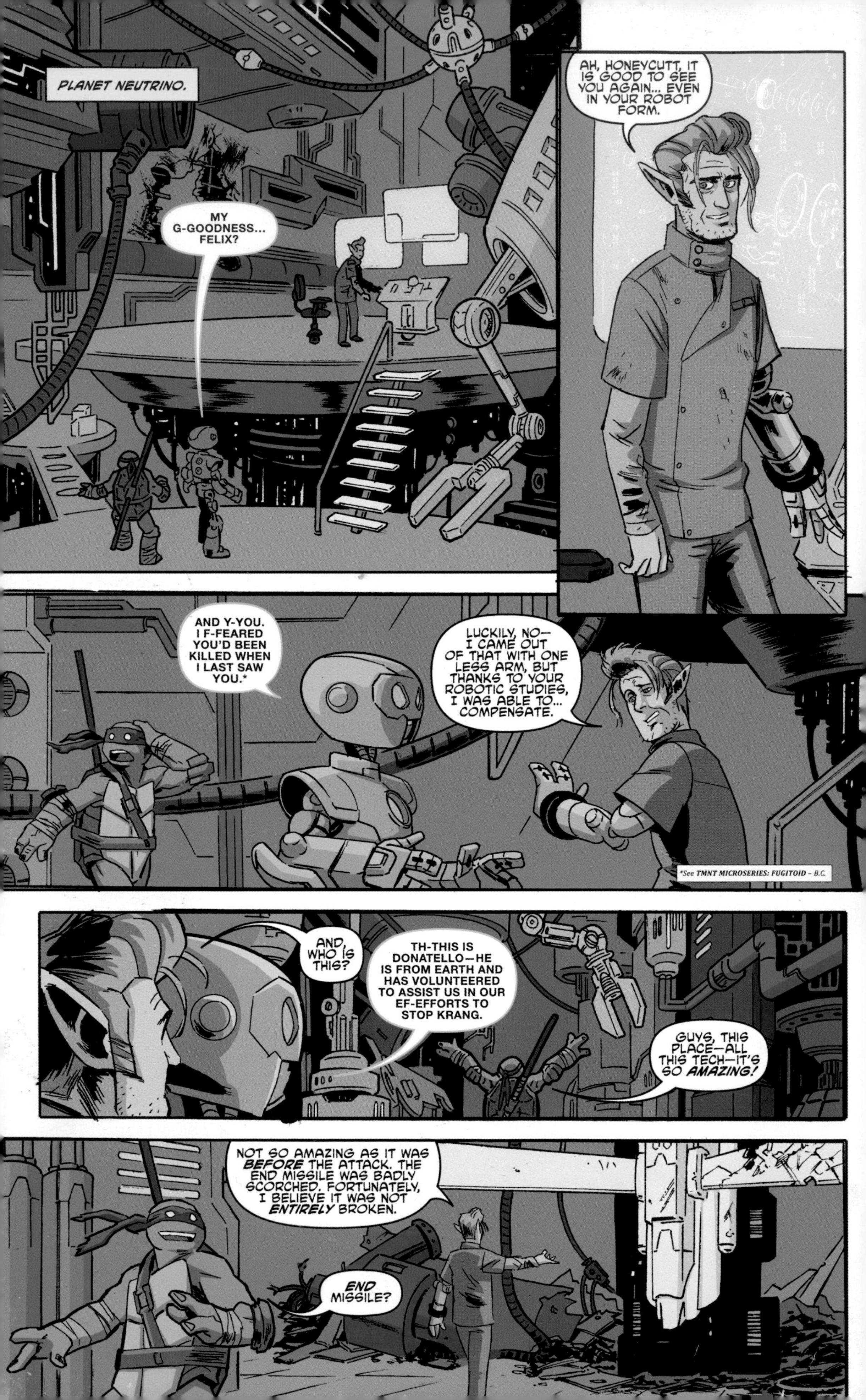
PLANET NEUTRINO.
MY G-GOODNESS... FELIX?
AH, HONEYCUTT, IT IS GOOD TO SEE YOU AGAIN... EVEN IN YOUR ROBOT FORM.
AND Y-YOU. I F-FEARED YOU'D BEEN KILLED WHEN I LAST SAW YOU.*
LUCKILY, NO— I CAME OUT OF THAT WITH ONE LESS ARM, BUT THANKS TO YOUR ROBOTIC STUDIES, I WAS ABLE TO... COMPENSATE.
*See TMNT MICROSERIES: FUGITOID – B.C.
AND, WHO IS THIS?
TH-THIS IS DONATELLO—HE IS FROM EARTH AND HAS VOLUNTEERED TO ASSIST US IN OUR EF-EFFORTS TO STOP KRANG.
GUYS, THIS PLACE—ALL THIS TECH—IT'S SO AMAZING!
NOT SO AMAZING AS IT WAS BEFORE THE ATTACK. THE END MISSILE WAS BADLY SCORCHED. FORTUNATELY, I BELIEVE IT WAS NOT ENTIRELY BROKEN.
END MISSILE?

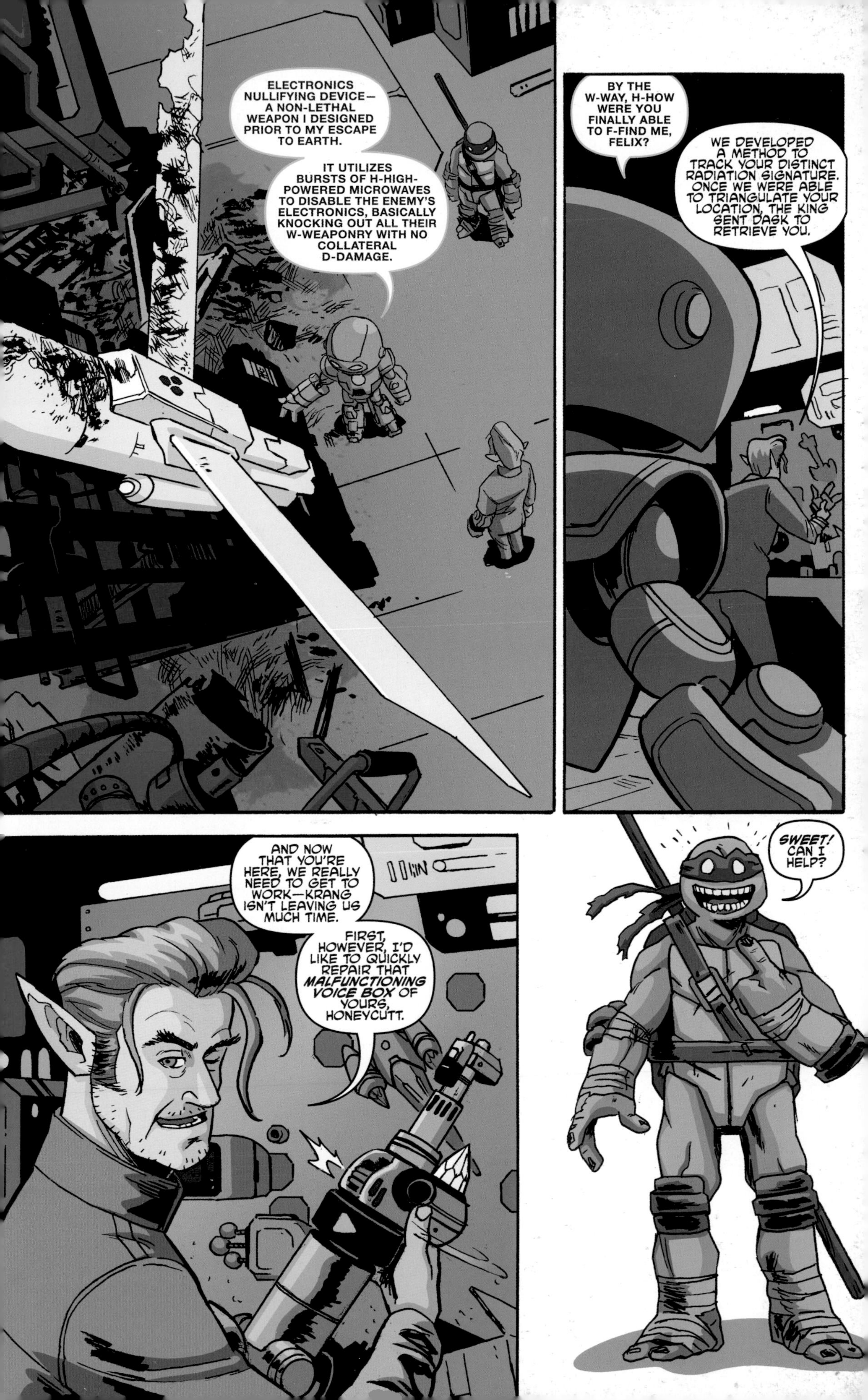
ELECTRONICS NULLIFYING DEVICE— A NON-LETHAL WEAPON I DESIGNED PRIOR TO MY ESCAPE TO EARTH.
IT UTILIZES BURSTS OF H-HIGH-POWERED MICROWAVES TO DISABLE THE ENEMY'S ELECTRONICS, BASICALLY KNOCKING OUT ALL THEIR W-WEAPONRY WITH NO COLLATERAL D-DAMAGE.
BY THE W-WAY, H-HOW WERE YOU FINALLY ABLE TO F-FIND ME, FELIX?
WE DEVELOPED A METHOD TO TRACK YOUR DISTINCT RADIATION SIGNATURE. ONCE WE WERE ABLE TO TRIANGULATE YOUR LOCATION, THE KING SENT DASK TO RETRIEVE YOU.
AND NOW THAT YOU'RE HERE, WE REALLY NEED TO GET TO WORK—KRANG ISN'T LEAVING US MUCH TIME.
FIRST, HOWEVER, I'D LIKE TO QUICKLY REPAIR THAT *MALFUNCTIONING VOICE BOX* OF YOURS, HONEYCUTT.
SWEET! CAN I HELP?

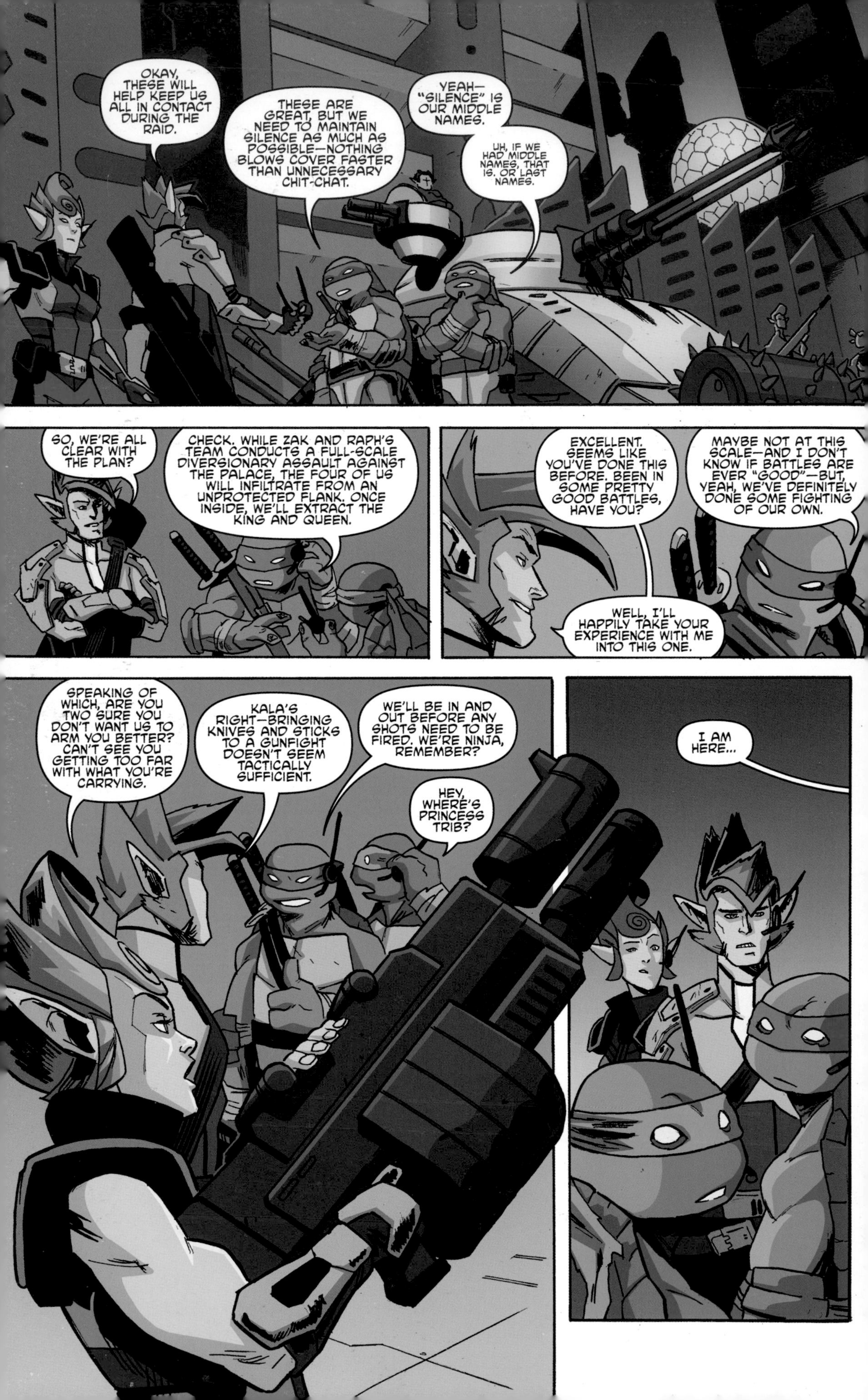
OKAY, THESE WILL HELP KEEP US ALL IN CONTACT DURING THE RAID.
THESE ARE GREAT, BUT WE NEED TO MAINTAIN SILENCE AS MUCH AS POSSIBLE—NOTHING BLOWS COVER FASTER THAN UNNECESSARY CHIT-CHAT.
YEAH— "SILENCE" IS OUR MIDDLE NAMES.
UH, IF WE HAD MIDDLE NAMES, THAT IS. OR LAST NAMES.
SO, WE'RE ALL CLEAR WITH THE PLAN?
CHECK. WHILE ZAK AND RAPH'S TEAM CONDUCTS A FULL-SCALE DIVERSIONARY ASSAULT AGAINST THE PALACE, THE FOUR OF US WILL INFILTRATE FROM AN UNPROTECTED FLANK. ONCE INSIDE, WE'LL EXTRACT THE KING AND QUEEN.
EXCELLENT. SEEMS LIKE YOU'VE DONE THIS BEFORE. BEEN IN SOME PRETTY GOOD BATTLES, HAVE YOU?
MAYBE NOT AT THIS SCALE—AND I DON'T KNOW IF BATTLES ARE EVER "GOOD"—BUT, YEAH, WE'VE DEFINITELY DONE SOME FIGHTING OF OUR OWN.
WELL, I'LL HAPPILY TAKE YOUR EXPERIENCE WITH ME INTO THIS ONE.
SPEAKING OF WHICH, ARE YOU TWO SURE YOU DON'T WANT US TO ARM YOU BETTER? CAN'T SEE YOU GETTING TOO FAR WITH WHAT YOU'RE CARRYING.
KALA'S RIGHT—BRINGING KNIVES AND STICKS TO A GUNFIGHT DOESN'T SEEM TACTICALLY SUFFICIENT.
WE'LL BE IN AND OUT BEFORE ANY SHOTS NEED TO BE FIRED. WE'RE NINJA, REMEMBER?
HEY, WHERE'S PRINCESS TRIB?
I AM HERE...

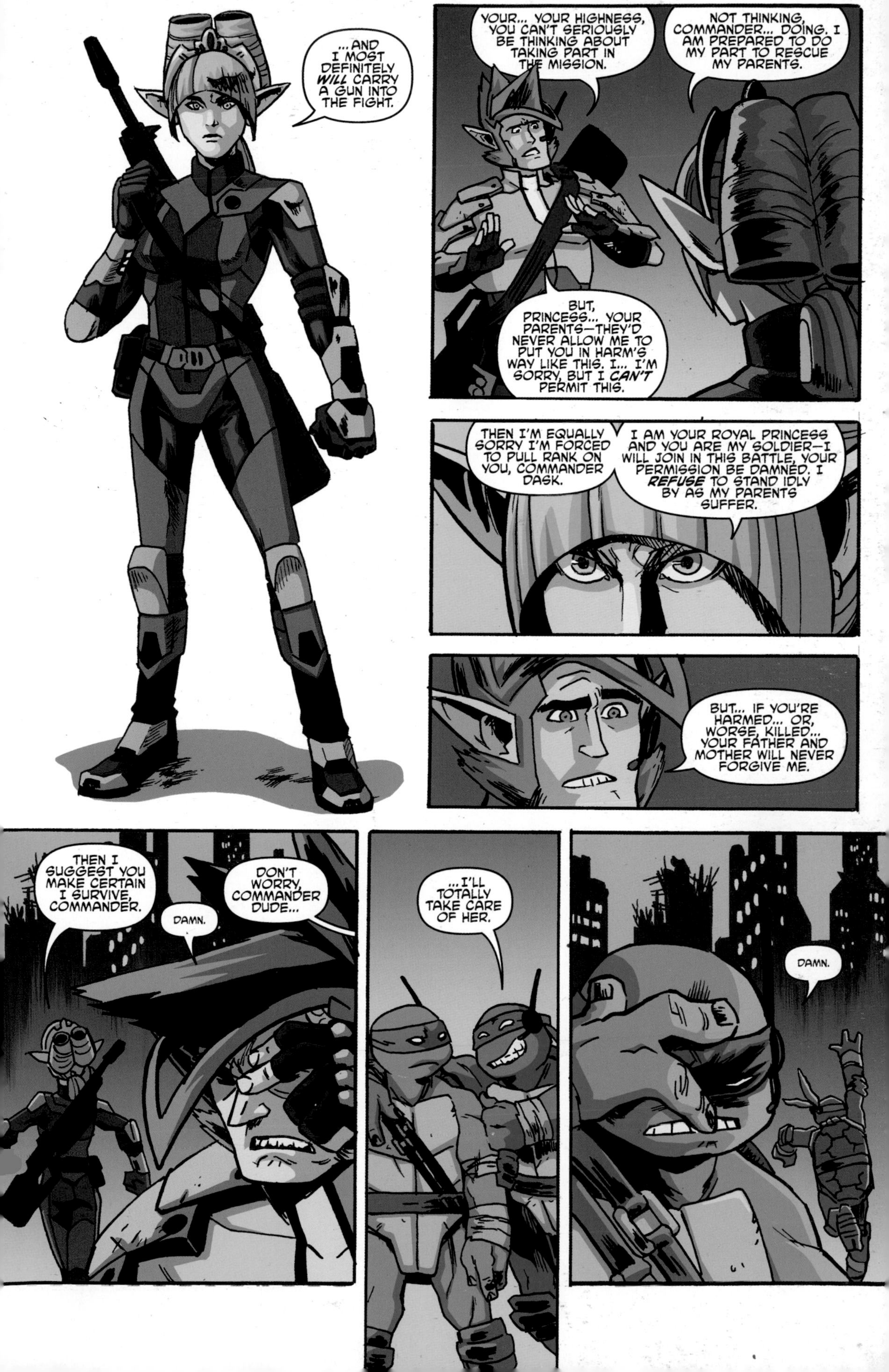
...AND I MOST DEFINITELY WILL CARRY A GUN INTO THE FIGHT.
YOUR... YOUR HIGHNESS, YOU CAN'T SERIOUSLY BE THINKING ABOUT TAKING PART IN THE MISSION.
NOT THINKING, COMMANDER... DOING. I AM PREPARED TO DO MY PART TO RESCUE MY PARENTS.
BUT, PRINCESS... YOUR PARENTS—THEY'D NEVER ALLOW ME TO PUT YOU IN HARM'S WAY LIKE THIS. I... I'M SORRY, BUT I CAN'T PERMIT THIS.
THEN I'M EQUALLY SORRY I'M FORCED TO PULL RANK ON YOU, COMMANDER DASK.
I AM YOUR ROYAL PRINCESS AND YOU ARE MY SOLDIER—I WILL JOIN IN THIS BATTLE, YOUR PERMISSION BE DAMNED. I REFUSE TO STAND IDLY BY AS MY PARENTS SUFFER.
BUT... IF YOU'RE HARMED... OR, WORSE, KILLED... YOUR FATHER AND MOTHER WILL NEVER FORGIVE ME.
THEN I SUGGEST YOU MAKE CERTAIN I SURVIVE, COMMANDER.
DAMN.
DON'T WORRY, COMMANDER DUDE...
...I'LL TOTALLY TAKE CARE OF HER.
DAMN.

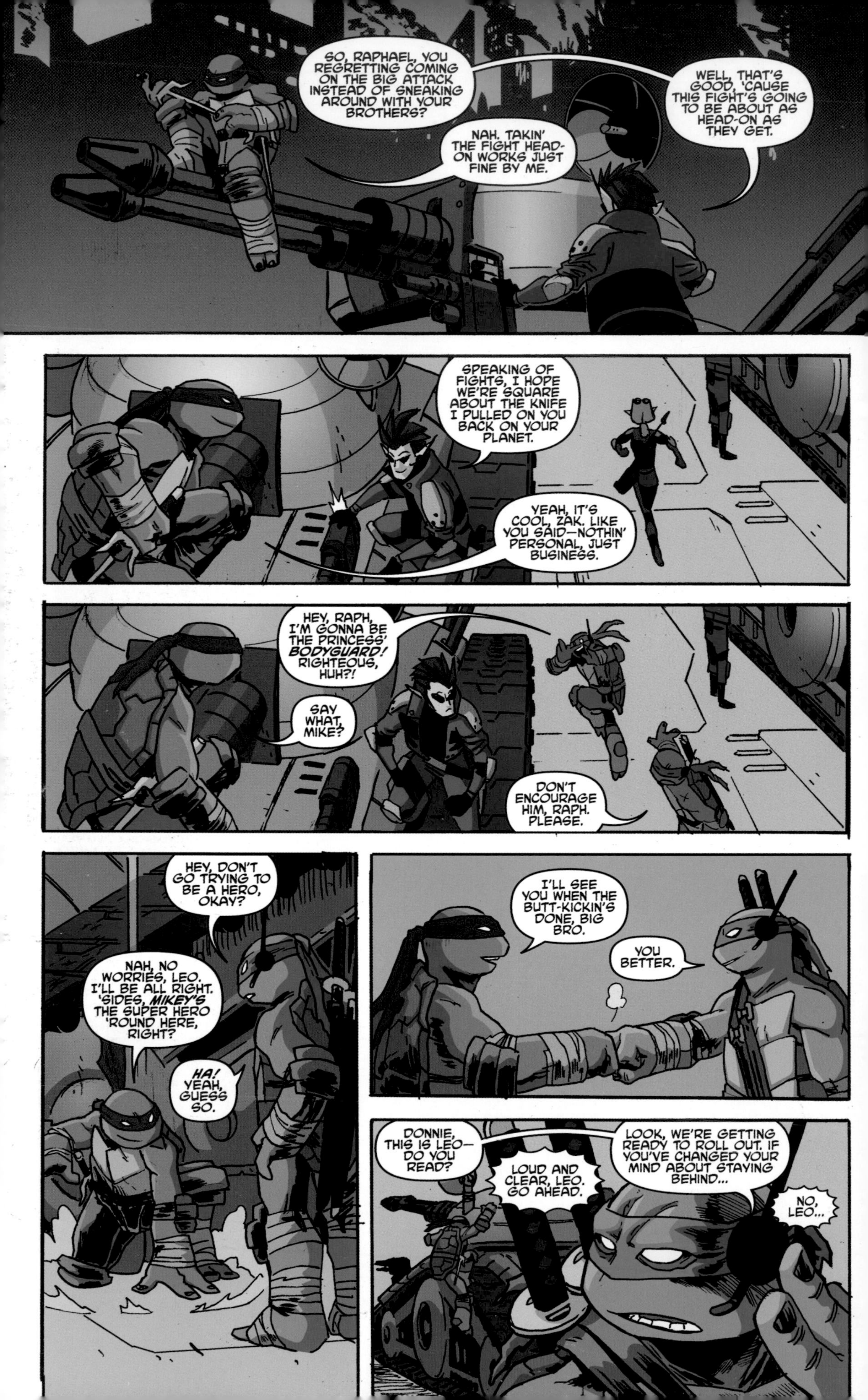
SO, RAPHAEL, YOU REGRETTING COMING ON THE BIG ATTACK INSTEAD OF SNEAKING AROUND WITH YOUR BROTHERS?
NAH. TAKIN' THE FIGHT HEAD-ON WORKS JUST FINE BY ME.
WELL, THAT'S GOOD, 'CAUSE THIS FIGHT'S GOING TO BE ABOUT AS HEAD-ON AS THEY GET.
SPEAKING OF FIGHTS, I HOPE WE'RE SQUARE ABOUT THE KNIFE I PULLED ON YOU BACK ON YOUR PLANET.
YEAH, IT'S COOL, ZAK. LIKE YOU SAID—NOTHIN' PERSONAL, JUST BUSINESS.
HEY, RAPH, I'M GONNA BE THE PRINCESS' BODYGUARD! RIGHTEOUS, HUH?!
SAY WHAT, MIKE?
DON'T ENCOURAGE HIM, RAPH. PLEASE.
HEY, DON'T GO TRYING TO BE A HERO, OKAY?
NAH, NO WORRIES, LEO. I'LL BE ALL RIGHT. 'SIDES, MIKEY'S THE SUPER HERO 'ROUND HERE, RIGHT?
HA! YEAH, GUESS SO.
I'LL SEE YOU WHEN THE BUTT-KICKIN'S DONE, BIG BRO.
YOU BETTER.
DONNIE, THIS IS LEO— DO YOU READ?
LOUD AND CLEAR, LEO. GO AHEAD.
LOOK, WE'RE GETTING READY TO ROLL OUT. IF YOU'VE CHANGED YOUR MIND ABOUT STAYING BEHIND...
NO, LEO...

...I'M RIGHT WHERE I NEED TO BE. YOU GUYS GO GET THE KING AND QUEEN AND I'LL SEE WHAT I CAN DO ABOUT SAVING EARTH.

I MUST THANK YOU BOTH AGAIN — HAVING A FUNCTIONAL VOICE BOX IS BEYOND RELIEF. I FEEL LIKE A NEW ROBOT.

SURE THING, PROFESSOR.

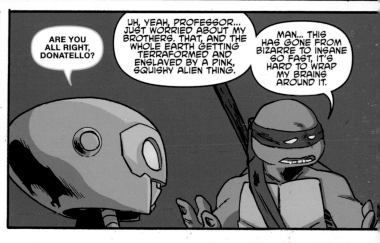

ARE YOU ALL RIGHT, DONATELLO?

UH, YEAH, PROFESSOR... JUST WORRIED ABOUT MY BROTHERS. THAT, AND THE WHOLE EARTH GETTING TERRAFORMED AND ENSLAVED BY A PINK, SQUISHY ALIEN THING.

MAN... THIS HAS GONE FROM BIZARRE TO INSANE SO FAST, IT'S HARD TO WRAP MY BRAINS AROUND IT.

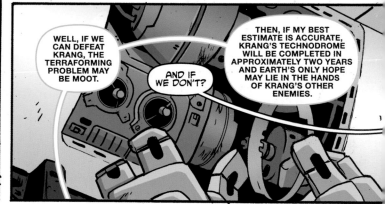

WELL, IF WE CAN DEFEAT KRANG, THE TERRAFORMING PROBLEM MAY BE MOOT.

AND IF WE DON'T?

THEN, IF MY BEST ESTIMATE IS ACCURATE, KRANG'S TECHNODROME WILL BE COMPLETED IN APPROXIMATELY TWO YEARS AND EARTH'S ONLY HOPE MAY LIE IN THE HANDS OF KRANG'S OTHER ENEMIES.

OTHER ENEMIES?

YES...

...EVEN AS CHET ALLEN, I FOUGHT AGAINST KRANG'S EVIL SCHEME IN WAYS THAT WERE BY NO MEANS HONORABLE, BUT ABSOLUTELY NECESSARY.

SADLY, IF WE LOSE THIS WAR, ONLY TIME WILL TELL IF MY EFFORTS WERE ENOUGH...

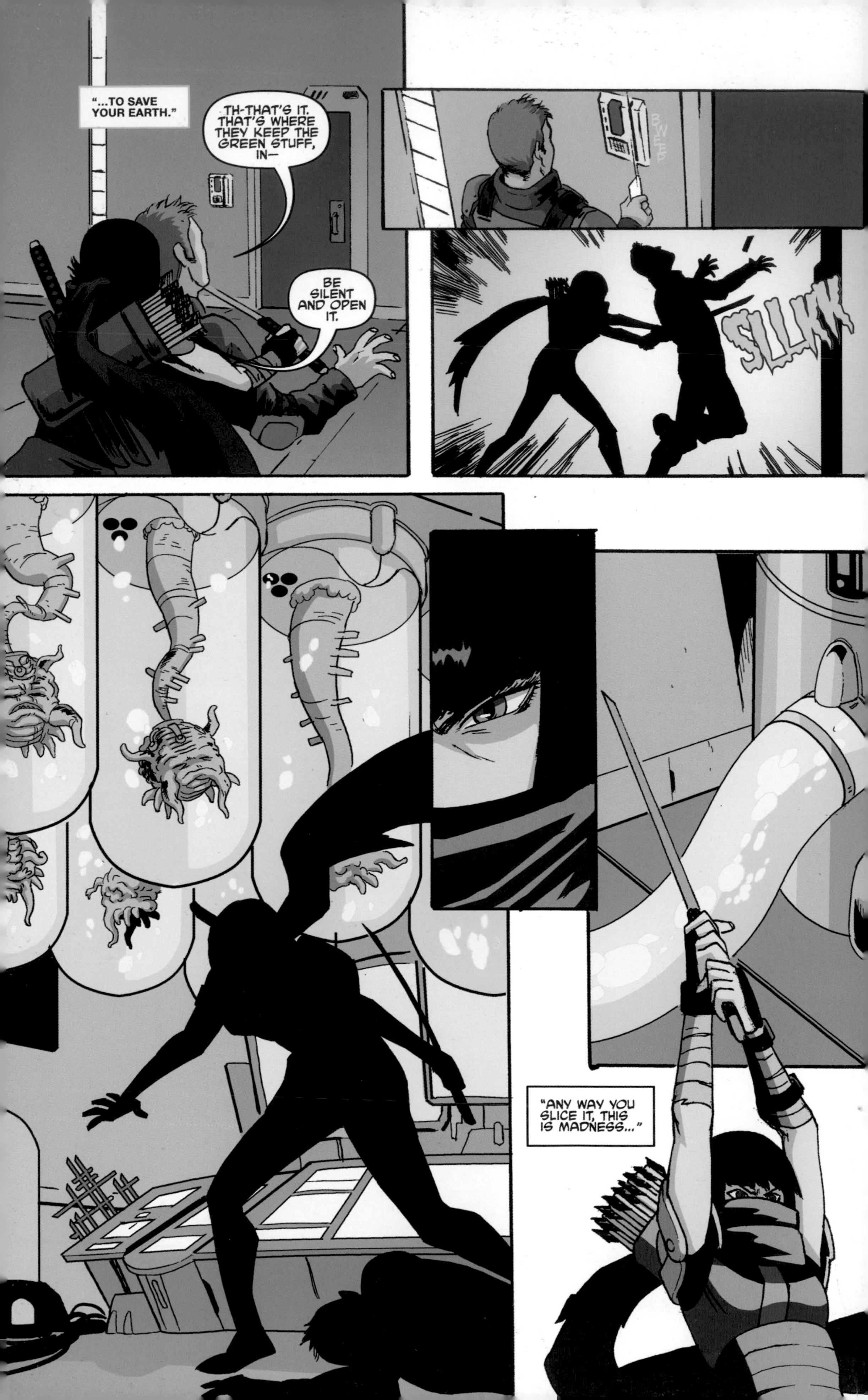
"...TO SAVE YOUR EARTH."
TH-THAT'S IT. THAT'S WHERE THEY KEEP THE GREEN STUFF, IN—
BE SILENT AND OPEN IT.
BWEEP
SLUKK
"ANY WAY YOU SLICE IT, THIS IS MADNESS..."

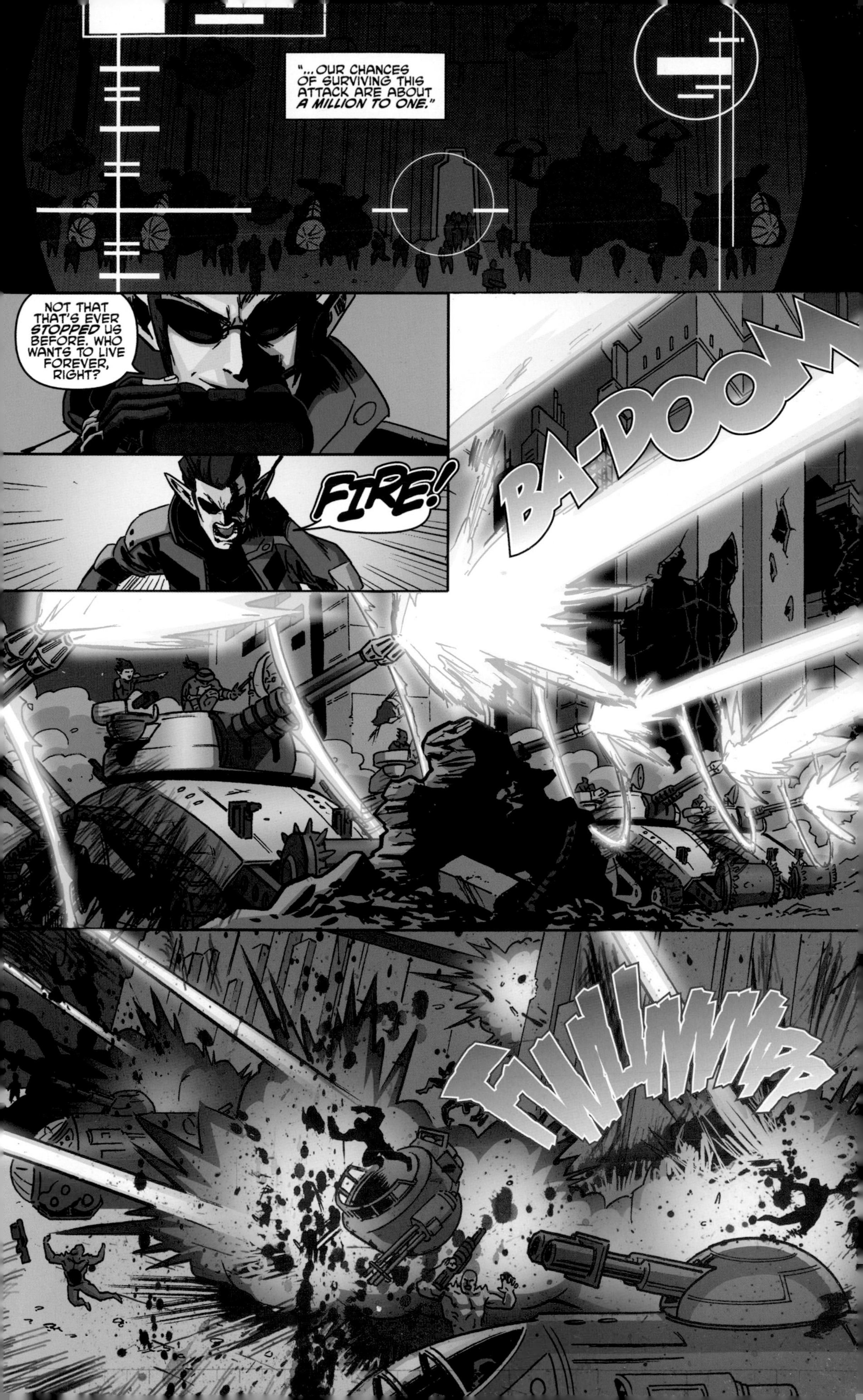
"...OUR CHANCES OF SURVIVING THIS ATTACK ARE ABOUT *A MILLION TO ONE.*"
NOT THAT THAT'S EVER *STOPPED* US BEFORE. WHO WANTS TO LIVE FOREVER, RIGHT?
BA-DOOM
FIRE!
FWUMMMB

WHAT IN BLAZES?!

CAPTAIN TRAGG, *SITREP!*

ON IT, GENERAL.

SERGEANT GRANITOR, WHAT THE *HELL* WAS THAT?

THE NRF ARE ATTACKING IN FORCE, CAPTAIN. ARMOR, ARTILLERY, GROUND TROOPS... YOU *NAME IT*, SIR.

LOOKS LIKE THEY'RE GONNA THROW *EVERYTHING* THEY GOT AT US TO TRY AND GET BACK THE KING AND QUEEN.

THE IDIOTS! THEY WOULD *DARE* FACE ME IN OPEN BATTLE RATHER THAN GIVE ME THAT WRETCHED ROBOT?

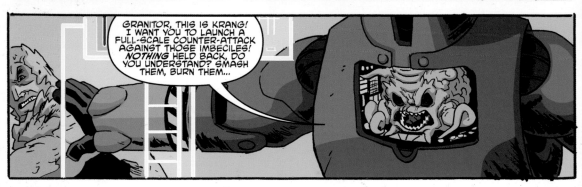

GRANITOR, THIS IS KRANG! I WANT YOU TO LAUNCH A FULL-SCALE COUNTER-ATTACK AGAINST THOSE IMBECILES! *NOTHING* HELD BACK, DO YOU UNDERSTAND? SMASH THEM, BURN THEM...

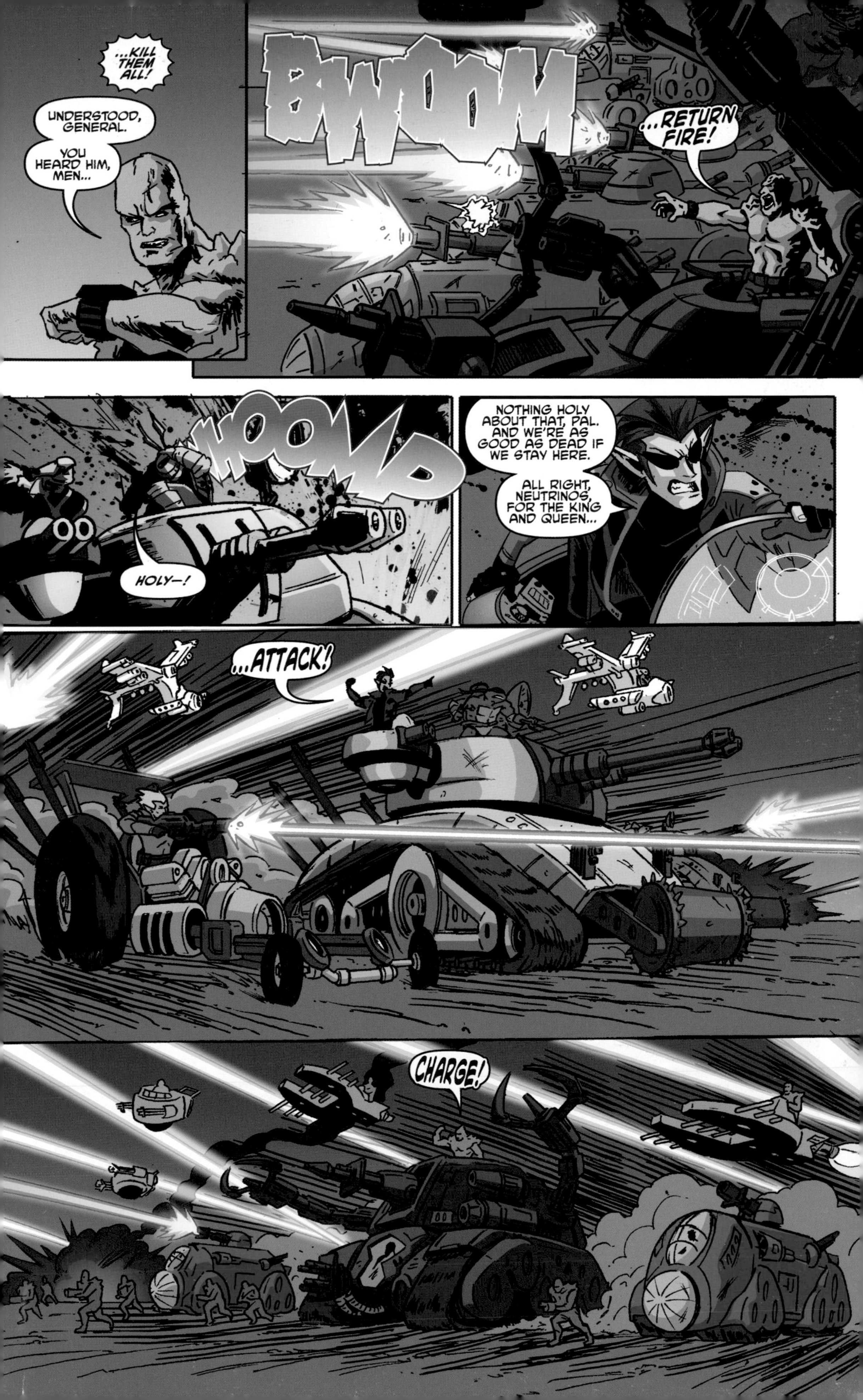
...KILL THEM ALL!
UNDERSTOOD, GENERAL.
YOU HEARD HIM, MEN...
BWOOM
...RETURN FIRE!
WHOOMP
HOLY—!
NOTHING HOLY ABOUT THAT, PAL. AND WE'RE AS GOOD AS DEAD IF WE STAY HERE.
ALL RIGHT, NEUTRINOS, FOR THE KING AND QUEEN...
...ATTACK!
CHARGE!

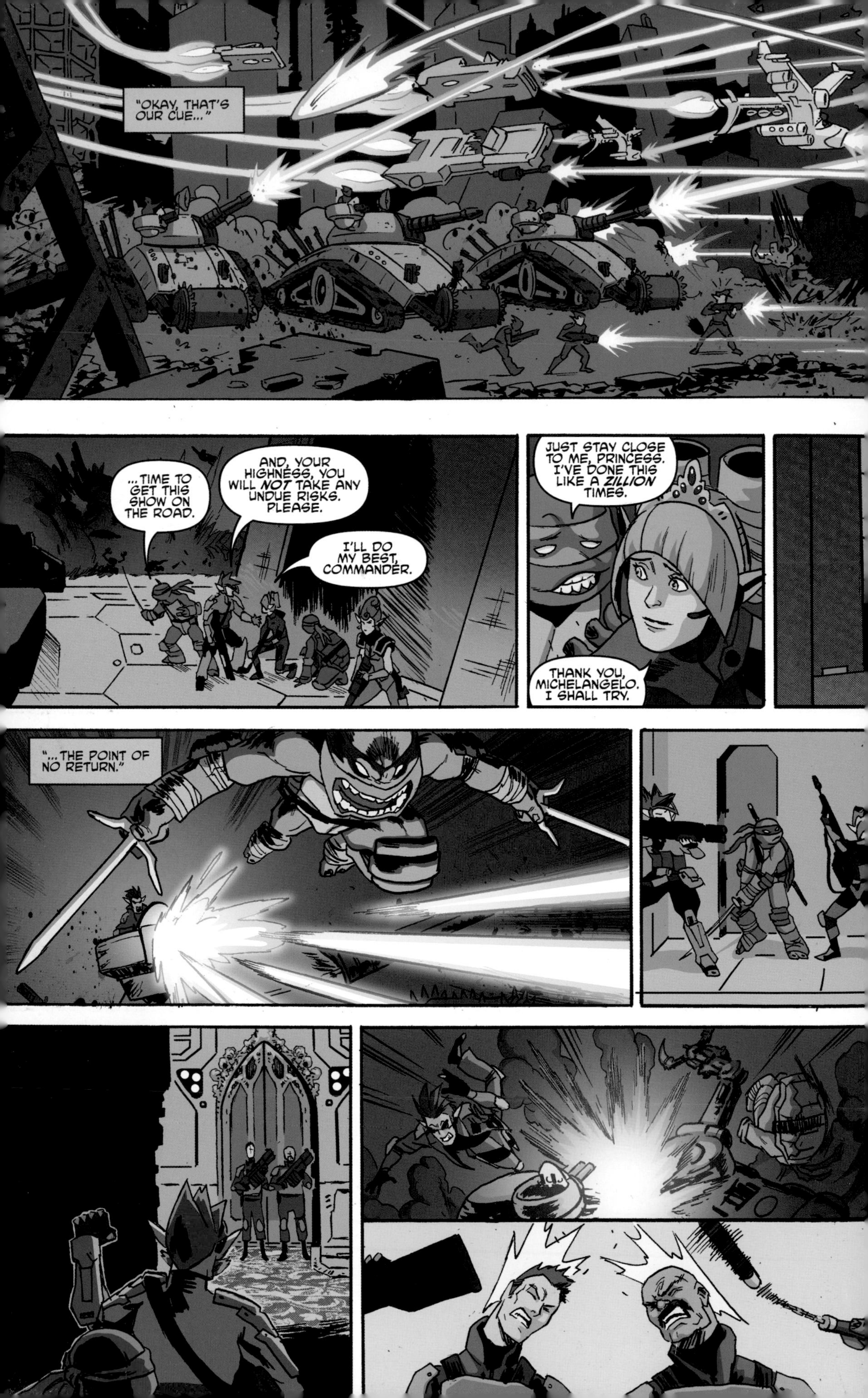
"OKAY, THAT'S OUR CUE..."
...TIME TO GET THIS SHOW ON THE ROAD.
AND, YOUR HIGHNESS, YOU WILL *NOT* TAKE ANY UNDUE RISKS. PLEASE.
I'LL DO MY BEST, COMMANDER.
JUST STAY CLOSE TO ME, PRINCESS. I'VE DONE THIS LIKE A *ZILLION* TIMES.
THANK YOU, MICHELANGELO. I SHALL TRY.
"...THE POINT OF NO RETURN."

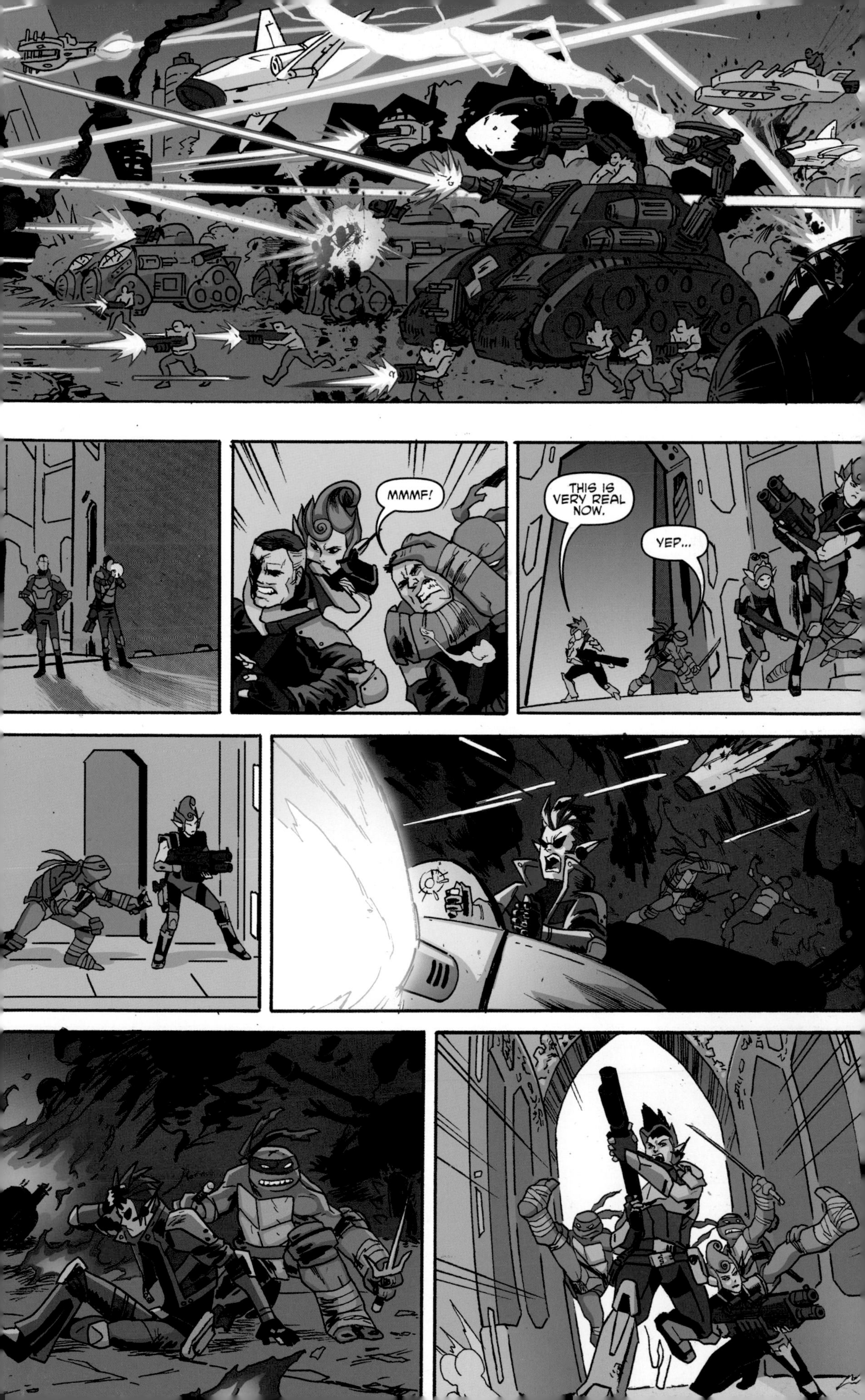
MMMF!
THIS IS VERY REAL NOW.
YEP...

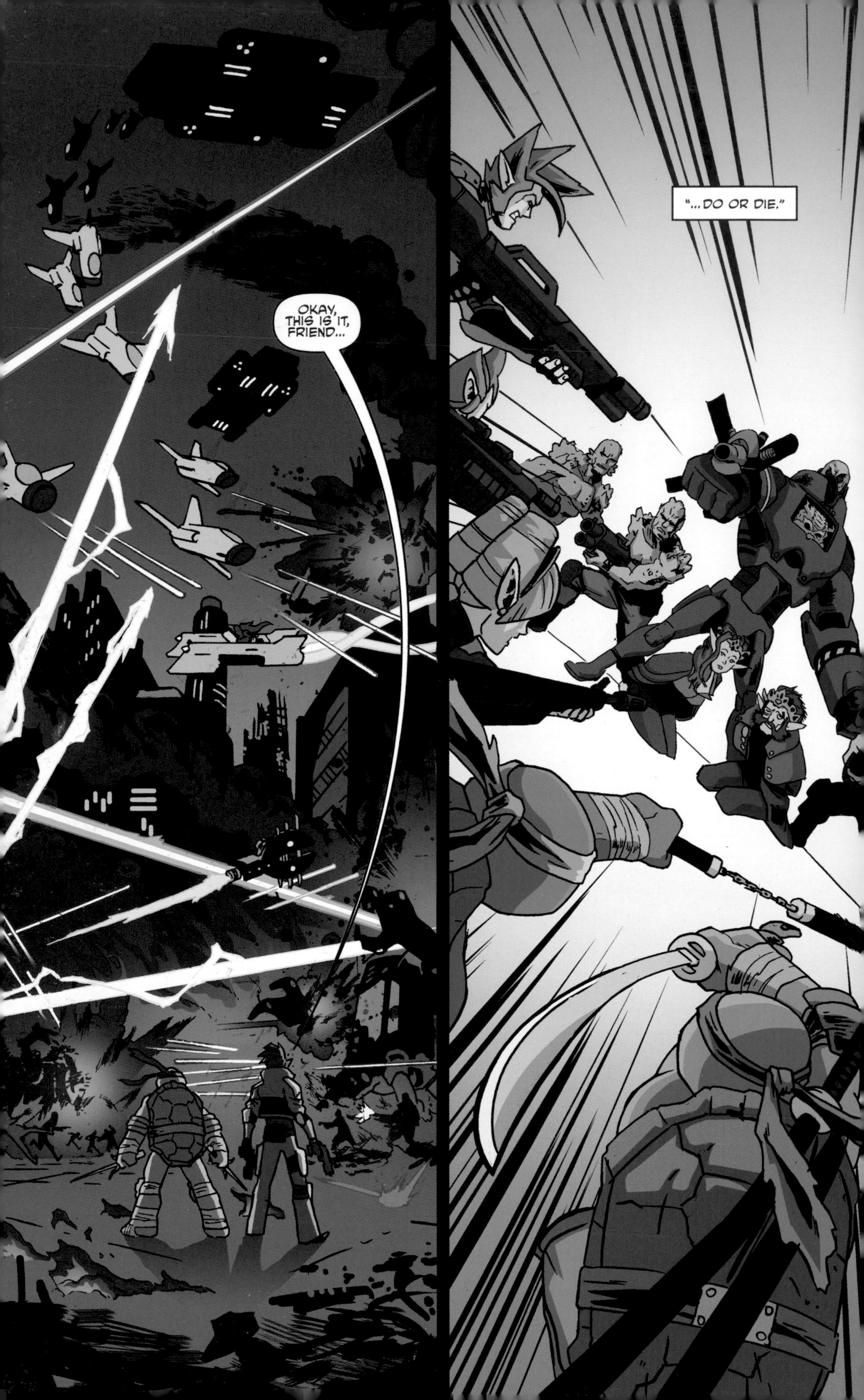
OKAY, THIS IS IT, FRIEND...
"...DO OR DIE."

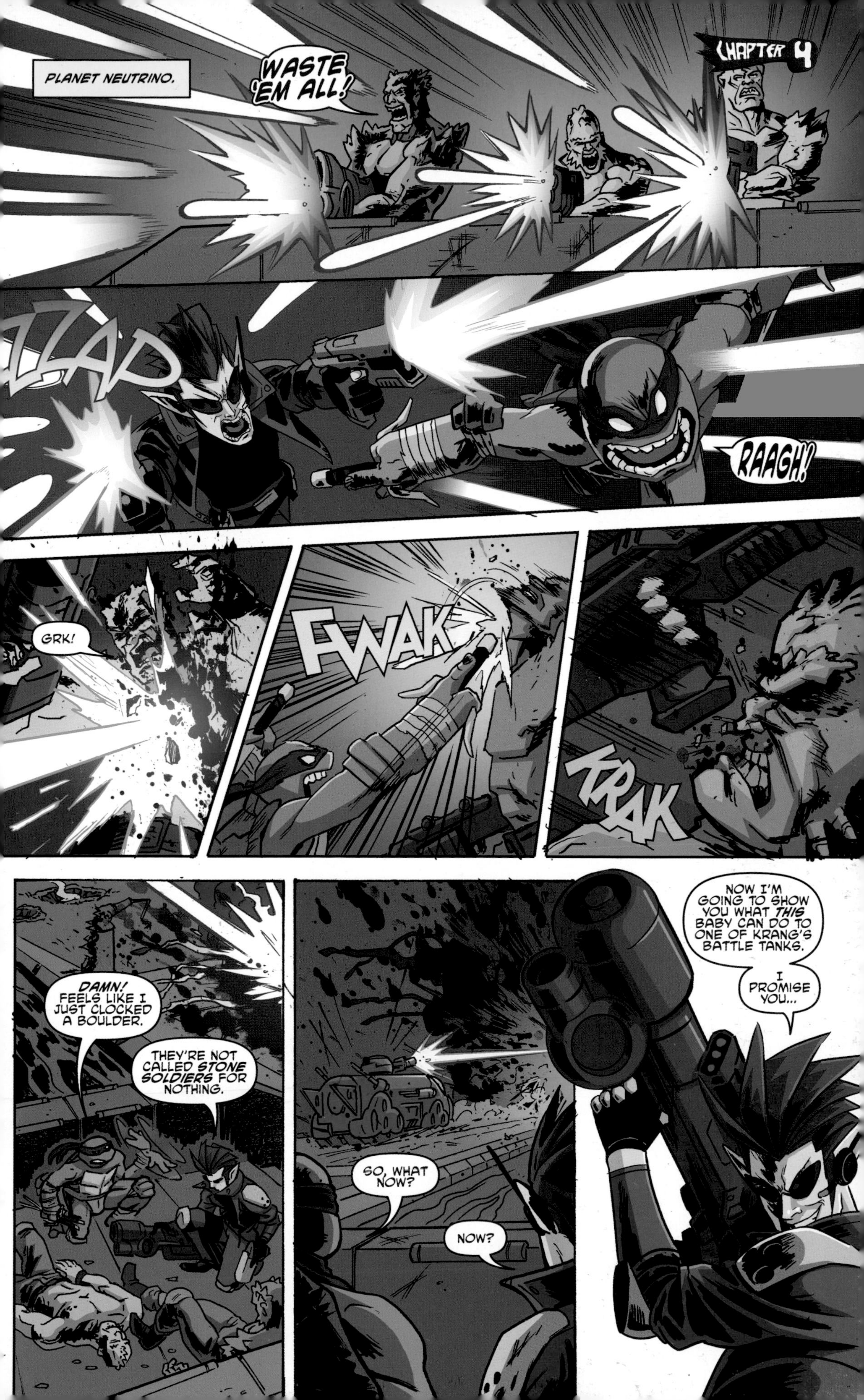

CHAPTER 4
PLANET NEUTRINO.
WASTE 'EM ALL!
ZZAP
RAAGH!
GRK!
FWAK
KRAK
DAMN! FEELS LIKE I JUST CLOCKED A BOULDER.
THEY'RE NOT CALLED STONE SOLDIERS FOR NOTHING.
SO, WHAT NOW?
NOW?
NOW I'M GOING TO SHOW YOU WHAT THIS BABY CAN DO TO ONE OF KRANG'S BATTLE TANKS.
I PROMISE YOU...

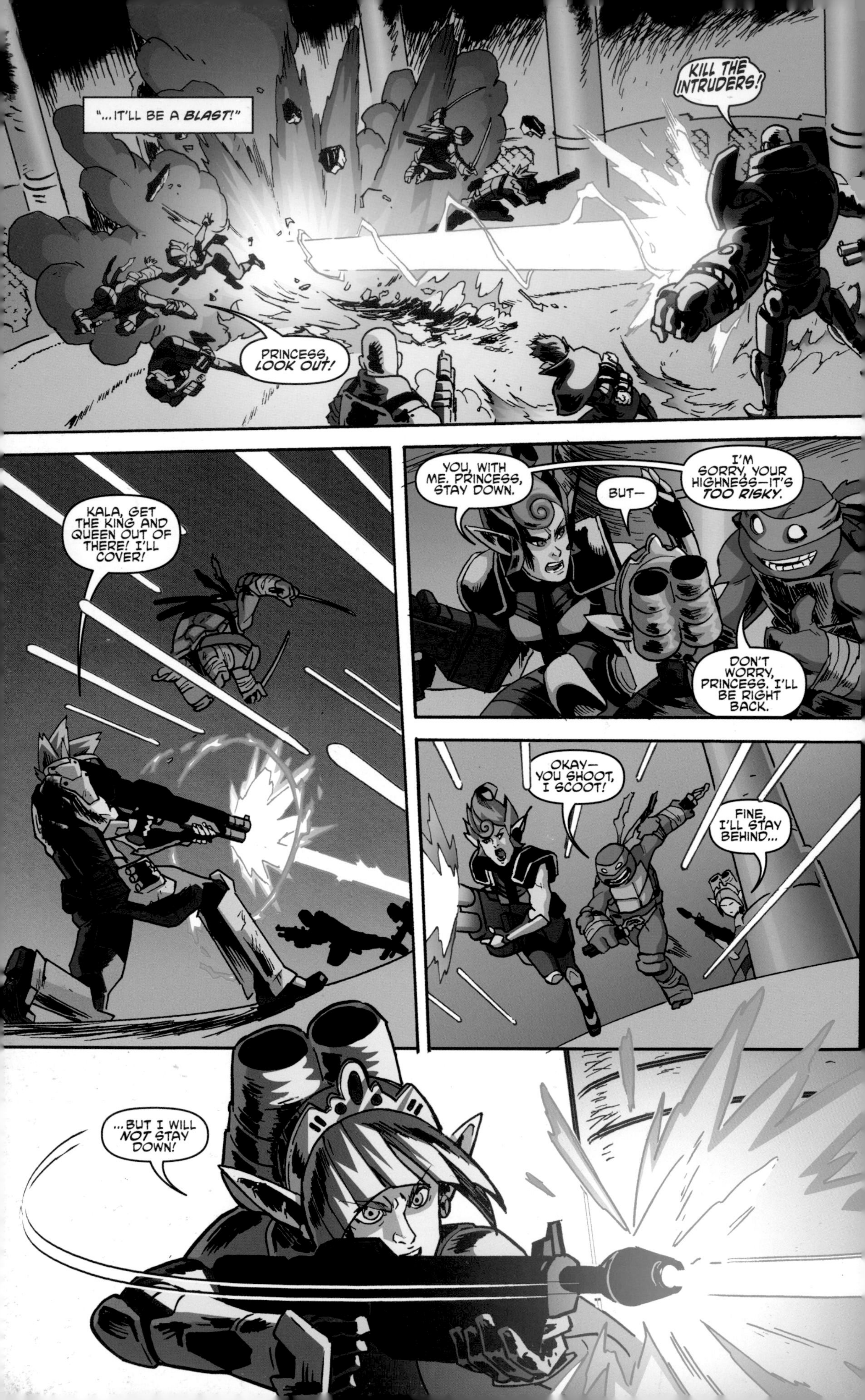
"...IT'LL BE A BLAST!"
KILL THE INTRUDERS!
PRINCESS, LOOK OUT!
KALA, GET THE KING AND QUEEN OUT OF THERE! I'LL COVER!
YOU, WITH ME. PRINCESS, STAY DOWN.
BUT—
I'M SORRY, YOUR HIGHNESS—IT'S TOO RISKY.
DON'T WORRY, PRINCESS. I'LL BE RIGHT BACK.
OKAY— YOU SHOOT, I SCOOT!
FINE, I'LL STAY BEHIND...
...BUT I WILL NOT STAY DOWN!

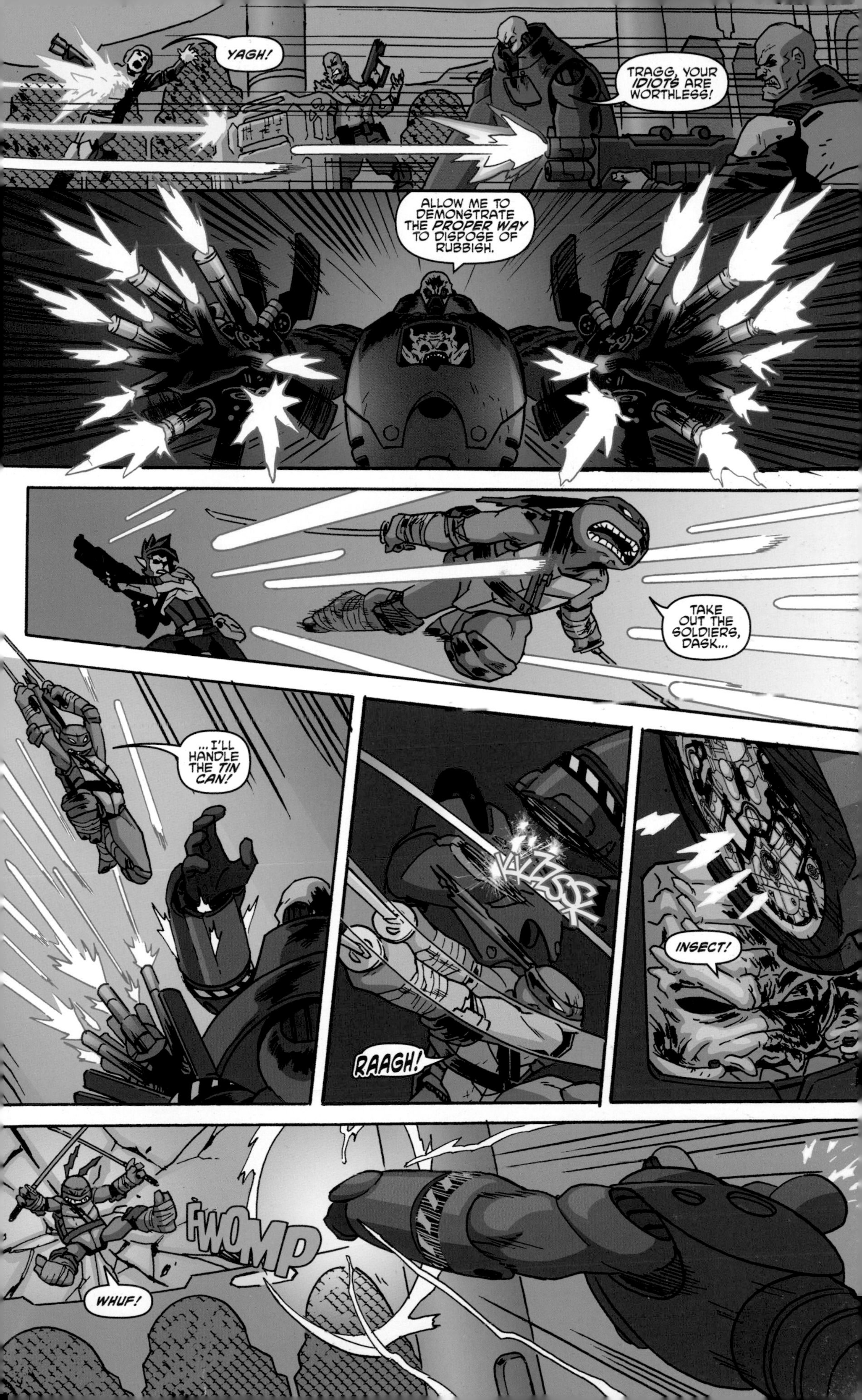
YAGH!
TRAGG, YOUR IDIOTS ARE WORTHLESS!
ALLOW ME TO DEMONSTRATE THE PROPER WAY TO DISPOSE OF RUBBISH.
TAKE OUT THE SOLDIERS, DASK...
...I'LL HANDLE THE TIN CAN!
RAAGH!
INSECT!
FWOMP
WHUF!

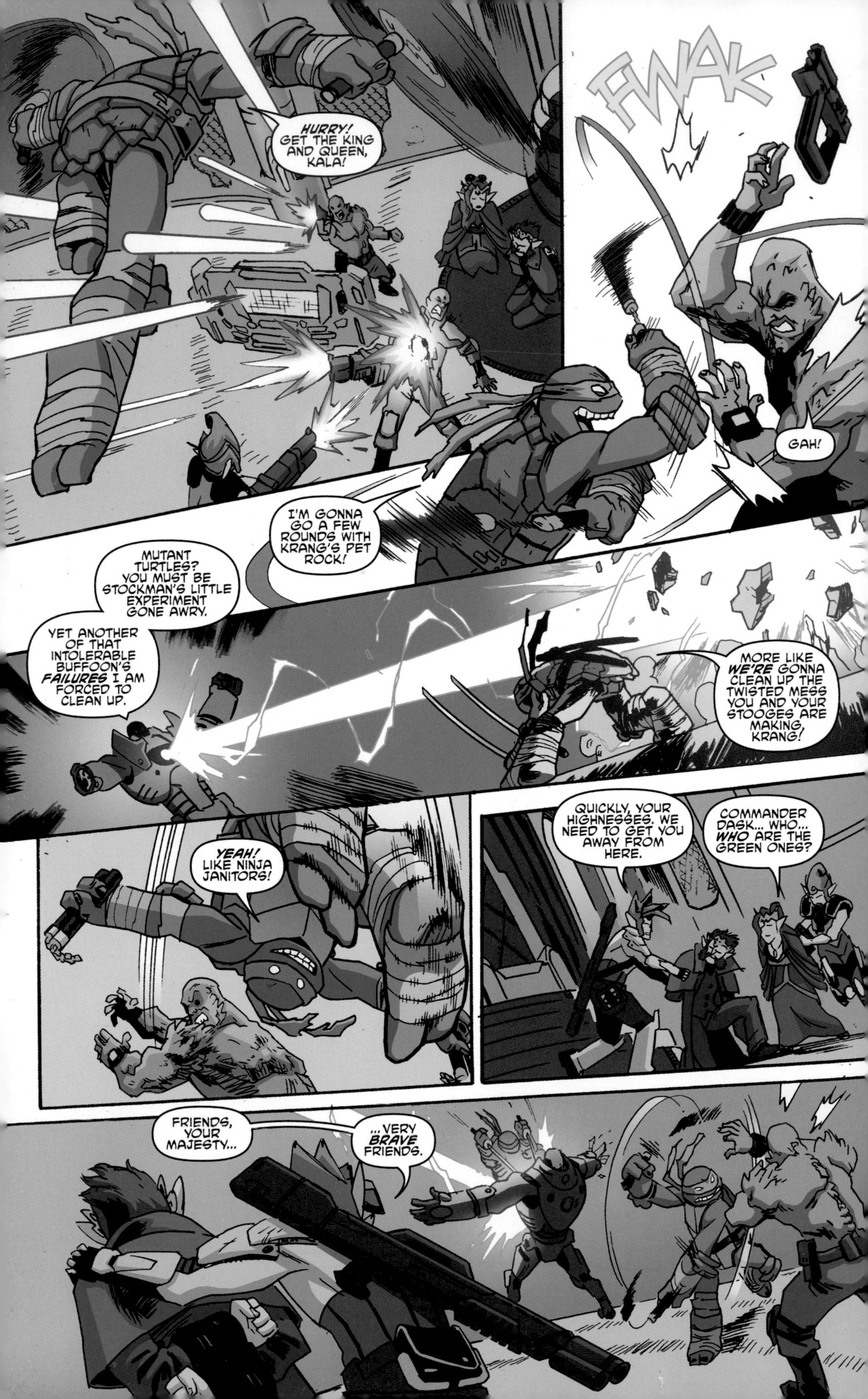
HURRY! GET THE KING AND QUEEN, KALA!
FWAK
GAH!
I'M GONNA GO A FEW ROUNDS WITH KRANG'S PET ROCK!
MUTANT TURTLES? YOU MUST BE STOCKMAN'S LITTLE EXPERIMENT GONE AWRY.
YET ANOTHER OF THAT INTOLERABLE BUFFOON'S FAILURES I AM FORCED TO CLEAN UP.
MORE LIKE WE'RE GONNA CLEAN UP THE TWISTED MESS YOU AND YOUR STOOGES ARE MAKING, KRANG!
YEAH! LIKE NINJA JANITORS!
QUICKLY, YOUR HIGHNESSES. WE NEED TO GET YOU AWAY FROM HERE.
COMMANDER DASK... WHO... WHO ARE THE GREEN ONES?
FRIENDS, YOUR MAJESTY...
...VERY BRAVE FRIENDS.

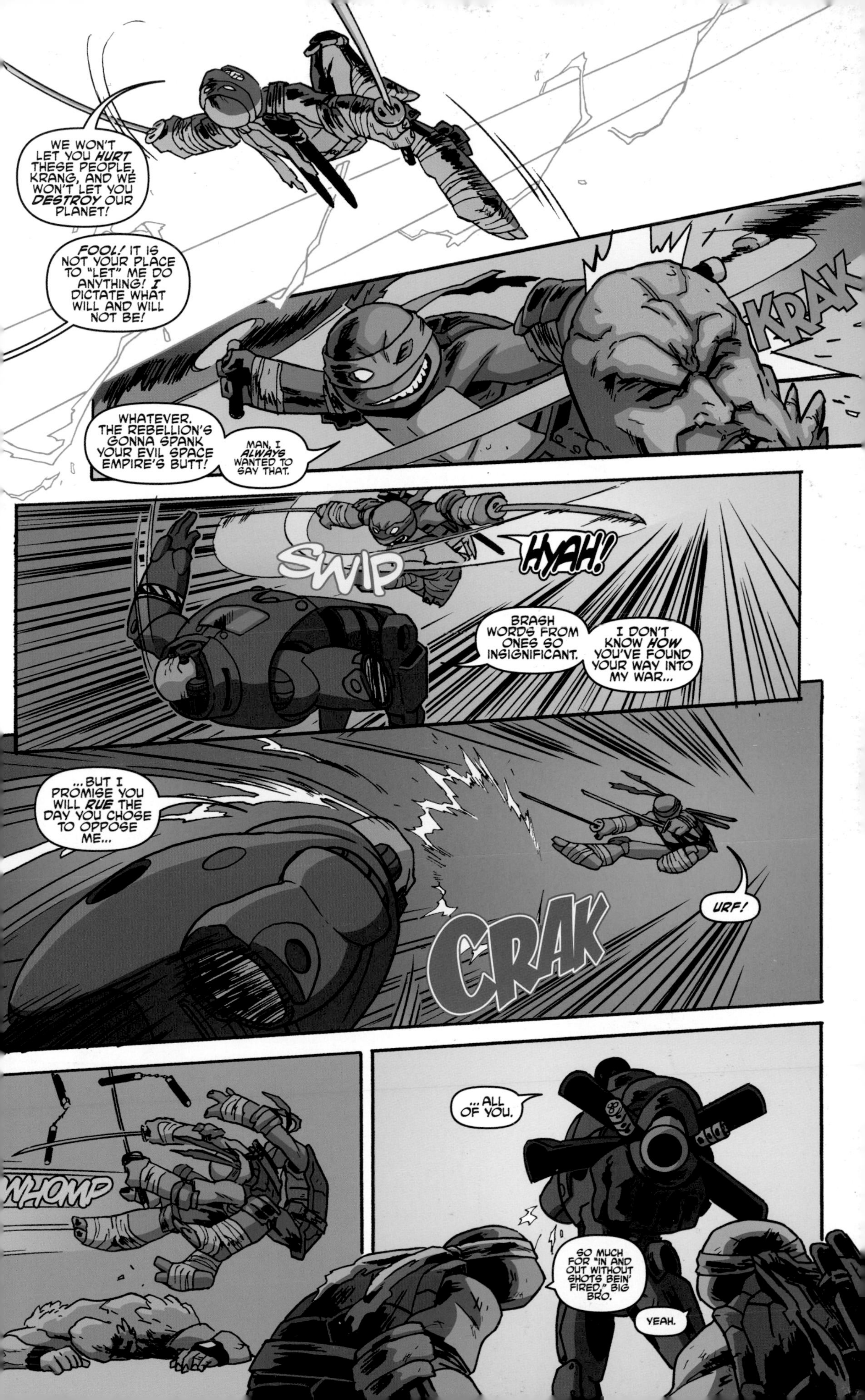
WE WON'T LET YOU *HURT* THESE PEOPLE, KRANG, AND WE WON'T LET YOU *DESTROY* OUR PLANET!
FOOL! IT IS NOT YOUR PLACE TO "LET" ME DO ANYTHING! *I* DICTATE WHAT WILL AND WILL NOT BE!
KRAK
WHATEVER. THE REBELLION'S GONNA SPANK YOUR EVIL SPACE EMPIRE'S BUTT!
MAN, I *ALWAYS* WANTED TO SAY THAT.
SWIP
HYAH!
BRASH WORDS FROM ONES SO INSIGNIFICANT.
I DON'T KNOW *HOW* YOU'VE FOUND YOUR WAY INTO MY WAR...
...BUT I PROMISE YOU WILL *RUE* THE DAY YOU CHOSE TO OPPOSE ME...
URF!
CRAK
WHOMP
...ALL OF YOU.
SO MUCH FOR "IN AND OUT WITHOUT SHOTS BEIN' FIRED," BIG BRO.
YEAH.

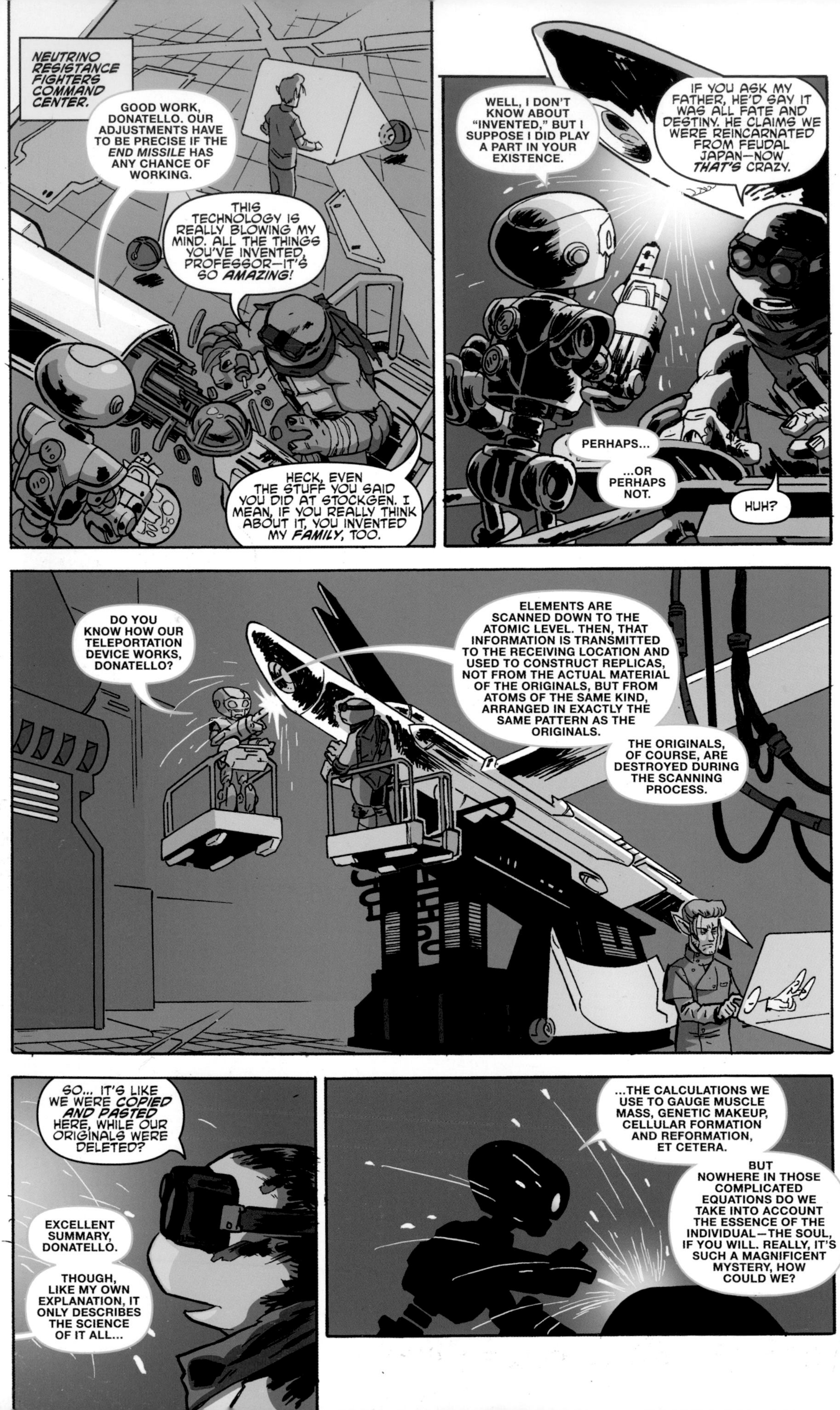
NEUTRINO RESISTANCE FIGHTERS COMMAND CENTER.
GOOD WORK, DONATELLO. OUR ADJUSTMENTS HAVE TO BE PRECISE IF THE END MISSILE HAS ANY CHANCE OF WORKING.
THIS TECHNOLOGY IS REALLY BLOWING MY MIND. ALL THE THINGS YOU'VE INVENTED, PROFESSOR—IT'S SO AMAZING!
HECK, EVEN THE STUFF YOU SAID YOU DID AT STOCKGEN. I MEAN, IF YOU REALLY THINK ABOUT IT, YOU INVENTED MY FAMILY, TOO.
WELL, I DON'T KNOW ABOUT "INVENTED," BUT I SUPPOSE I DID PLAY A PART IN YOUR EXISTENCE.
IF YOU ASK MY FATHER, HE'D SAY IT WAS ALL FATE AND DESTINY. HE CLAIMS WE WERE REINCARNATED FROM FEUDAL JAPAN—NOW THAT'S CRAZY.
PERHAPS...
...OR PERHAPS NOT.
HUH?
DO YOU KNOW HOW OUR TELEPORTATION DEVICE WORKS, DONATELLO?
ELEMENTS ARE SCANNED DOWN TO THE ATOMIC LEVEL. THEN, THAT INFORMATION IS TRANSMITTED TO THE RECEIVING LOCATION AND USED TO CONSTRUCT REPLICAS, NOT FROM THE ACTUAL MATERIAL OF THE ORIGINALS, BUT FROM ATOMS OF THE SAME KIND, ARRANGED IN EXACTLY THE SAME PATTERN AS THE ORIGINALS.
THE ORIGINALS, OF COURSE, ARE DESTROYED DURING THE SCANNING PROCESS.
SO... IT'S LIKE WE WERE COPIED AND PASTED HERE, WHILE OUR ORIGINALS WERE DELETED?
EXCELLENT SUMMARY, DONATELLO.
THOUGH, LIKE MY OWN EXPLANATION, IT ONLY DESCRIBES THE SCIENCE OF IT ALL...
...THE CALCULATIONS WE USE TO GAUGE MUSCLE MASS, GENETIC MAKEUP, CELLULAR FORMATION AND REFORMATION, ET CETERA.
BUT NOWHERE IN THOSE COMPLICATED EQUATIONS DO WE TAKE INTO ACCOUNT THE ESSENCE OF THE INDIVIDUAL—THE SOUL, IF YOU WILL. REALLY, IT'S SUCH A MAGNIFICENT MYSTERY, HOW COULD WE?

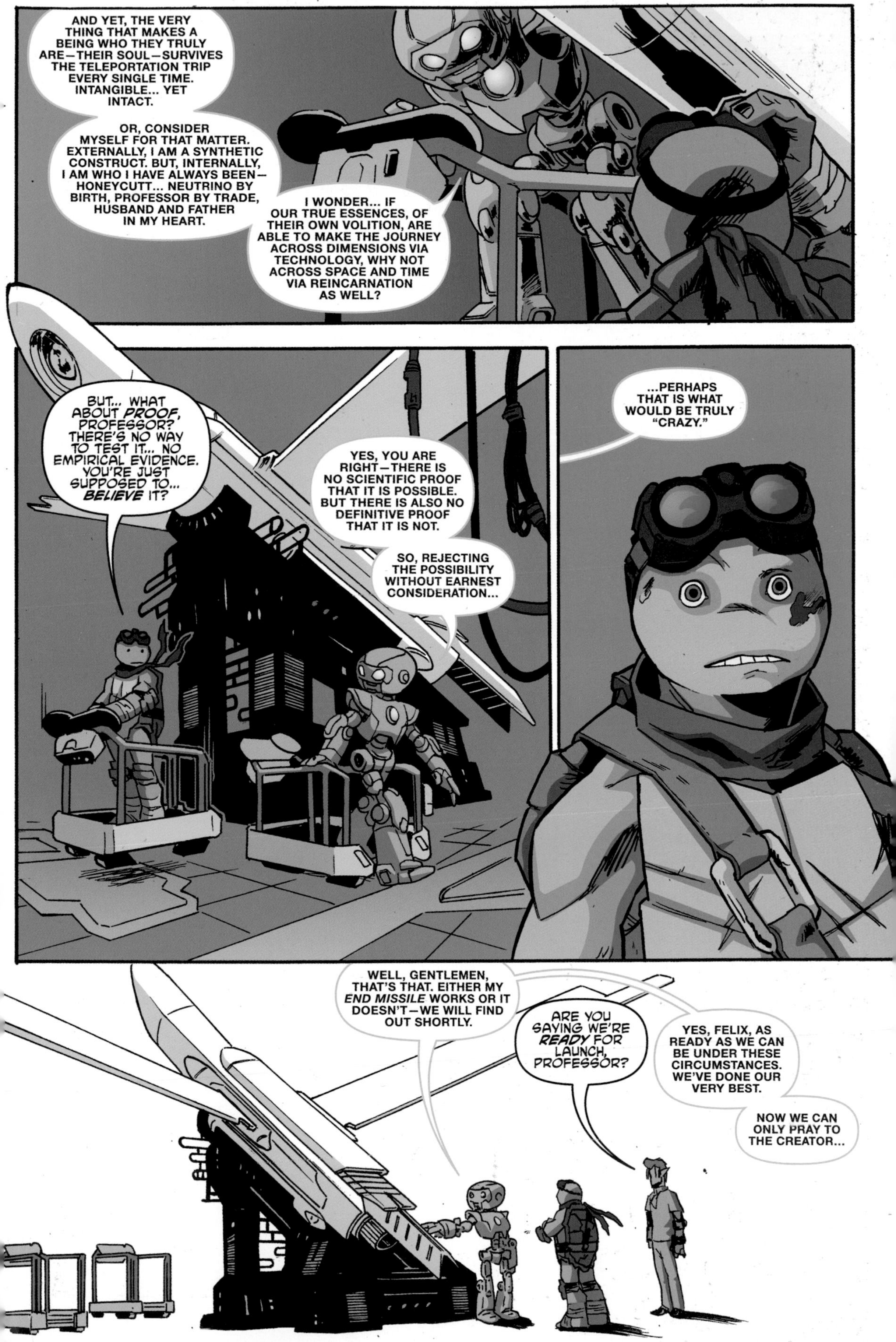
AND YET, THE VERY THING THAT MAKES A BEING WHO THEY TRULY ARE—THEIR SOUL—SURVIVES THE TELEPORTATION TRIP EVERY SINGLE TIME. INTANGIBLE... YET INTACT.
OR, CONSIDER MYSELF FOR THAT MATTER. EXTERNALLY, I AM A SYNTHETIC CONSTRUCT. BUT, INTERNALLY, I AM WHO I HAVE ALWAYS BEEN—HONEYCUTT... NEUTRINO BY BIRTH, PROFESSOR BY TRADE, HUSBAND AND FATHER IN MY HEART.
I WONDER... IF OUR TRUE ESSENCES, OF THEIR OWN VOLITION, ARE ABLE TO MAKE THE JOURNEY ACROSS DIMENSIONS VIA TECHNOLOGY, WHY NOT ACROSS SPACE AND TIME VIA REINCARNATION AS WELL?
BUT... WHAT ABOUT PROOF, PROFESSOR? THERE'S NO WAY TO TEST IT... NO EMPIRICAL EVIDENCE. YOU'RE JUST SUPPOSED TO... BELIEVE IT?
YES, YOU ARE RIGHT—THERE IS NO SCIENTIFIC PROOF THAT IT IS POSSIBLE. BUT THERE IS ALSO NO DEFINITIVE PROOF THAT IT IS NOT.
SO, REJECTING THE POSSIBILITY WITHOUT EARNEST CONSIDERATION...
...PERHAPS THAT IS WHAT WOULD BE TRULY "CRAZY."
WELL, GENTLEMEN, THAT'S THAT. EITHER MY END MISSILE WORKS OR IT DOESN'T—WE WILL FIND OUT SHORTLY.
ARE YOU SAYING WE'RE READY FOR LAUNCH, PROFESSOR?
YES, FELIX, AS READY AS WE CAN BE UNDER THESE CIRCUMSTANCES. WE'VE DONE OUR VERY BEST.
NOW WE CAN ONLY PRAY TO THE CREATOR...

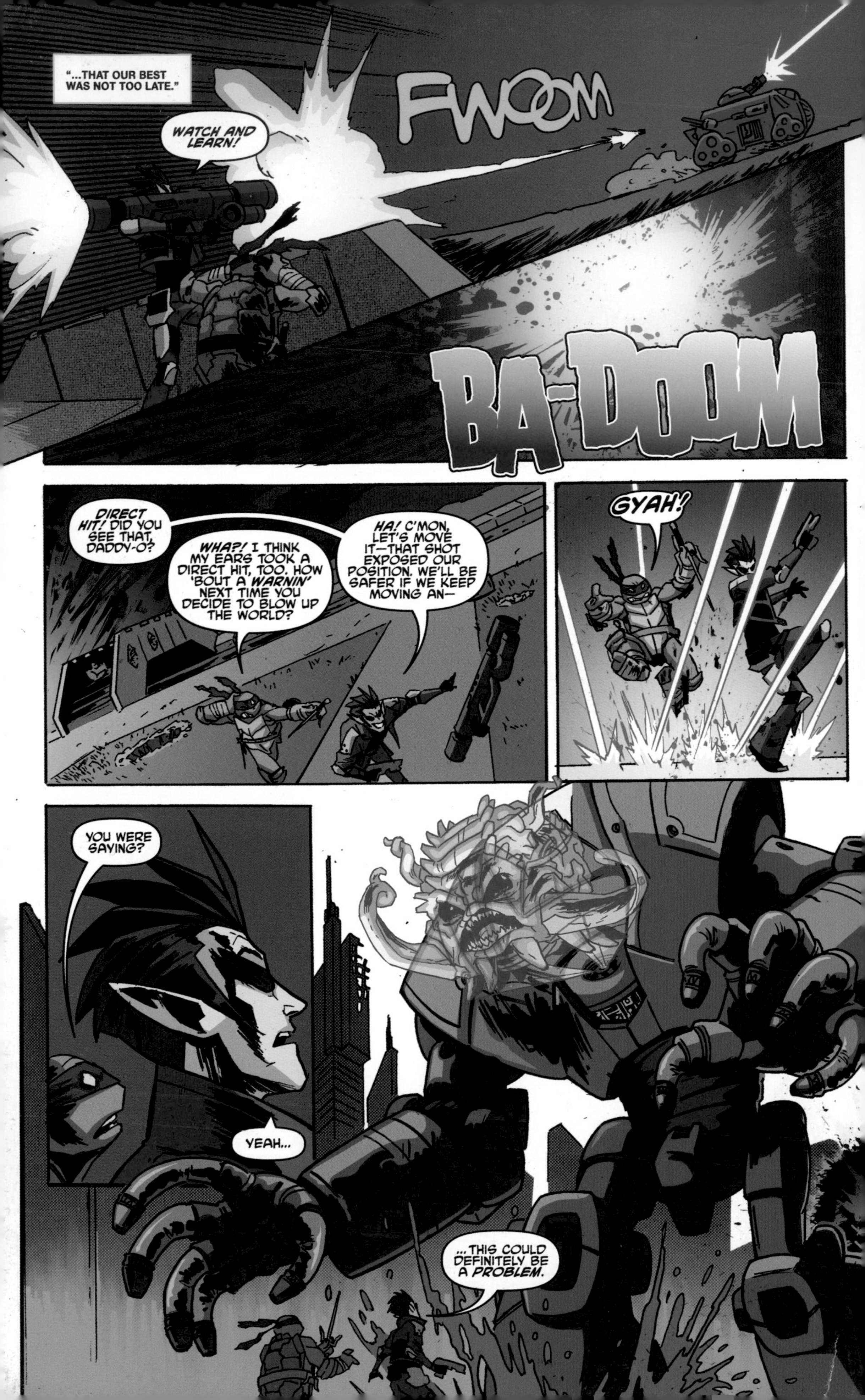
"...THAT OUR BEST WAS NOT TOO LATE."
WATCH AND LEARN!
FWOOM
BA-DOOM
DIRECT HIT! DID YOU SEE THAT, DADDY-O?
WHA?! I THINK MY EARS TOOK A DIRECT HIT, TOO. HOW 'BOUT A WARNIN' NEXT TIME YOU DECIDE TO BLOW UP THE WORLD?
HA! C'MON, LET'S MOVE IT--THAT SHOT EXPOSED OUR POSITION. WE'LL BE SAFER IF WE KEEP MOVING AN--
GYAH!
YOU WERE SAYING?
YEAH...
...THIS COULD DEFINITELY BE A PROBLEM.

BURNOW ISLAND.

CENTRAL, THIS IS BLOCK M. WE'VE GOT A *PROBLEM* HERE, OVER.

BLOCK M, THIS IS CENTRAL— WHAT'S THE *SITUATION*, OVER?

WE'VE HAD A *BREACH* AT THE CRYO-STASIS CHAMBER. THERE'S A MAN DOWN OUTSIDE AND—

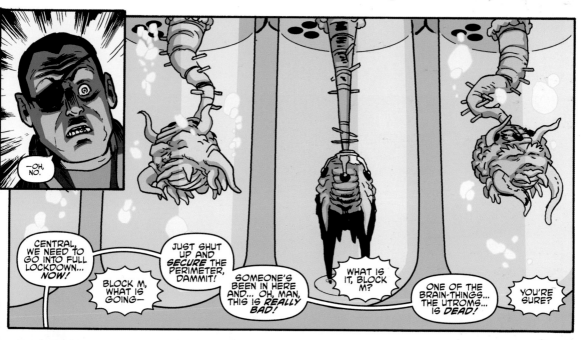

—OH, NO.

CENTRAL, WE NEED TO GO INTO FULL LOCKDOWN... *NOW!*

BLOCK M, WHAT IS GOING—

JUST SHUT UP AND *SECURE* THE PERIMETER, DAMMIT!

SOMEONE'S BEEN IN HERE AND... OH, MAN, THIS IS *REALLY BAD!*

WHAT IS IT, BLOCK M?

ONE OF THE BRAIN-THINGS... THE UTROMS... IS *DEAD!*

YOU'RE SURE?

YEAH, I'M *SURE*—IT'S JUST HANGING LIMP AND ALL ITS OOZE IS GONE!

IF WHOEVER DID THIS GETS AWAY, KRANG'S GONNA KILL *US*, TOO!

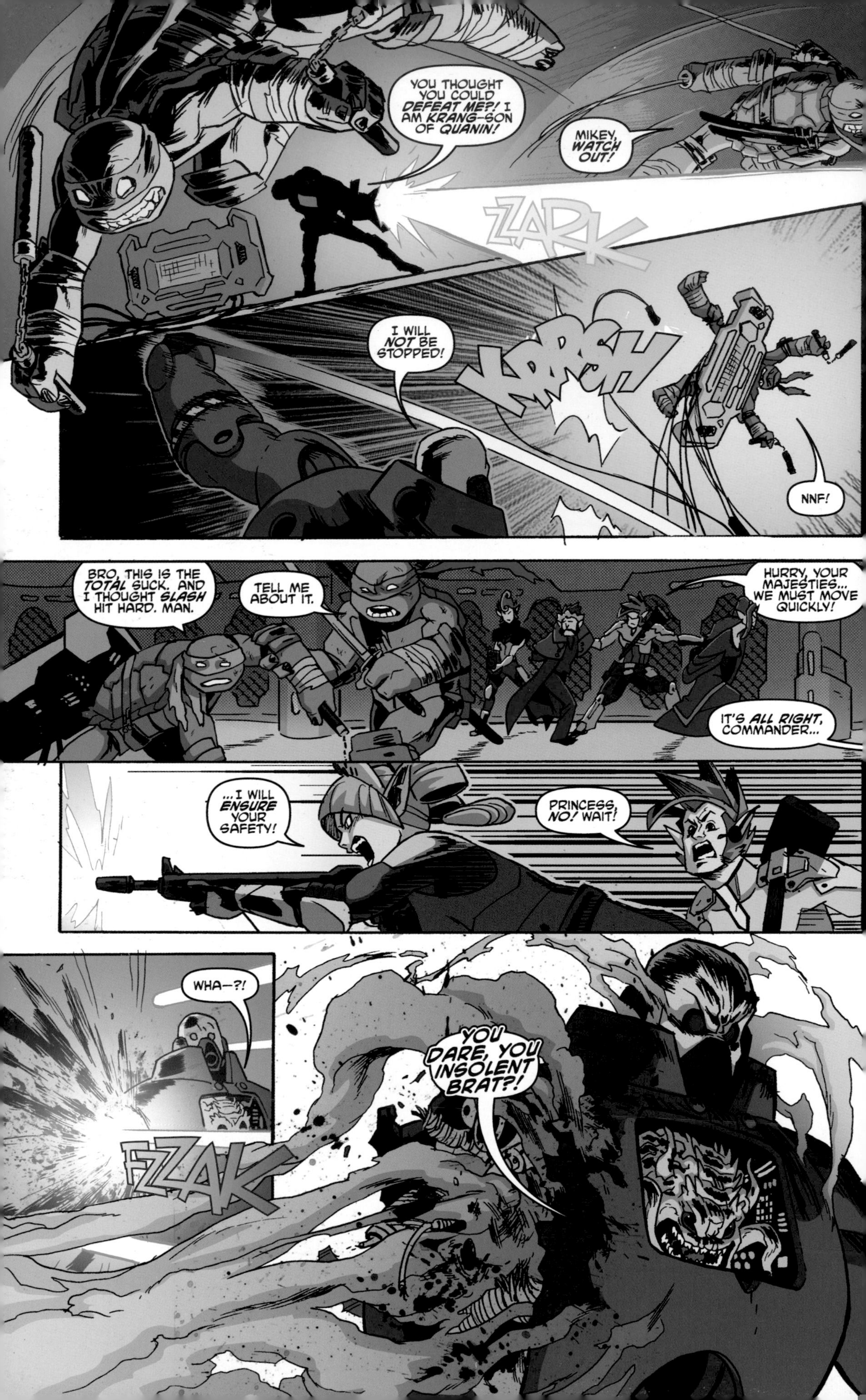
YOU THOUGHT YOU COULD DEFEAT ME?! I AM KRANG--SON OF QUANIN!
MIKEY, WATCH OUT!
ZZARK
I WILL NOT BE STOPPED!
KRRSH
NNF!
BRO, THIS IS THE TOTAL SUCK. AND I THOUGHT SLASH HIT HARD. MAN.
TELL ME ABOUT IT.
HURRY, YOUR MAJESTIES... WE MUST MOVE QUICKLY!
IT'S ALL RIGHT, COMMANDER...
...I WILL ENSURE YOUR SAFETY!
PRINCESS, NO! WAIT!
WHA--?!
FZZAK
YOU DARE, YOU INSOLENT BRAT?!

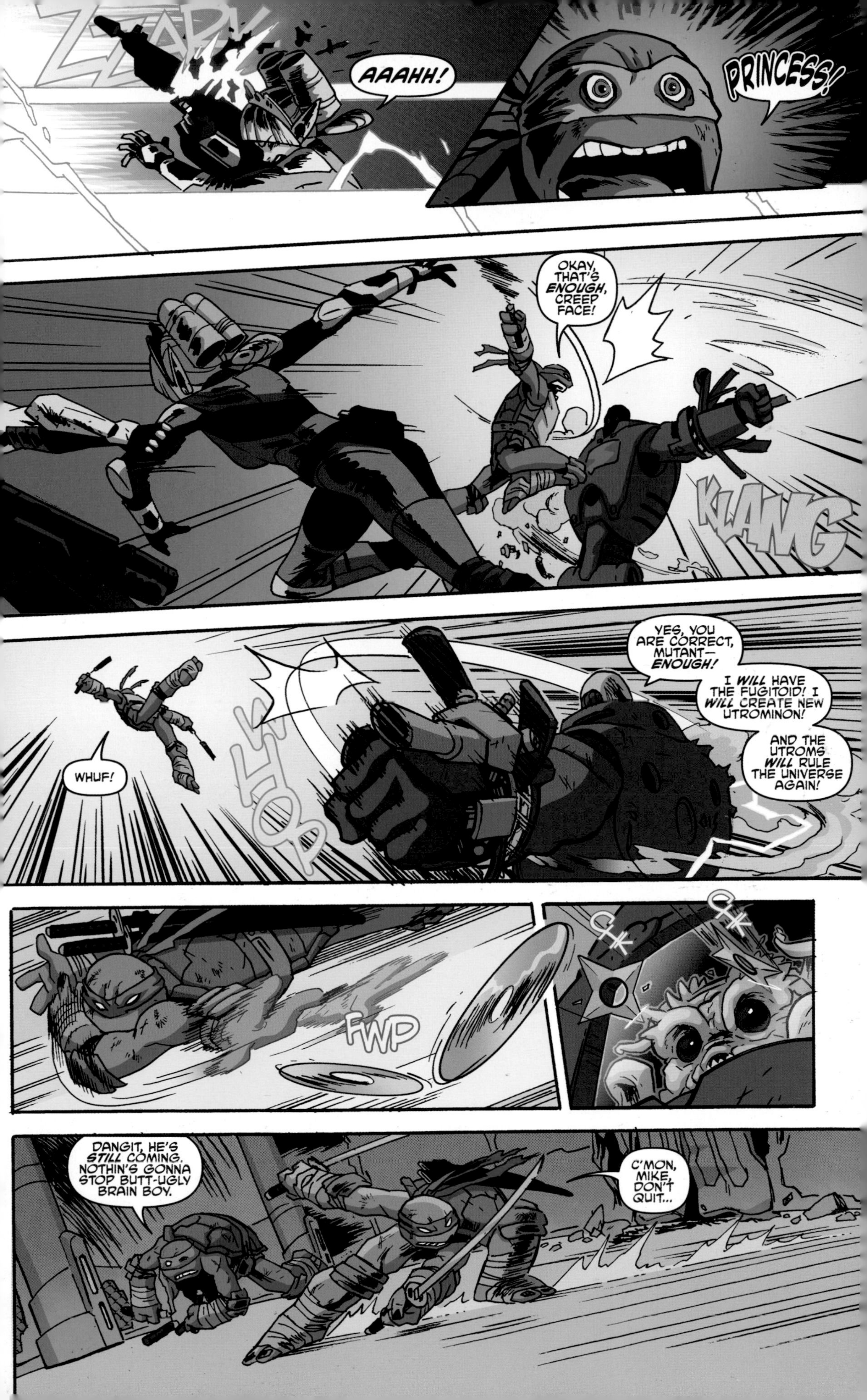
ZZZAP!
AAAHH!
PRINCESS!
OKAY, THAT'S ENOUGH, CREEP FACE!
KLANG
YES, YOU ARE CORRECT, MUTANT— ENOUGH!
I WILL HAVE THE FUGITOID! I WILL CREATE NEW UTROMINON!
AND THE UTROMS WILL RULE THE UNIVERSE AGAIN!
WHUF!
KLHOP
FWP
CHK
CHK
DANGIT, HE'S STILL COMING. NOTHIN'S GONNA STOP BUTT-UGLY BRAIN BOY.
C'MON, MIKE, DON'T QUIT...

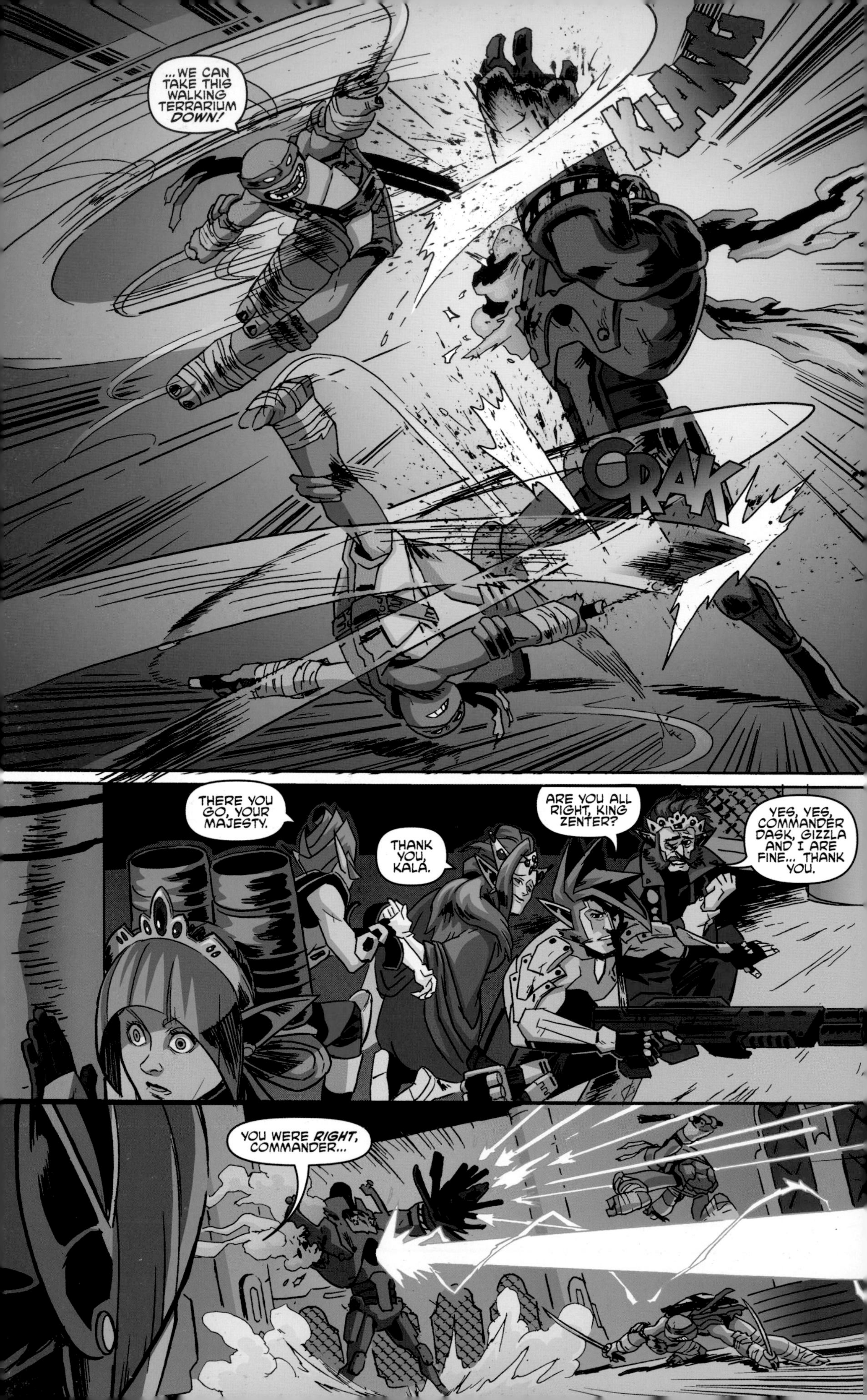

...WE CAN TAKE THIS WALKING TERRARIUM DOWN!
KLANG
CRAK
THERE YOU GO, YOUR MAJESTY.
THANK YOU, KALA.
ARE YOU ALL RIGHT, KING ZENTER?
YES, YES, COMMANDER DASK. GIZZLA AND I ARE FINE... THANK YOU.
YOU WERE RIGHT, COMMANDER...

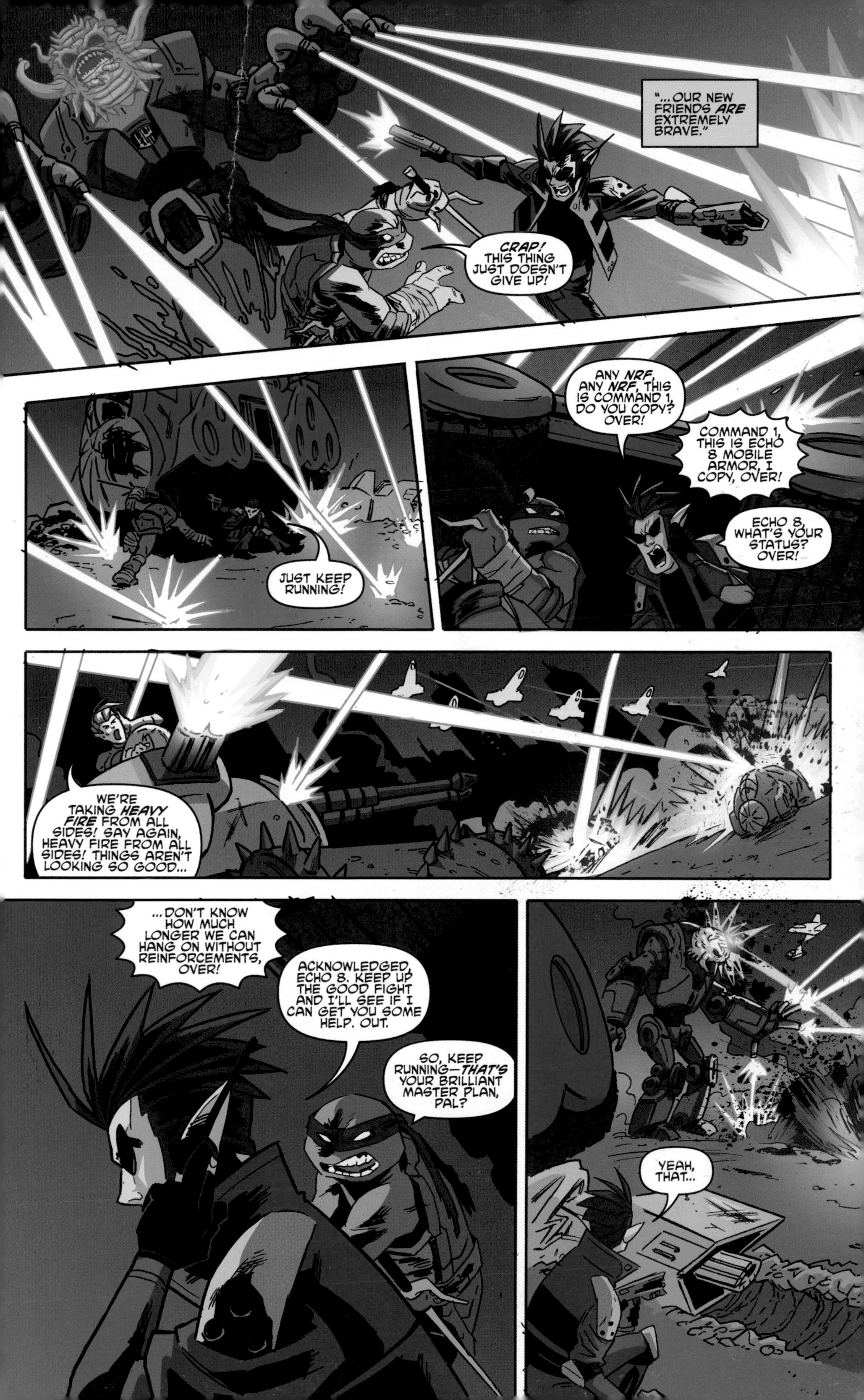
"...OUR NEW FRIENDS *ARE* EXTREMELY BRAVE."
CRAP! THIS THING JUST DOESN'T GIVE UP!
JUST KEEP RUNNING!
ANY *NRF*, ANY *NRF*, THIS IS COMMAND 1, DO YOU COPY? OVER!
COMMAND 1, THIS IS ECHO 8 MOBILE ARMOR, I COPY, OVER!
ECHO 8, WHAT'S YOUR STATUS? OVER!
WE'RE TAKING *HEAVY FIRE* FROM ALL SIDES! SAY AGAIN, HEAVY FIRE FROM ALL SIDES! THINGS AREN'T LOOKING SO GOOD...
...DON'T KNOW HOW MUCH LONGER WE CAN HANG ON WITHOUT REINFORCEMENTS, OVER!
ACKNOWLEDGED, ECHO 8. KEEP UP THE GOOD FIGHT AND I'LL SEE IF I CAN GET YOU SOME HELP. OUT.
SO, KEEP RUNNING—*THAT'S* YOUR BRILLIANT MASTER PLAN, PAL?
YEAH, THAT...

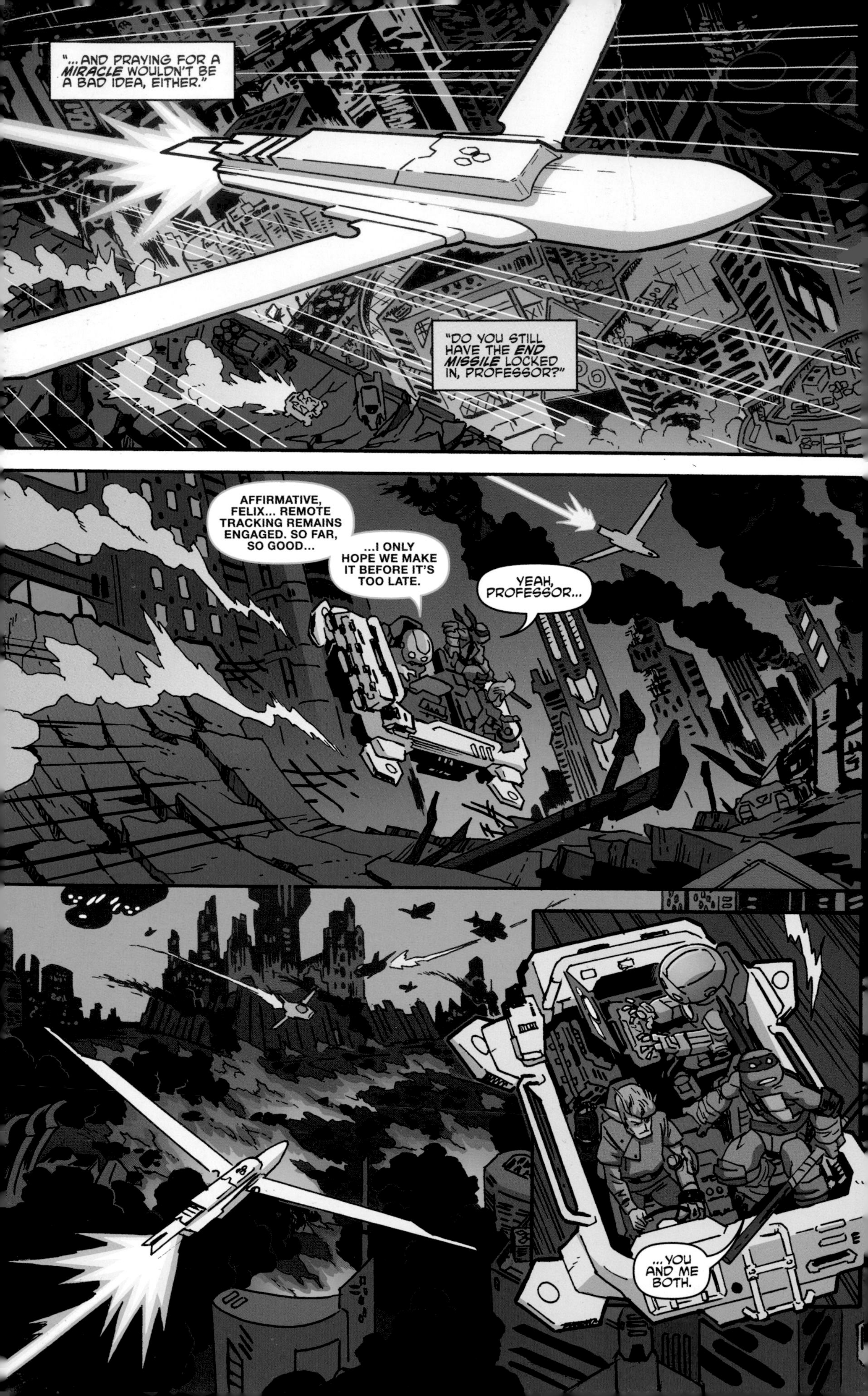
"...AND PRAYING FOR A MIRACLE WOULDN'T BE A BAD IDEA, EITHER."
"DO YOU STILL HAVE THE END MISSILE LOCKED IN, PROFESSOR?"
AFFIRMATIVE, FELIX... REMOTE TRACKING REMAINS ENGAGED. SO FAR, SO GOOD...
...I ONLY HOPE WE MAKE IT BEFORE IT'S TOO LATE.
YEAH, PROFESSOR...
...YOU AND ME BOTH.

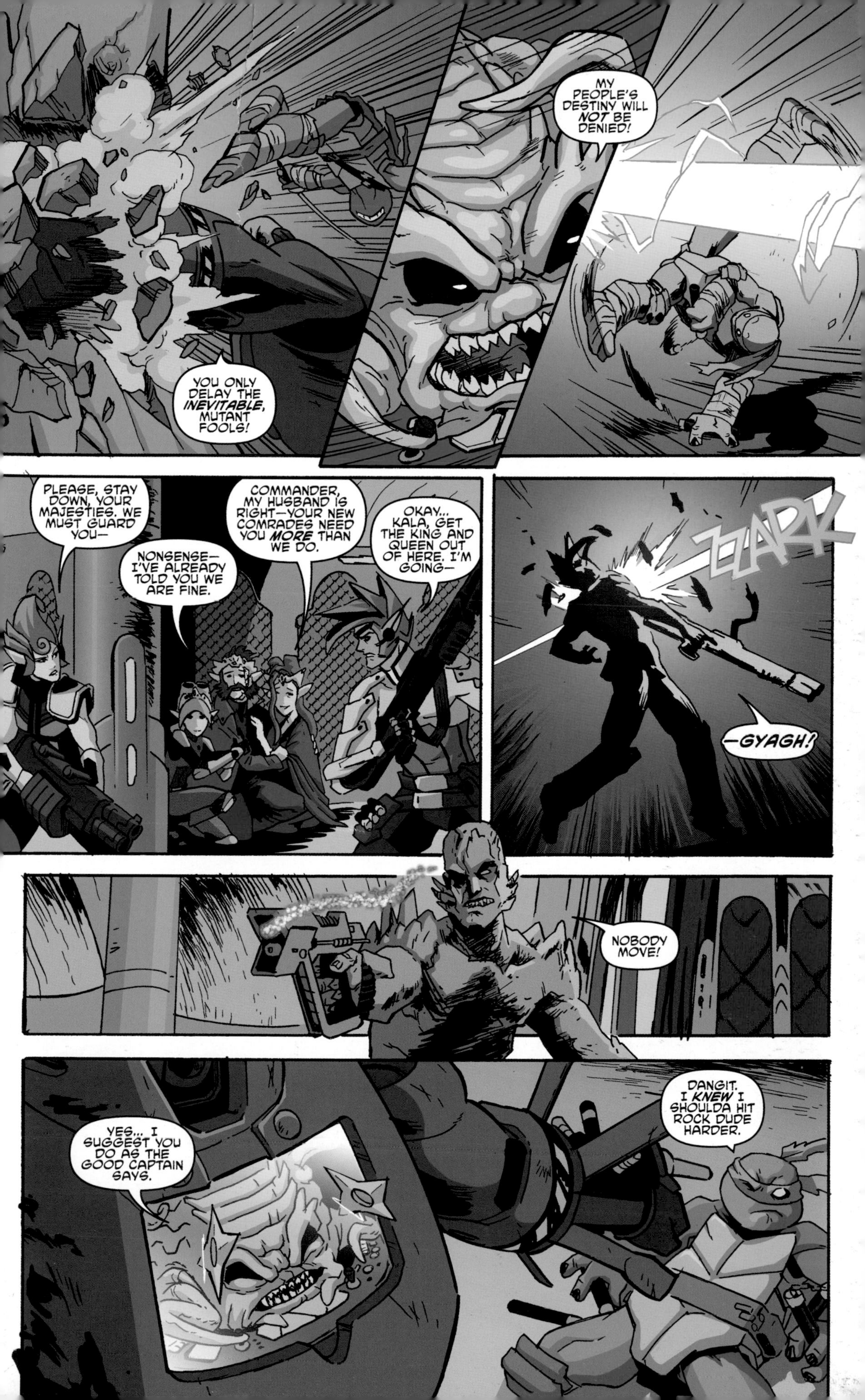
YOU ONLY DELAY THE *INEVITABLE*, MUTANT FOOLS!
MY PEOPLE'S DESTINY WILL *NOT* BE DENIED!
PLEASE, STAY DOWN, YOUR MAJESTIES. WE MUST GUARD YOU—
NONSENSE—I'VE ALREADY TOLD YOU WE ARE FINE.
COMMANDER, MY HUSBAND IS RIGHT—YOUR NEW COMRADES NEED YOU *MORE* THAN WE DO.
OKAY... KALA, GET THE KING AND QUEEN OUT OF HERE. I'M GOING—
ZZARK
—GYAGH!
NOBODY MOVE!
YES... I SUGGEST YOU DO AS THE GOOD CAPTAIN SAYS.
DANGIT. I *KNEW* I SHOULDA HIT ROCK DUDE HARDER.

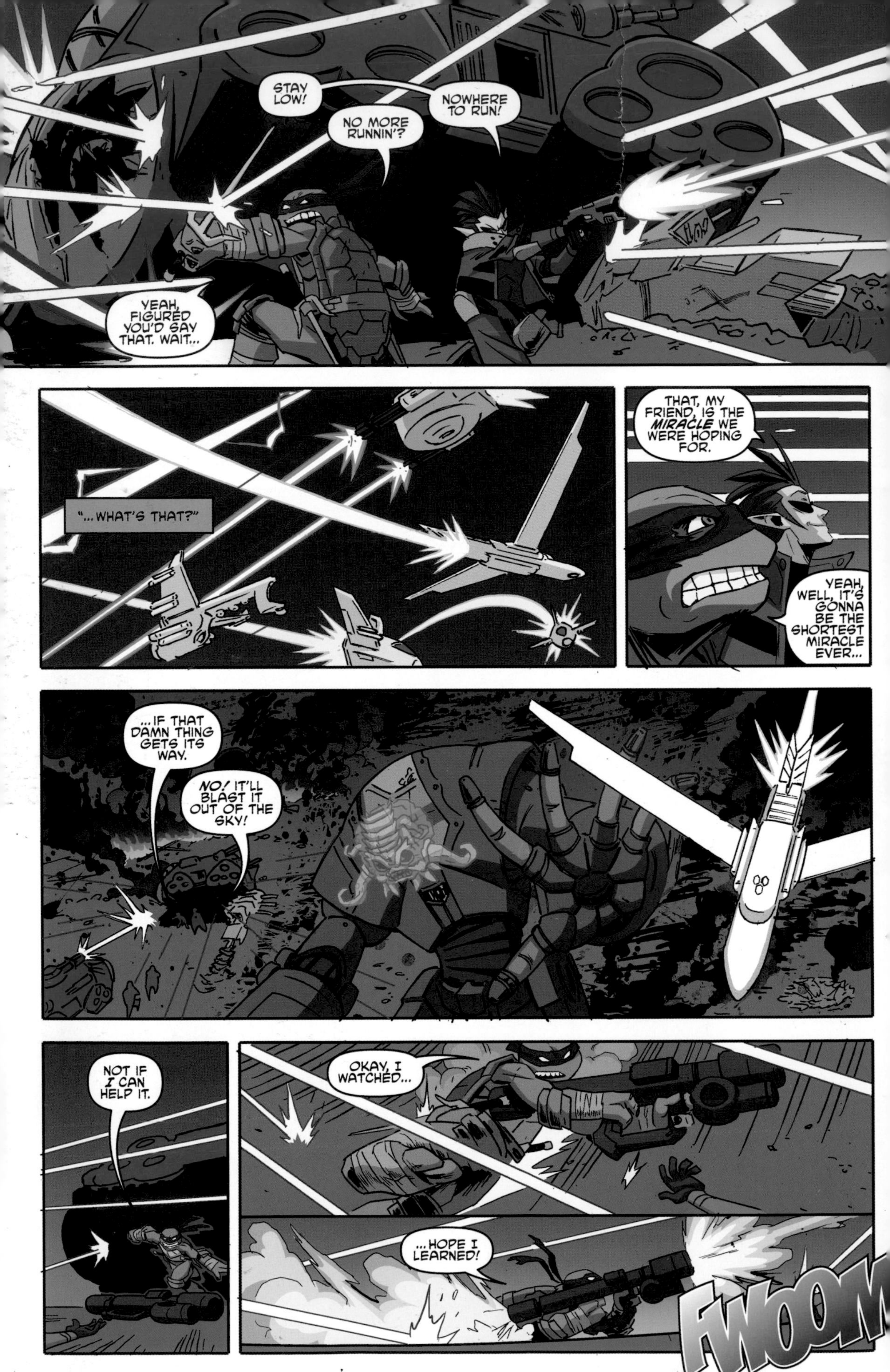
STAY LOW!
NO MORE RUNNIN'?
NOWHERE TO RUN!
YEAH, FIGURED YOU'D SAY THAT. WAIT...
"...WHAT'S THAT?"
THAT, MY FRIEND, IS THE MIRACLE WE WERE HOPING FOR.
YEAH, WELL, IT'S GONNA BE THE SHORTEST MIRACLE EVER...
...IF THAT DAMN THING GETS ITS WAY.
NO! IT'LL BLAST IT OUT OF THE SKY!
NOT IF I CAN HELP IT.
OKAY, I WATCHED...
...HOPE I LEARNED!
FWOOM

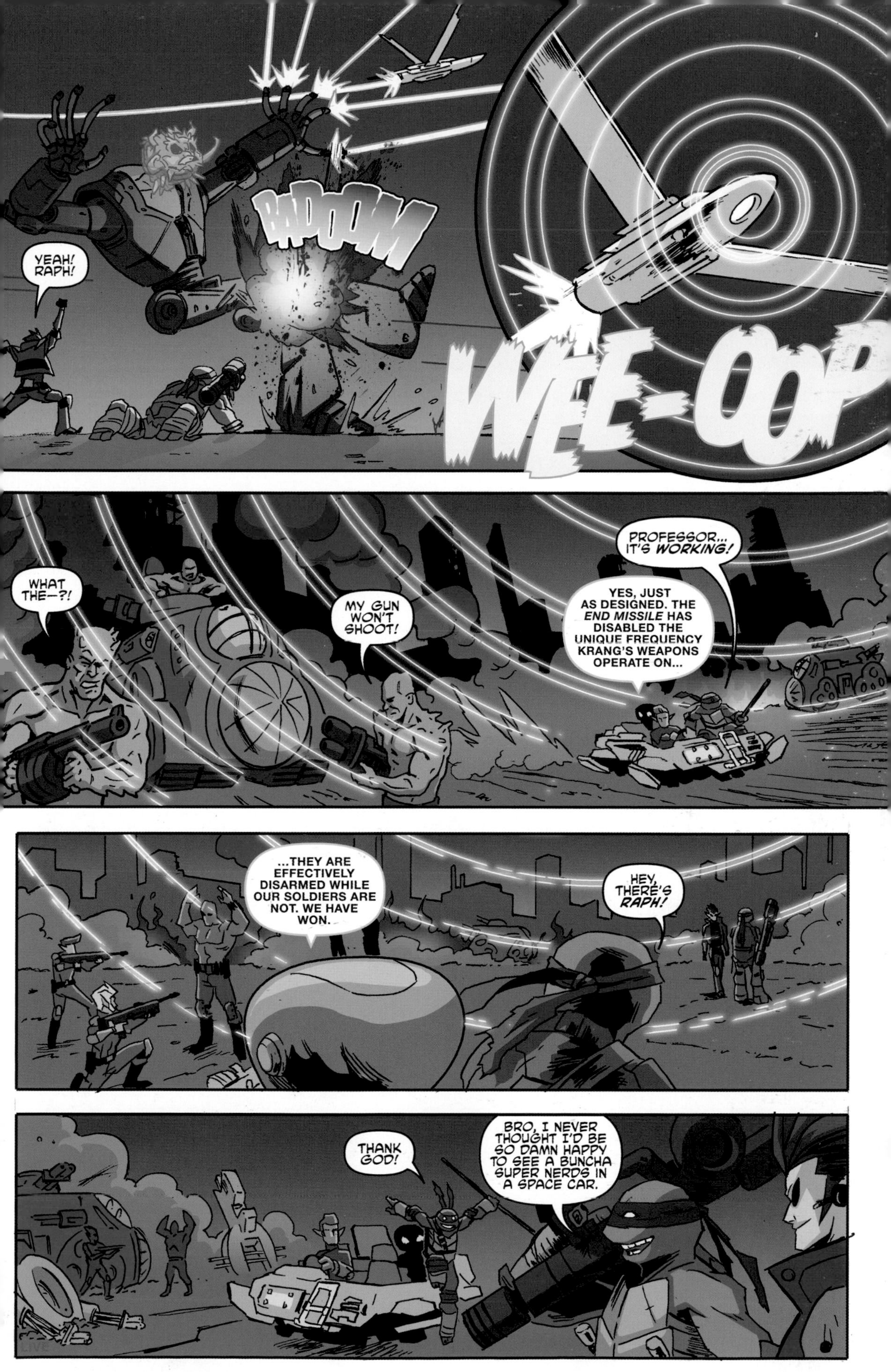
YEAH! RAPH!
BADOOM
WEE-OOP
WHAT THE--?!
MY GUN WON'T SHOOT!
PROFESSOR... IT'S *WORKING!*
YES, JUST AS DESIGNED. THE *END MISSILE* HAS DISABLED THE UNIQUE FREQUENCY KRANG'S WEAPONS OPERATE ON...
...THEY ARE EFFECTIVELY DISARMED WHILE OUR SOLDIERS ARE NOT. WE HAVE WON.
HEY, THERE'S *RAPH!*
THANK GOD!
BRO, I NEVER THOUGHT I'D BE SO DAMN HAPPY TO SEE A BUNCHA SUPER NERDS IN A SPACE CAR.

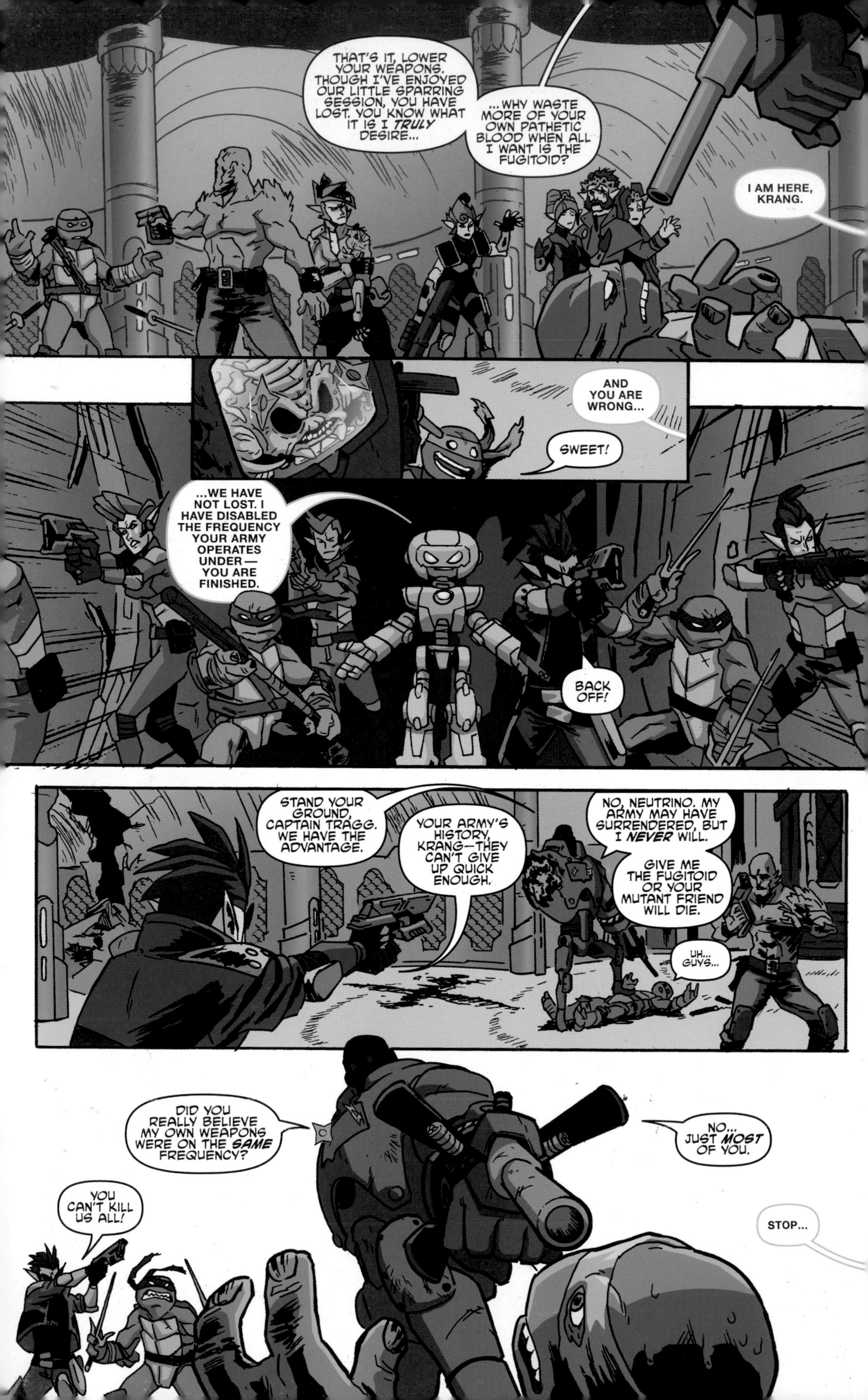
THAT'S IT, LOWER YOUR WEAPONS. THOUGH I'VE ENJOYED OUR LITTLE SPARRING SESSION, YOU HAVE LOST. YOU KNOW WHAT IT IS I TRULY DESIRE...
...WHY WASTE MORE OF YOUR OWN PATHETIC BLOOD WHEN ALL I WANT IS THE FUGITOID?
I AM HERE, KRANG.
AND YOU ARE WRONG...
SWEET!
...WE HAVE NOT LOST. I HAVE DISABLED THE FREQUENCY YOUR ARMY OPERATES UNDER— YOU ARE FINISHED.
BACK OFF!
STAND YOUR GROUND, CAPTAIN TRAGG. WE HAVE THE ADVANTAGE.
YOUR ARMY'S HISTORY, KRANG—THEY CAN'T GIVE UP QUICK ENOUGH.
NO, NEUTRINO. MY ARMY MAY HAVE SURRENDERED, BUT I NEVER WILL.
GIVE ME THE FUGITOID OR YOUR MUTANT FRIEND WILL DIE.
UH... GUYS...
DID YOU REALLY BELIEVE MY OWN WEAPONS WERE ON THE SAME FREQUENCY?
NO... JUST MOST OF YOU.
YOU CAN'T KILL US ALL!
STOP...

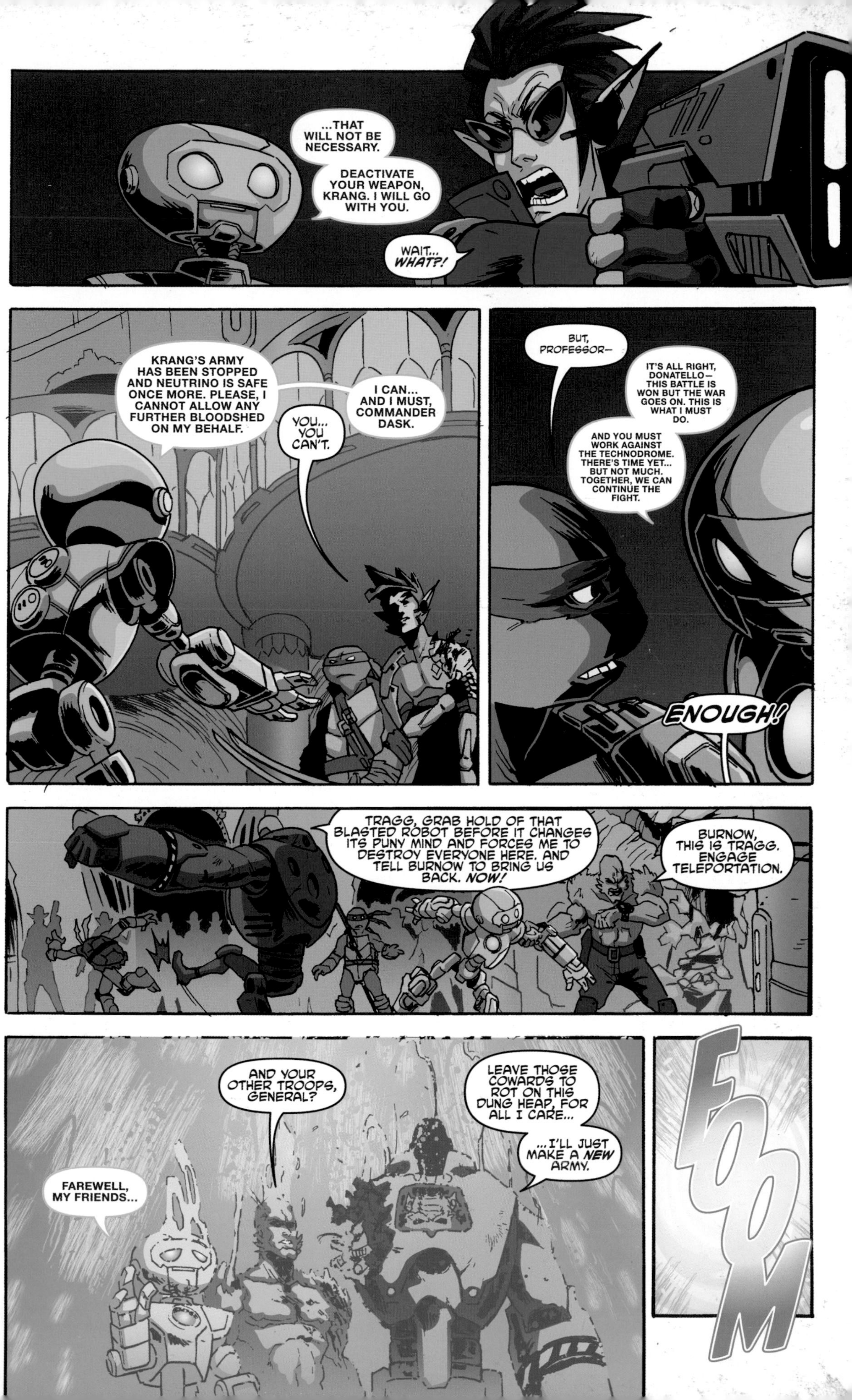

...THAT WILL NOT BE NECESSARY.
DEACTIVATE YOUR WEAPON, KRANG. I WILL GO WITH YOU.
WAIT... WHAT?!
KRANG'S ARMY HAS BEEN STOPPED AND NEUTRINO IS SAFE ONCE MORE. PLEASE, I CANNOT ALLOW ANY FURTHER BLOODSHED ON MY BEHALF.
YOU... YOU CAN'T.
I CAN... AND I MUST, COMMANDER DASK.
BUT, PROFESSOR—
IT'S ALL RIGHT, DONATELLO— THIS BATTLE IS WON BUT THE WAR GOES ON. THIS IS WHAT I MUST DO.
AND YOU MUST WORK AGAINST THE TECHNODROME. THERE'S TIME YET... BUT NOT MUCH. TOGETHER, WE CAN CONTINUE THE FIGHT.
ENOUGH!
TRAGG, GRAB HOLD OF THAT BLASTED ROBOT BEFORE IT CHANGES ITS PUNY MIND AND FORCES ME TO DESTROY EVERYONE HERE. AND TELL BURNOW TO BRING US BACK. NOW!
BURNOW, THIS IS TRAGG. ENGAGE TELEPORTATION.
FAREWELL, MY FRIENDS...
AND YOUR OTHER TROOPS, GENERAL?
LEAVE THOSE COWARDS TO ROT ON THIS DUNG HEAP, FOR ALL I CARE...
...I'LL JUST MAKE A NEW ARMY.
FOOM

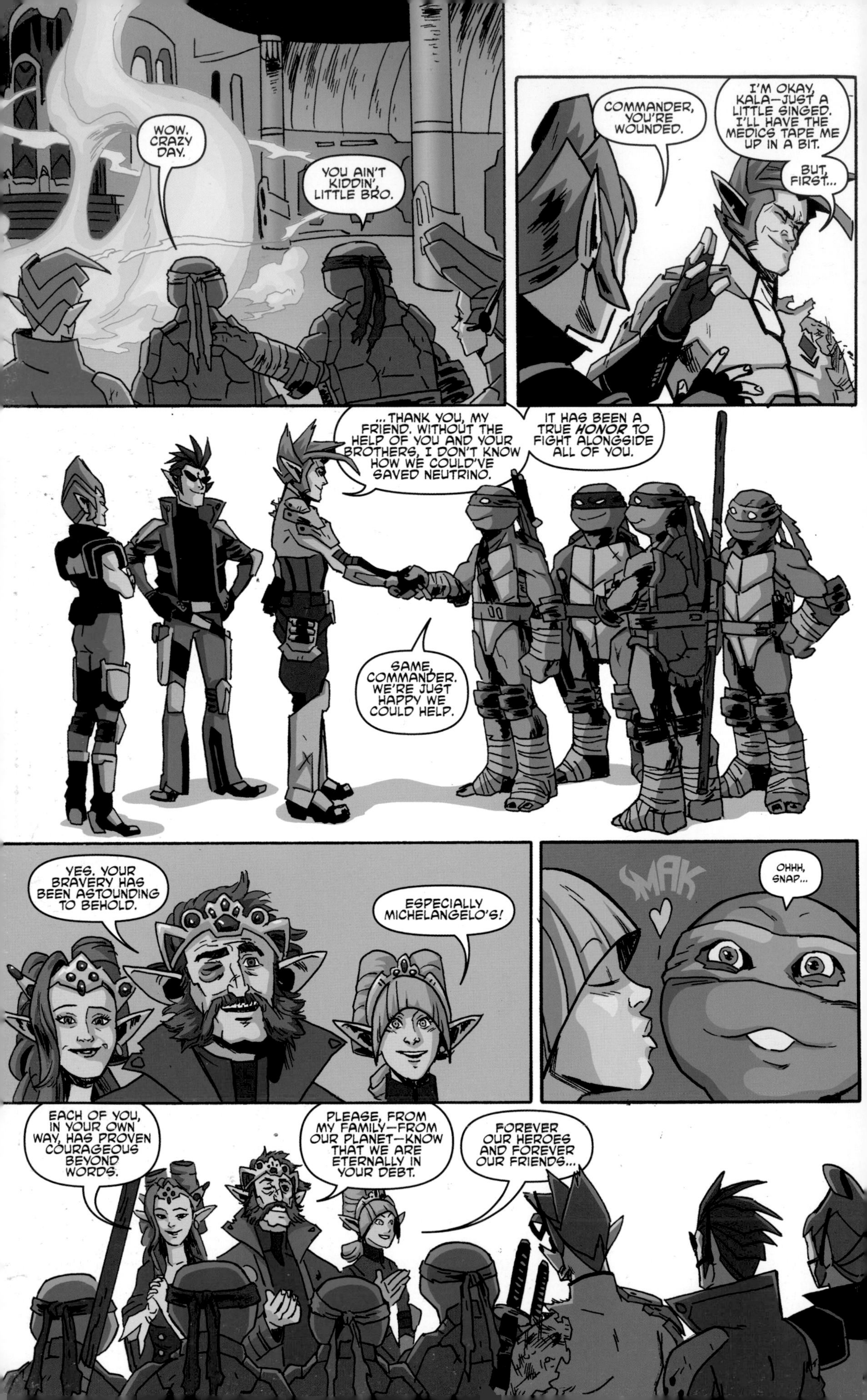
WOW. CRAZY DAY.
YOU AIN'T KIDDIN', LITTLE BRO.
COMMANDER, YOU'RE WOUNDED.
I'M OKAY, KALA—JUST A LITTLE SINGED. I'LL HAVE THE MEDICS TAPE ME UP IN A BIT.
BUT, FIRST...
...THANK YOU, MY FRIEND. WITHOUT THE HELP OF YOU AND YOUR BROTHERS, I DON'T KNOW HOW WE COULD'VE SAVED NEUTRINO.
IT HAS BEEN A TRUE *HONOR* TO FIGHT ALONGSIDE ALL OF YOU.
SAME, COMMANDER. WE'RE JUST HAPPY WE COULD HELP.
YES. YOUR BRAVERY HAS BEEN ASTOUNDING TO BEHOLD.
ESPECIALLY MICHELANGELO'S!
SMAK
OHHH, SNAP...
EACH OF YOU, IN YOUR OWN WAY, HAS PROVEN COURAGEOUS BEYOND WORDS.
PLEASE, FROM MY FAMILY—FROM OUR PLANET—KNOW THAT WE ARE ETERNALLY IN YOUR DEBT.
FOREVER OUR HEROES AND FOREVER OUR FRIENDS...

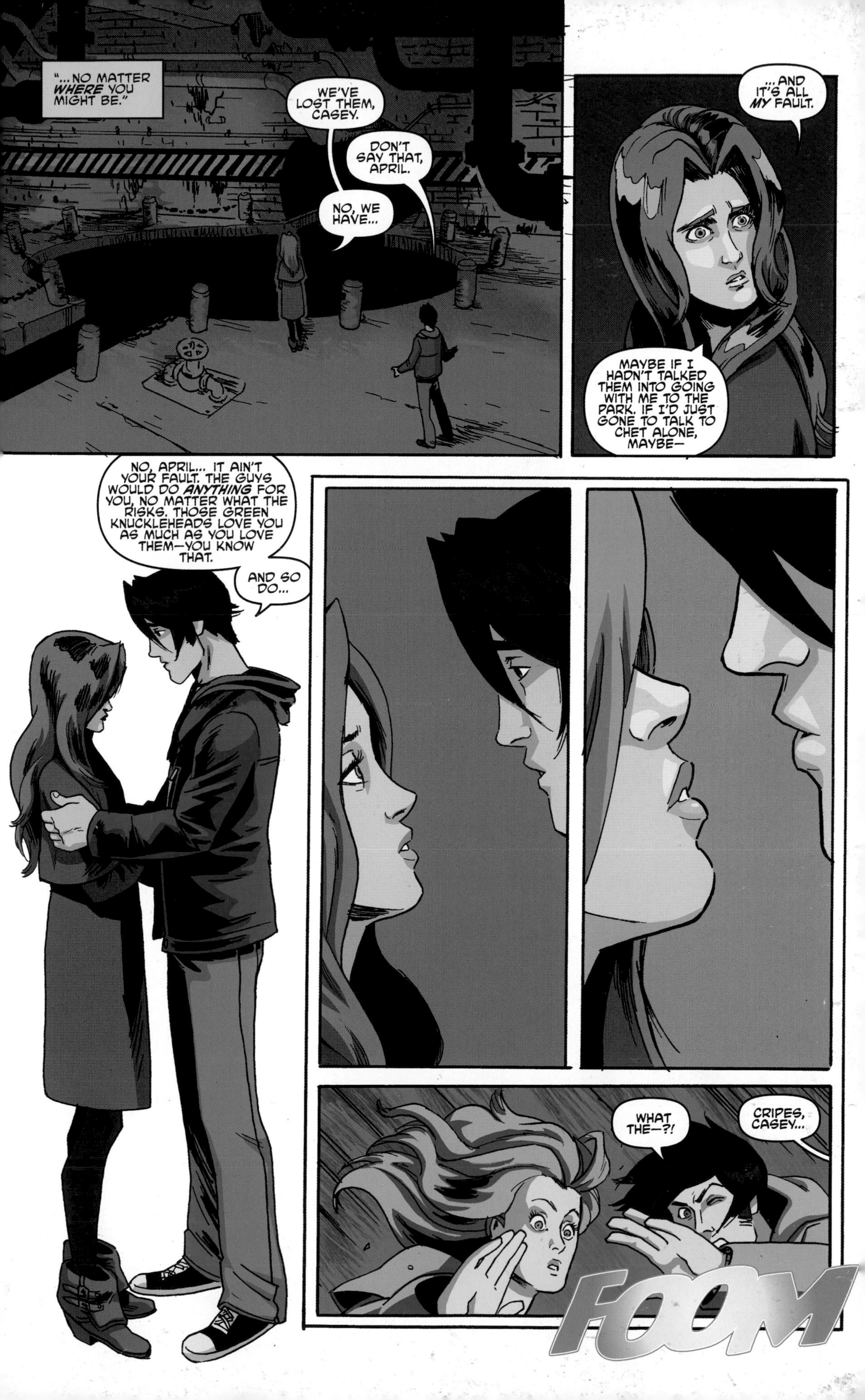
"...NO MATTER *WHERE* YOU MIGHT BE."
WE'VE LOST THEM, CASEY.
DON'T SAY THAT, APRIL.
NO, WE HAVE...
...AND IT'S ALL *MY* FAULT.
MAYBE IF I HADN'T TALKED THEM INTO GOING WITH ME TO THE PARK. IF I'D JUST GONE TO TALK TO CHET ALONE, MAYBE—
NO, APRIL... IT AIN'T YOUR FAULT. THE GUYS WOULD DO *ANYTHING* FOR YOU, NO MATTER WHAT THE RISKS. THOSE GREEN KNUCKLEHEADS LOVE YOU AS MUCH AS YOU LOVE THEM—YOU KNOW THAT.
AND SO DO...
WHAT THE—?!
CRIPES, CASEY...
FOOM

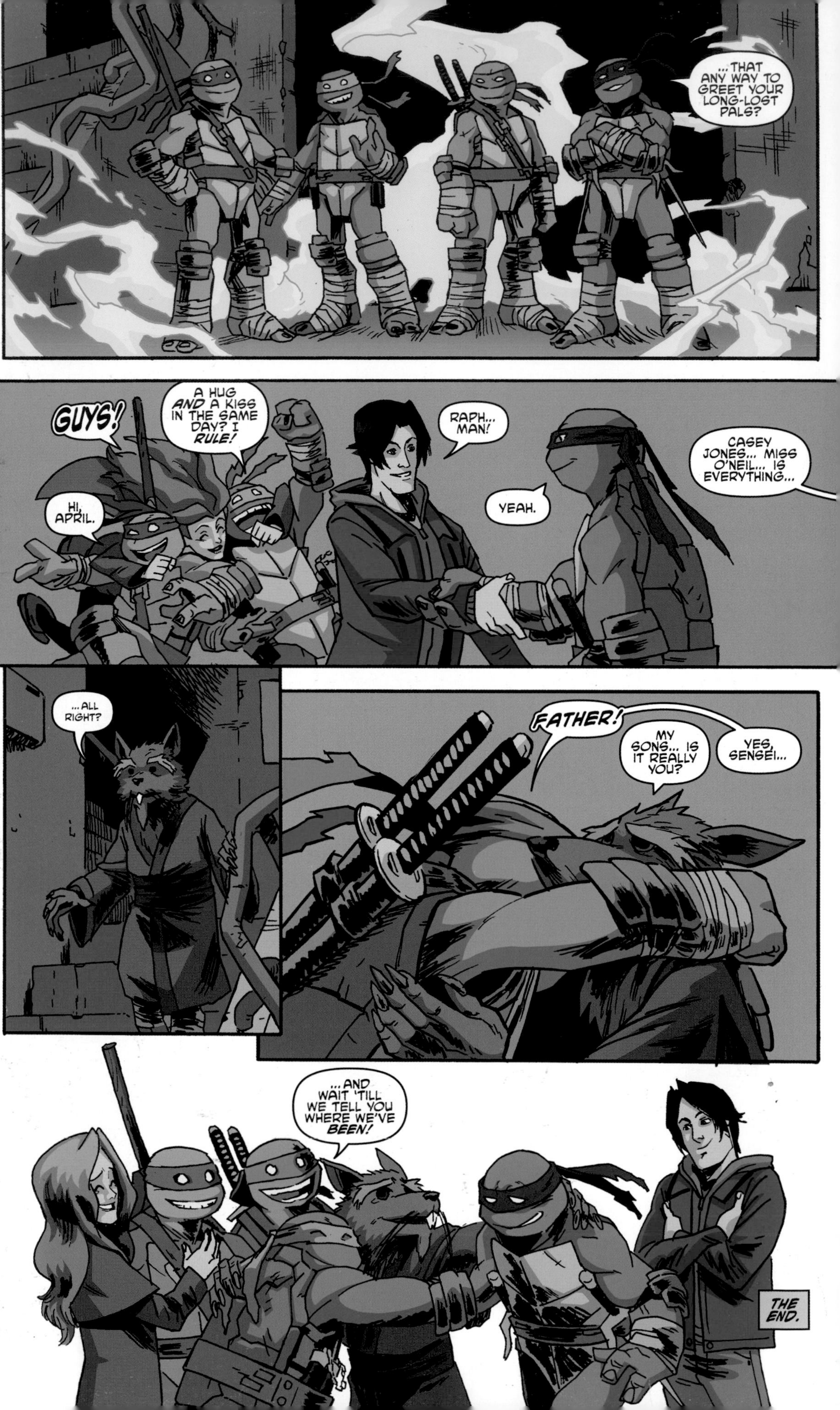
...THAT ANY WAY TO GREET YOUR LONG-LOST PALS?
GUYS!
A HUG AND A KISS IN THE SAME DAY? I RULE!
HI, APRIL.
RAPH... MAN!
YEAH.
CASEY JONES... MISS O'NEIL... IS EVERYTHING...
...ALL RIGHT?
FATHER!
MY SONS... IS IT REALLY YOU?
YES, SENSEI...
...AND WAIT 'TILL WE TELL YOU WHERE WE'VE BEEN!
THE END.

ART GALLERY

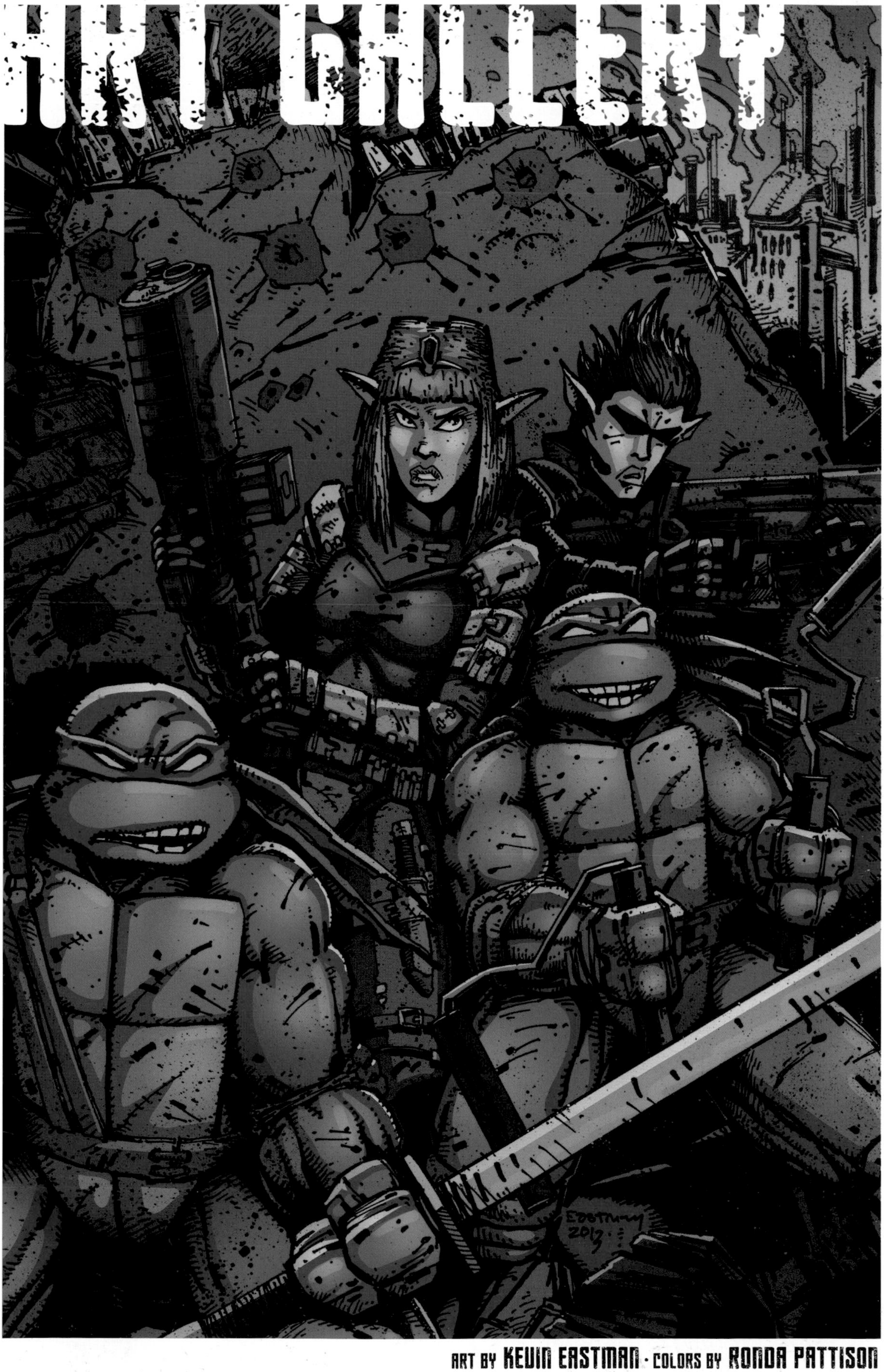

ART BY KEVIN EASTMAN · COLORS BY RONDA PATTISON

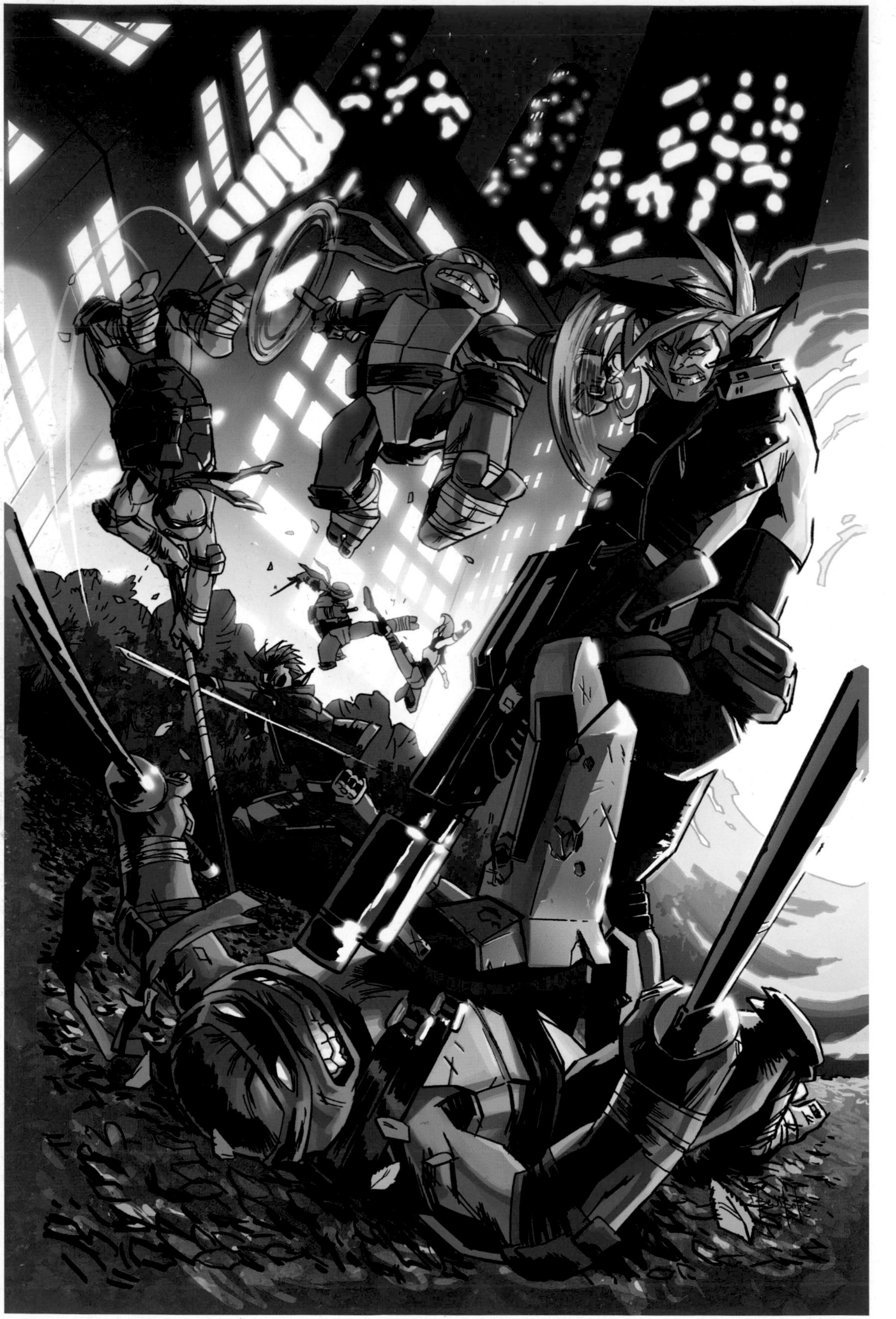

THIS PAGE AND OPPOSITE PAGE: ART BY **BEN BATES**

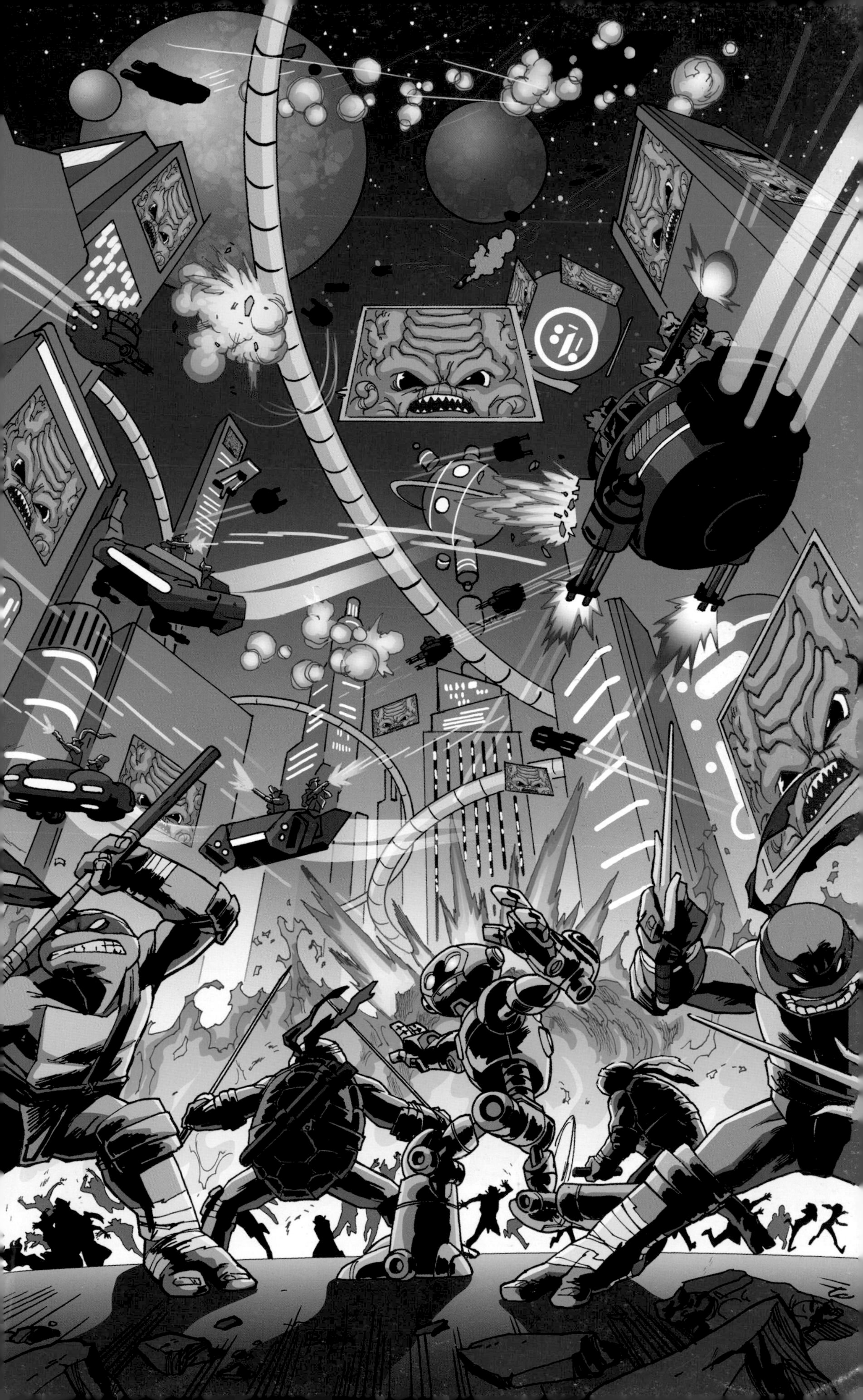

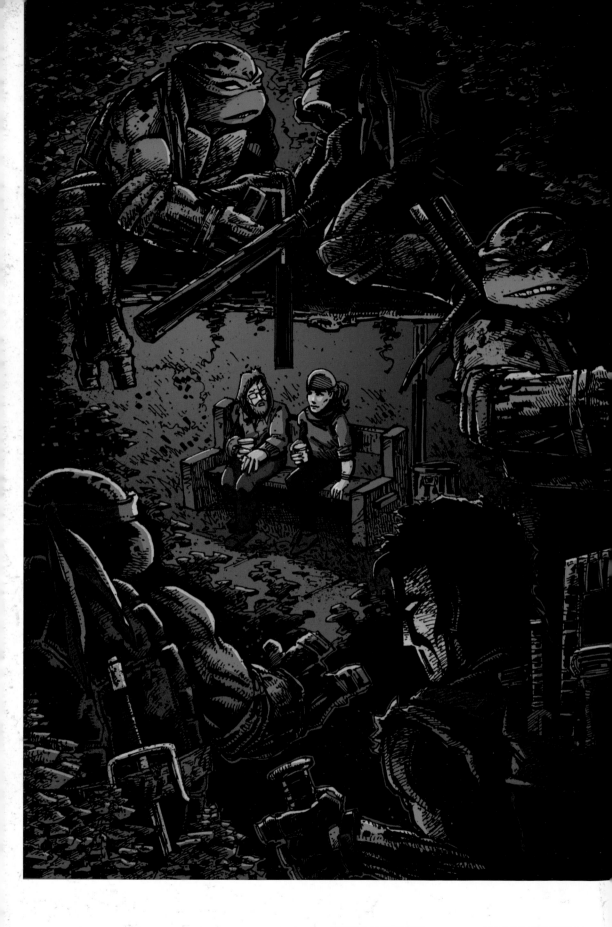

THIS PAGE AND OPPOSITE PAGE: ART BY KEVIN EASTMAN · COLORS BY RONDA PATTISON

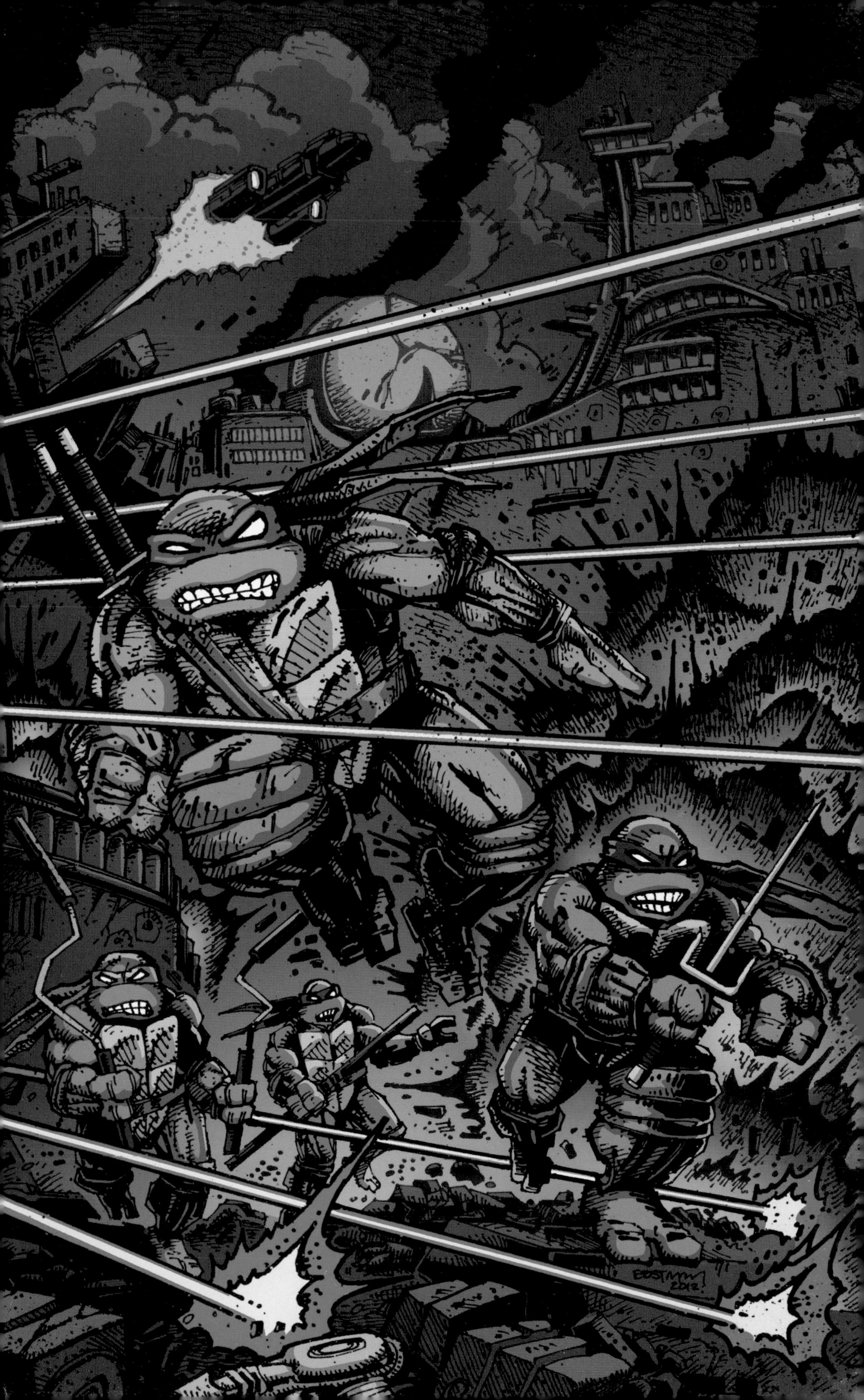

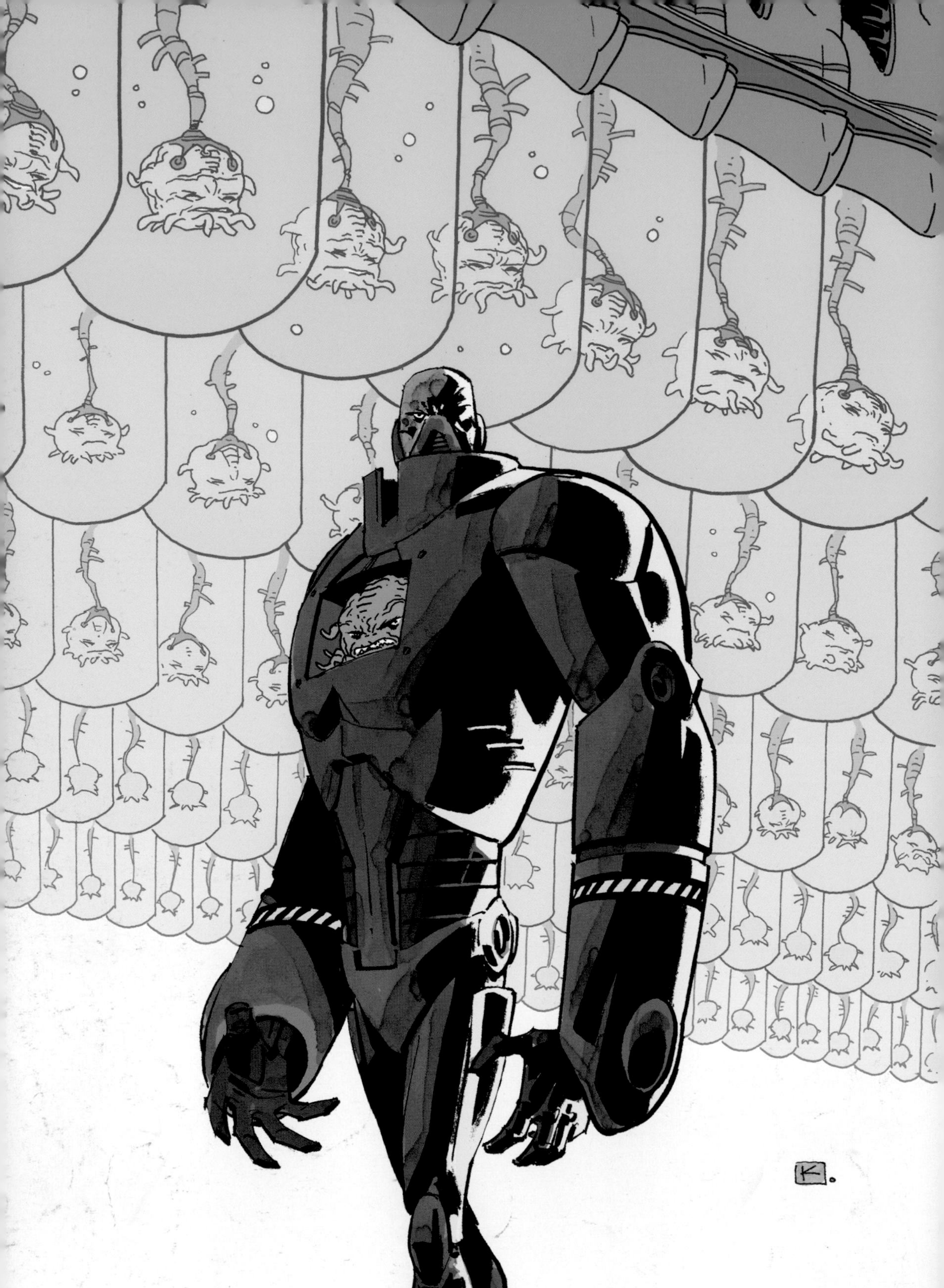

ART BY ANDY KUHN

OPPOSITE PAGE: ART BY MARK TORRES

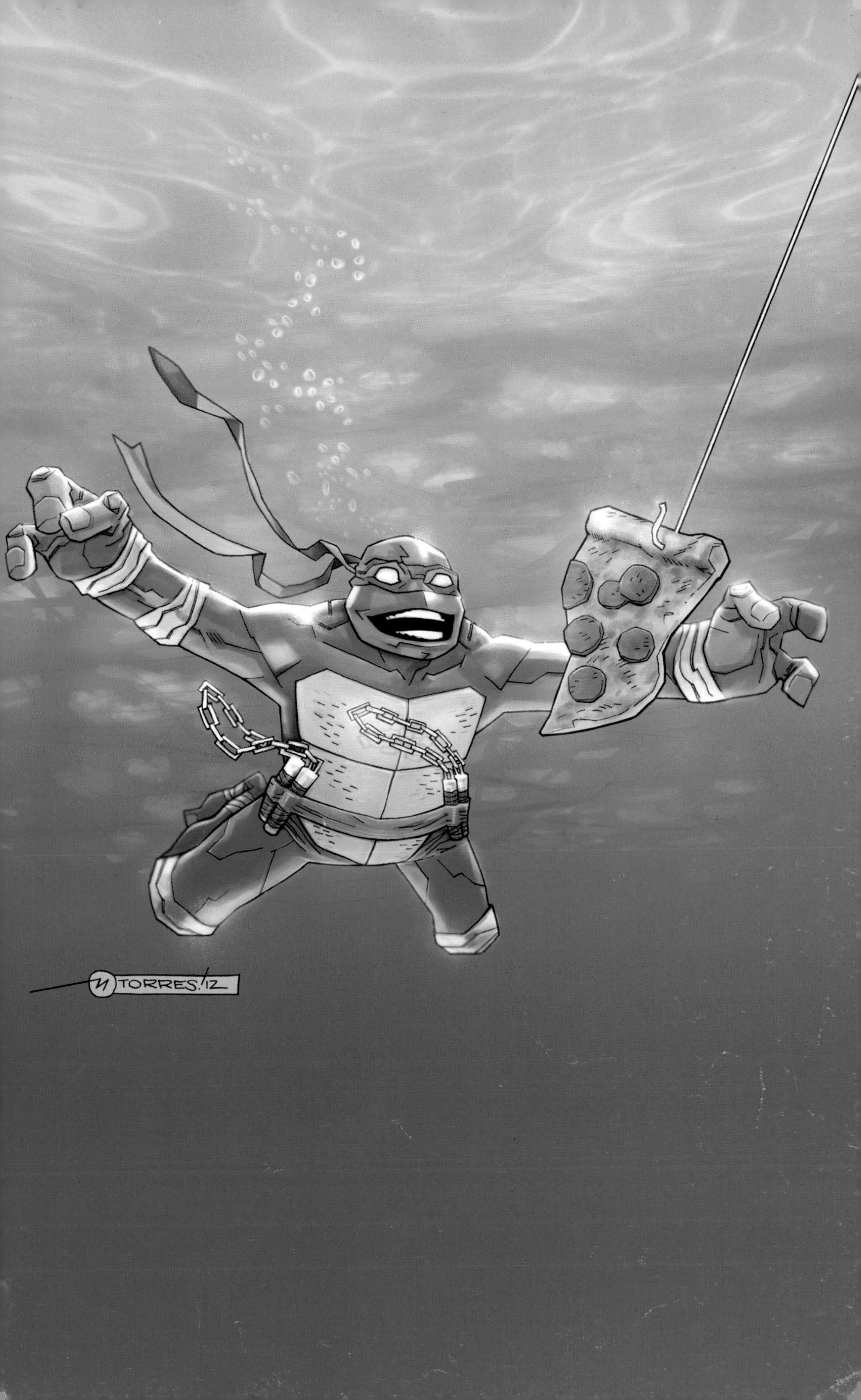
TORRES '12

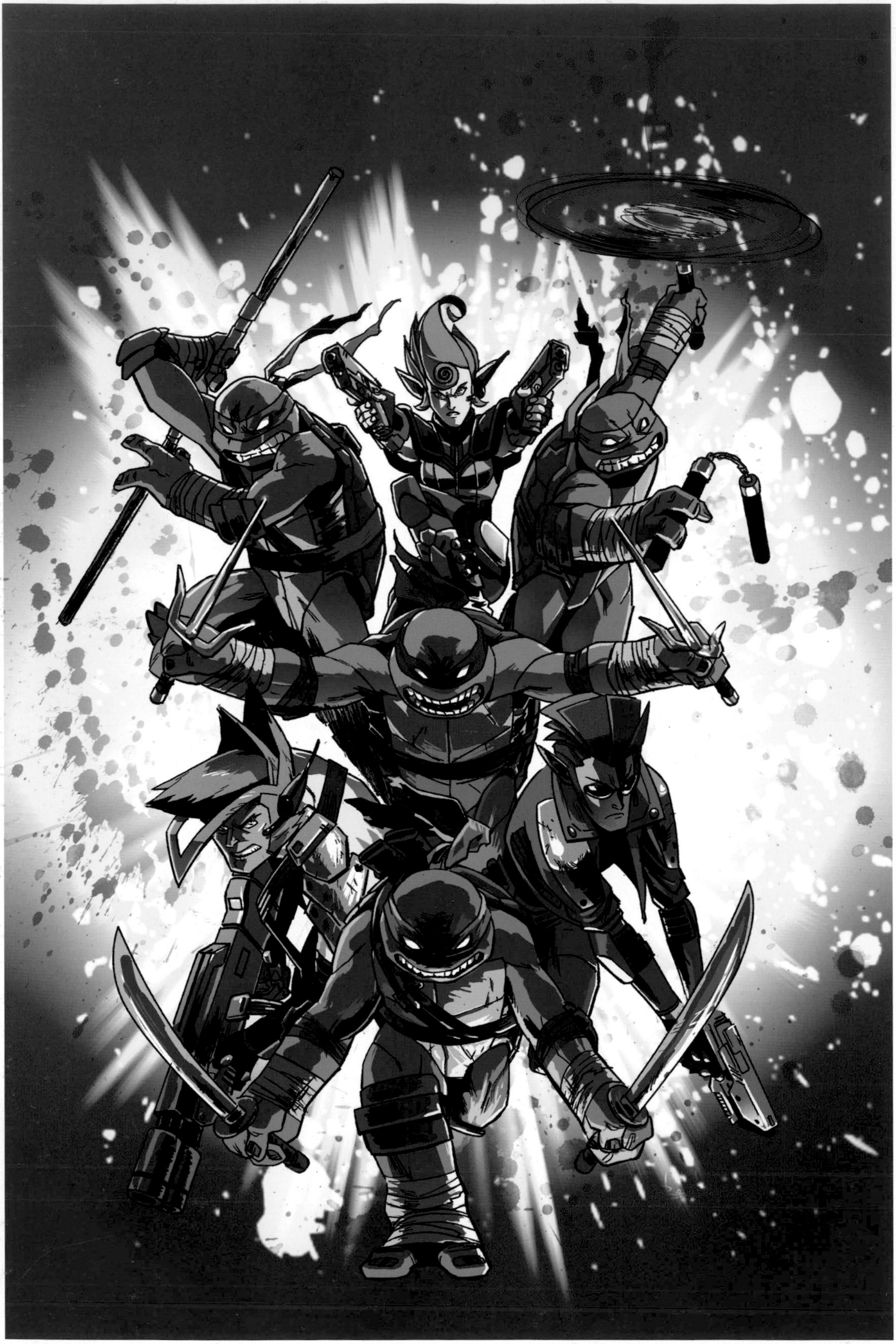

THIS PAGE AND OPPOSITE PAGE: ART BY BEN BATES

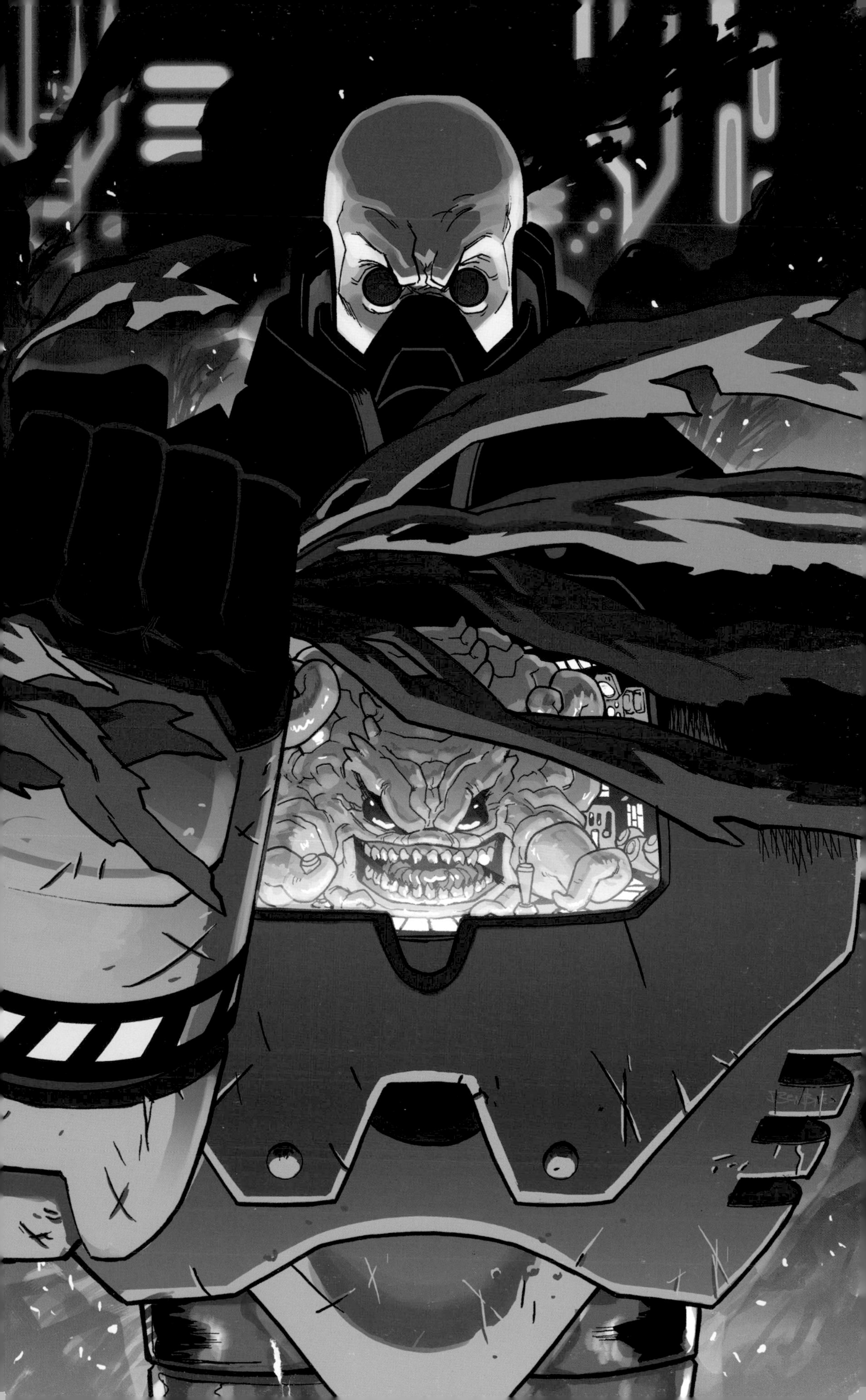

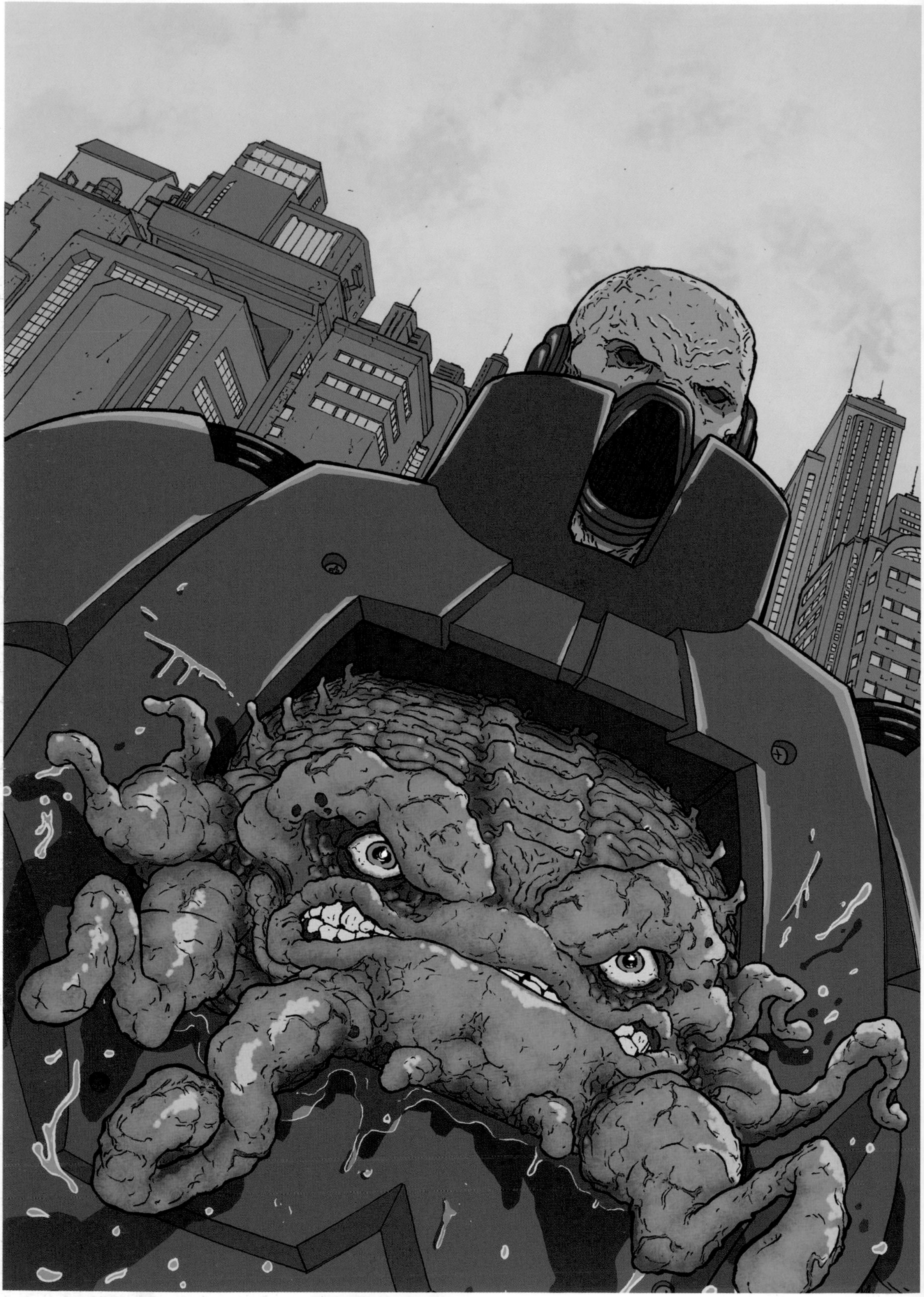

ART BY NICK PITARRA · COLORS BY MEGAN WILSON

OPPOSITE PAGE: ART BY LANGDON FOSS

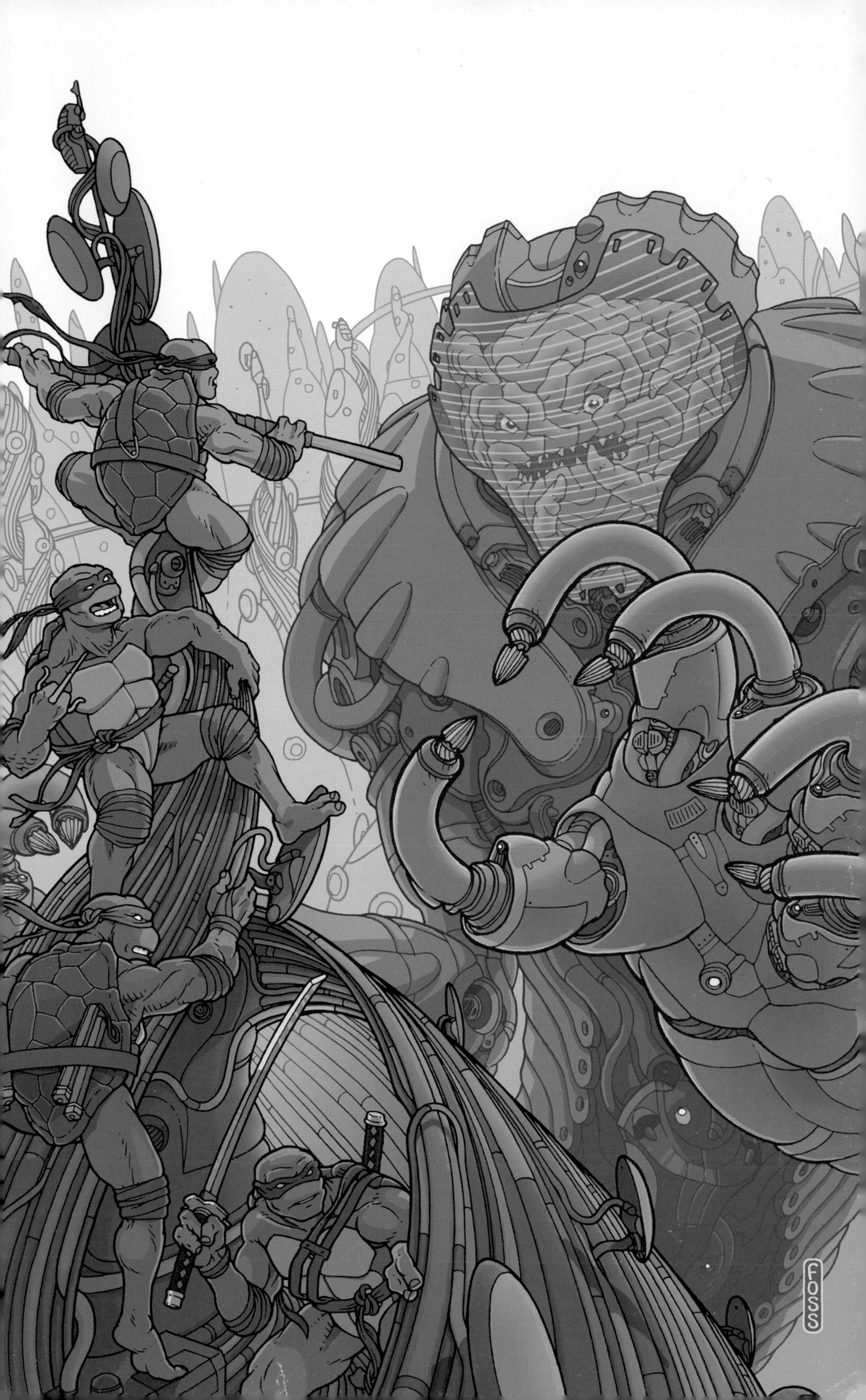
FOSS

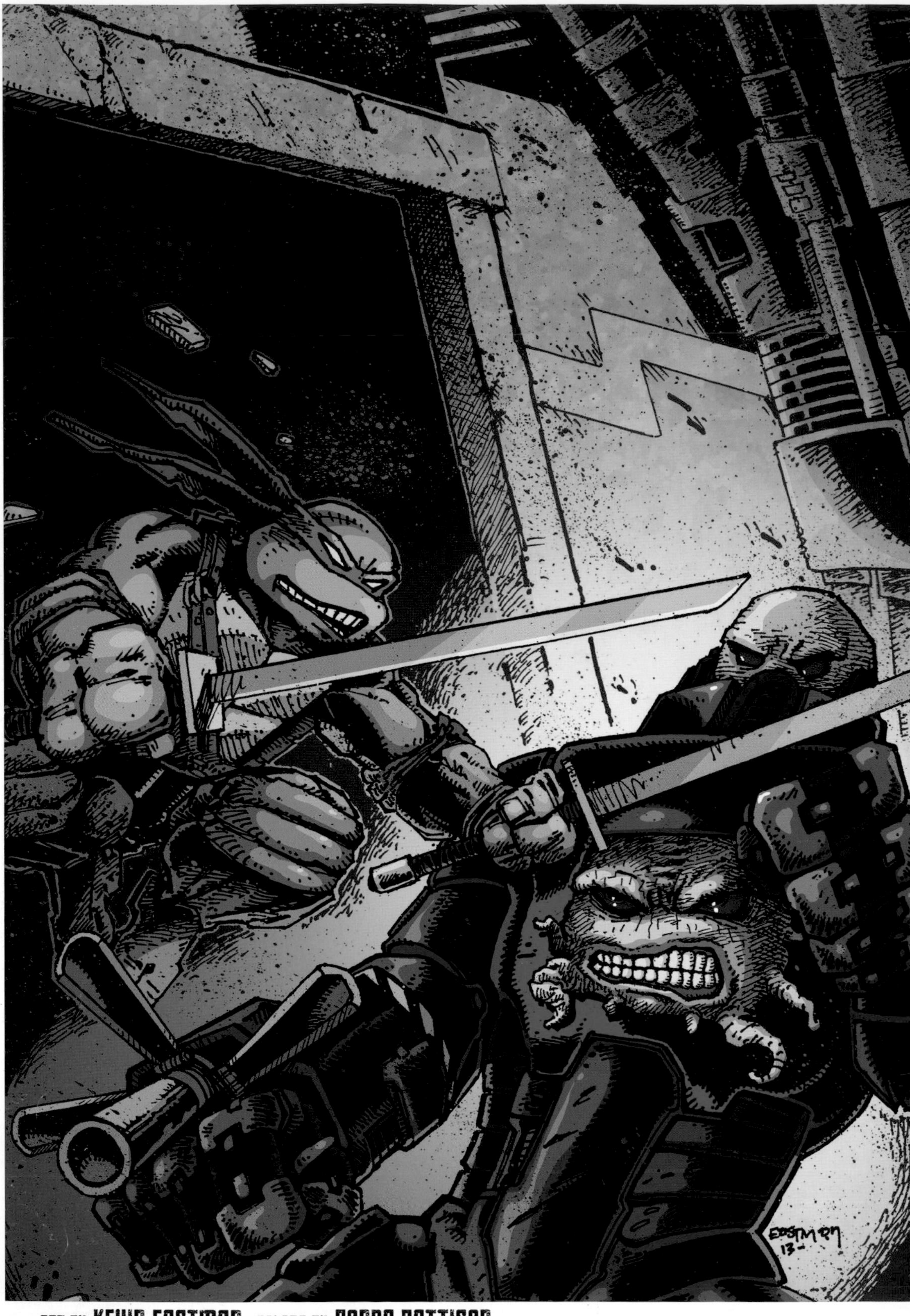

ART BY **KEVIN EASTMAN** · COLORS BY **RONDA PATTISON**

OPPOSITE PAGE: ART BY **BEN BATES**

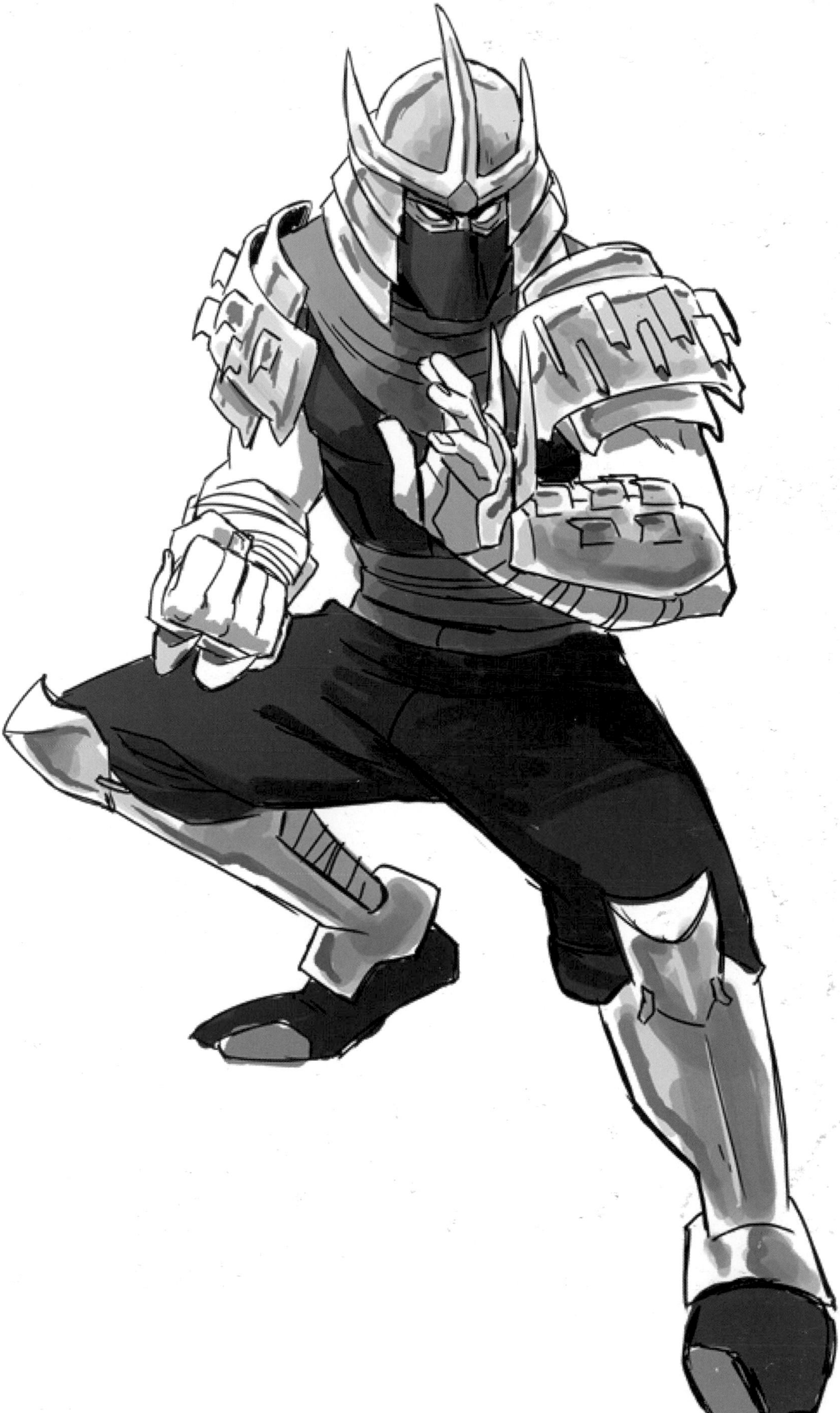

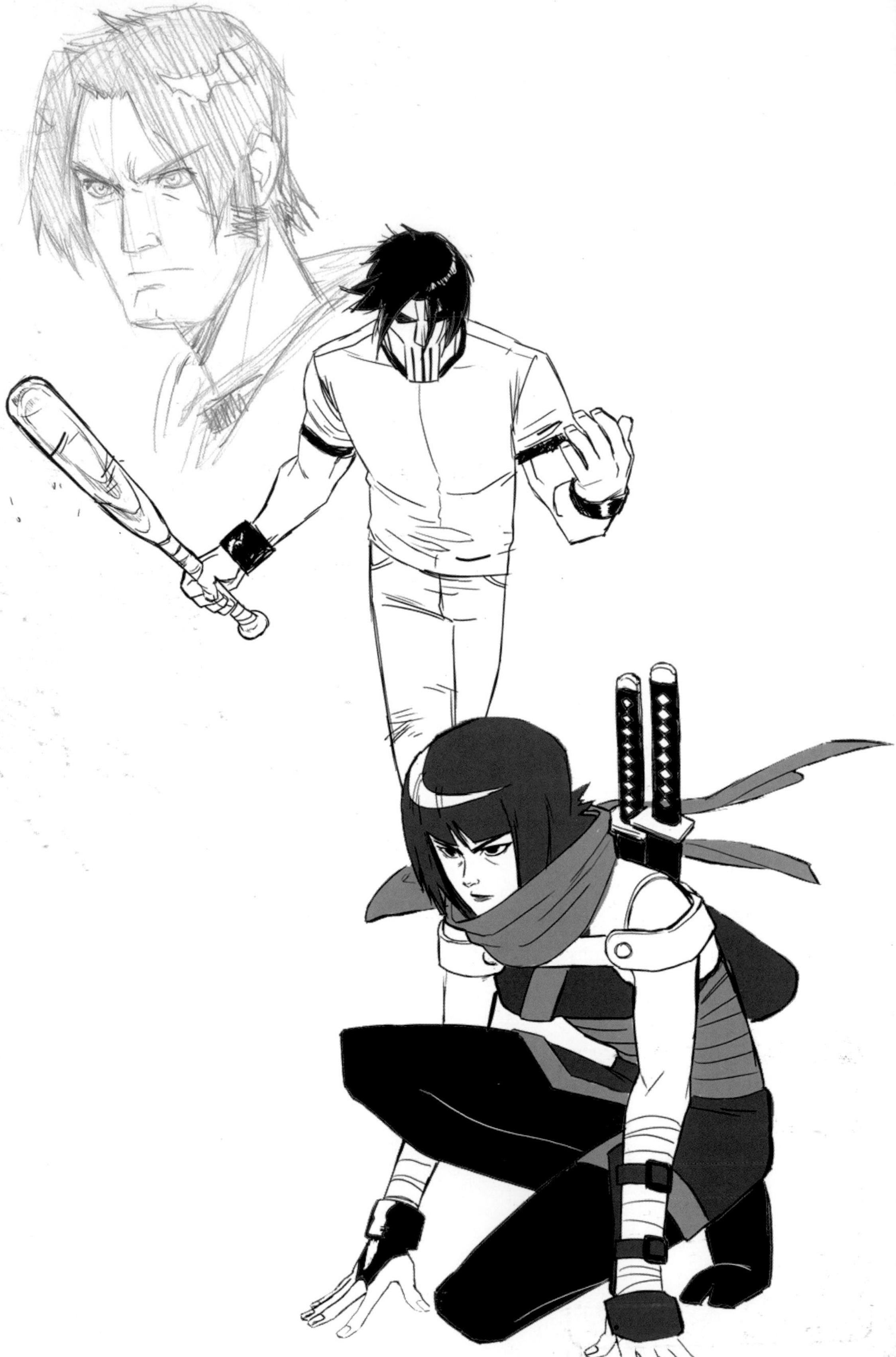

THIS PAGE AND OPPOSITE PAGE: ART BY BEN BATES

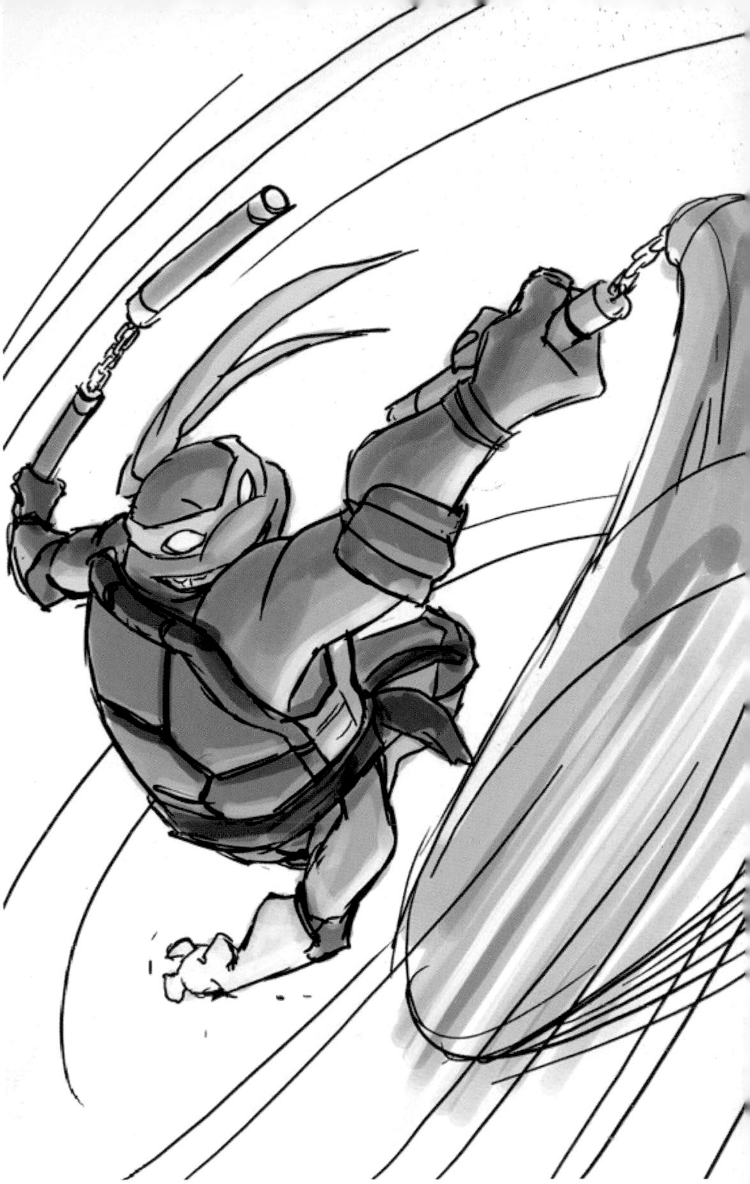

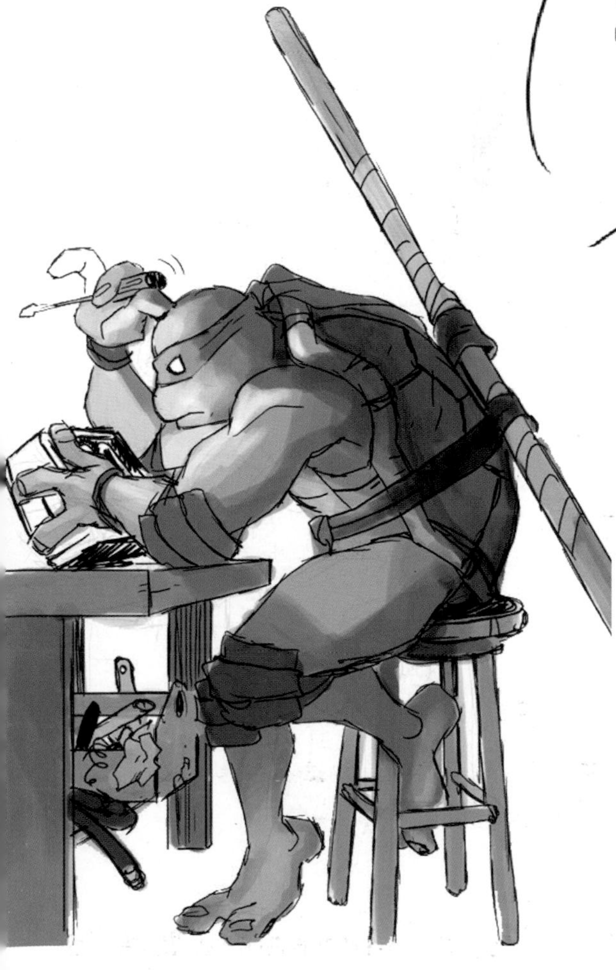

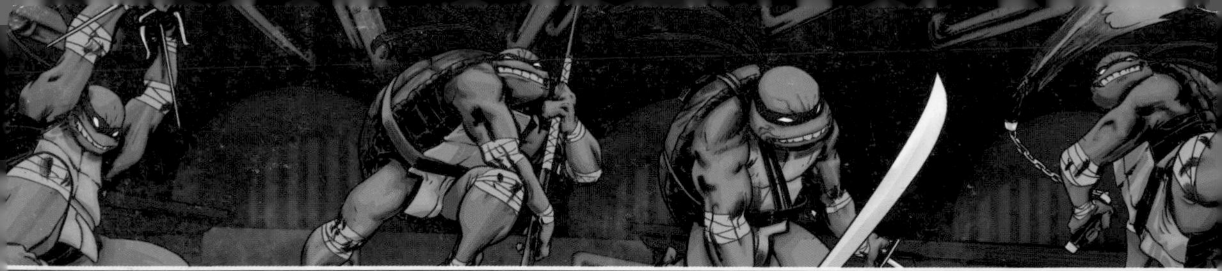

TEENAGE MUTANT NINJA TURTLES

MORE TURTLE ACTION!

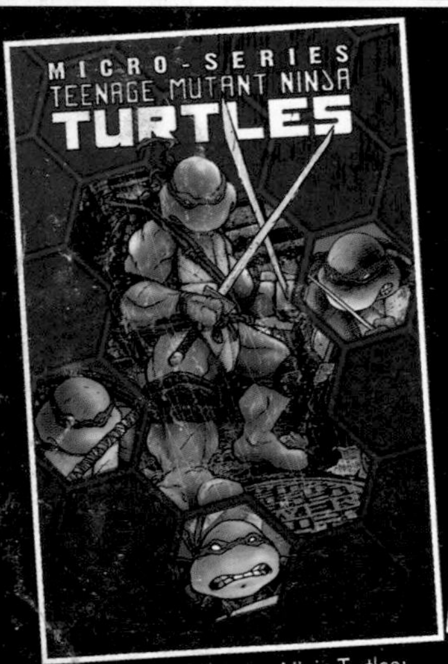
MICRO-SERIES
TEENAGE MUTANT NINJA
TURTLES

Teenage Mutant Ninja Turtles:
Micro-Series, Vol. 1
ISBN: 978-1-61377-232-4

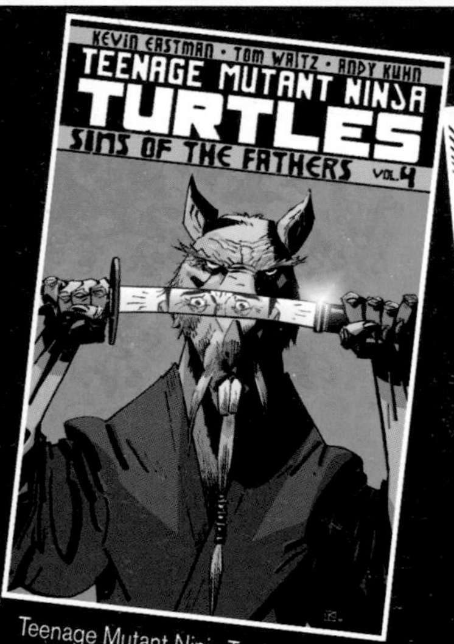
KEVIN EASTMAN • TOM WALTZ • ANDY KUHN
TEENAGE MUTANT NINJA
TURTLES
SINS OF THE FATHERS VOL. 4

Teenage Mutant Ninja Turtles, Vol. 4:
Sins of the Fathers
ISBN: 978-1-61377-568-4

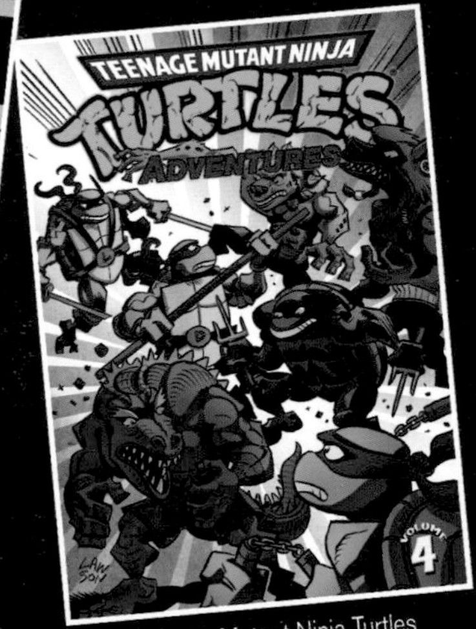
TEENAGE MUTANT NINJA
TURTLES
ADVENTURES
VOLUME 4

Teenage Mutant Ninja Turtles
Adventures, Vol. 4
ISBN: 978-1-61377-591-2

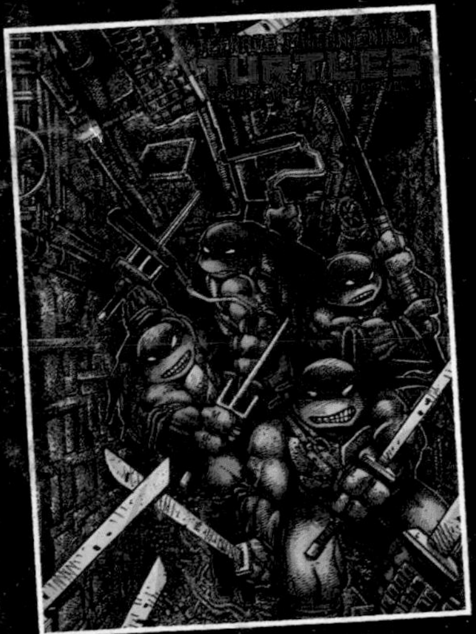

Teenage Mutant Ninja Turtles:
The Ultimate Collection, Vol. 4
ISBN: 978-1-61377-496-0

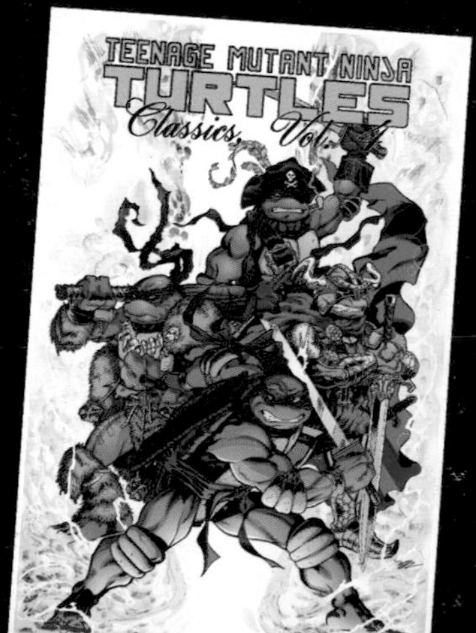
TEENAGE MUTANT NINJA
TURTLES
Classics, Vol. 4

Teenage Mutant Ninja Turtles
Classics, Vol. 4
ISBN: 978-1-61377-567-7

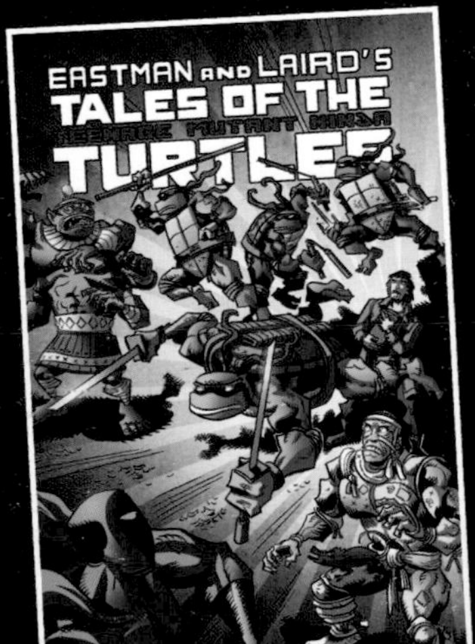
EASTMAN AND LAIRD'S
TALES OF THE
TEENAGE MUTANT NINJA
TURTLES

Tales of the Teenage Mutant
Ninja Turtles, Vol. 1
ISBN: 978-1-61377-416-8

ON SALE NOW

www.idwpublishing.com

IDW

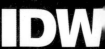